美国语文
— ★ 我喜欢这样的自己 ★ —

[美] 埃德温·埃尔德曼◎主编
尹吴娅琪 等◎译

苏州新闻出版集团
古吴轩出版社

图书在版编目（CIP）数据

美国语文. 我喜欢这样的自己 /（美）埃德温·埃尔德曼主编；尹昊娅琪等译. -- 苏州：古吴轩出版社，2016.12（2024.9重印）

ISBN 978-7-5546-0788-6

Ⅰ.①美… Ⅱ.①埃… ②尹… Ⅲ.①英语课—小学—美国—教材 Ⅳ.①G624.311

中国版本图书馆CIP数据核字(2016)第248041号

责任编辑：蒋丽华
见习编辑：薛　芳
策　　划：党霄羽
封面设计：沈加坤

书　　名：美国语文——我喜欢这样的自己
主　　编：[美]埃德温·埃尔德曼
译　　者：尹昊娅琪　等
出版发行：苏州新闻出版集团
　　　　　古吴轩出版社
　　　　　地址：苏州市八达街118号苏州新闻大厦30F
　　　　　电话：0512-65233679　　邮编：215123
出 版 人：王乐飞
印　　刷：天津旭非印刷有限公司
开　　本：690mm×980mm　1/16
印　　张：15.25
版　　次：2016年12月第1版
印　　次：2024年9月第2次印刷
书　　号：ISBN 978-7-5546-0788-6
定　　价：49.80元

如有印装质量问题，请与印刷厂联系．022-22520876

推荐序一

李江月

（伊利诺斯大学PHD，湖北省高考作文满分获得者）

我在美国留学的时候，不仅要承担繁重的学习任务，还要传道授业，帮自己的导师们带本科新生。那时候我就经常想，要是有一套全新的教材，难度适中，学生和教师都能在书中获得营养，让来自中国的学生既能学习原汁原味的地道的美式英语，又能对自己所学的专业有所帮助，还能和各个领域的大咖们谈笑风生，打破很多美国人觉得中国人就是书呆子的刻板印象，那该多好啊！

这部千呼万唤始出来的《美国语文》丛书，解决了大家英语学习和教学的需求。每一篇课文都有精美的翻译，译文都做到了信达雅，读起来让人感觉如沐春风，甚至有时候让人感动，让学习英语这个看上去很繁重很枯燥的历程充满了惊喜。

众所周知，英语是不断变化的语言，也许需要每个学习者终身不断地学习。本套书的英文原版，是由常青藤名校校长精编精选，汇集了许多名家的经典之作，所以我们每一位读者，不仅是学生，还包括老师和家长，都能在这样美妙的阅读中感受到自己的进步，得到切切实实的满足感。这些美丽的体验，是市面上一般读物难以给予我们的。

相比很多所谓"高屋建瓴"的语言学著作，这部丛书经历了实践的考验，是一部非常亲民和接地气的青少年读物，也是家长和老师很好的帮手。

很多时候，因为应试教育的需求，同学们不得不死记硬背许多文学大家的作品，但是他们并不理解这些作品。于是，虽然短期内成绩提高了，却在成年后丧失了对文学的爱好和学习的欲望。不论在中国还是美国，总能看到这样令人遗憾的现象。对此，我们觉得很可惜，学习文学本来应该是一种乐趣，而不应该是一种负担。我们希望孩子们开心地学，家长们愉快地陪伴他们学习，老师们欣喜地发现孩子们的进步，而不是扼杀他们的兴趣，阻碍他们进一步追求知识的脚步。

我们知道，很多文学大师虽然不是专门的儿童作家，但是他们并不是没有给孩子写过作品。本套书的一大亮点就是集结了很多大家笔下从未被翻译成汉语的遗珠之作——在各领域专门为孩子创作的作品。通过阅读本套书，孩子们能在书中了解到许多新奇的知识，坐在家里就环游世界，也为未来的学习打下扎实的基础。

本书主编埃德温·埃尔德曼先生，用他的智慧和孜孜不倦的努力，代替了我们在文山书海的盲目搜寻，就像我们的另一双眼睛，带我们遨游浩瀚的书海，获取人类文明的精华。

一言以蔽之，这套丛书是我用过的最好的美国语文学习、教学的教材，既可以用来自学，也可以用到课堂上。特此，我将这部丛书诚挚推荐给大家。让我们一起在《美国语文》的海洋里自由地冲浪吧！

推荐序二

曹海元

(MIT PHD)

迄今为止，阅读一直是我最大的爱好，而在现今残存的记忆里，我最早读到可以真正称得上书的，正是父亲给我的那套页面泛黄的《上下五千年》。我在脑海里至今仍旧清晰地记得那套书的封面，茕茕孑立的烽火台，赭红的城楼，残阳如血。华夏五千年那时而诡谲绵密时而波澜壮阔的历史也随着作者娓娓道来的小故事，奔涌到我充满好奇的内心，溅起了一片片波澜。虽然以我当时的阅历和见识无法理解许多深奥的名词和藏在历史故事背后深刻的道理，但是那套书唤起了我内心对于知识的渴望。阅读让我得以坐上时光机，身临其境般在华夏文明的浩瀚长河中自由穿梭，在我的心中种下了星星之火。正是这些星星点点的火种，照亮了我内心通往知识殿堂的道路，让阅读成了我生命中最大的乐趣，从而造就了我今天这副模样。

《上下五千年》那套书在我如今看来，也许简陋不堪，只是一些历史小故事汇编，但在当年那个懵懂少年看来却已然是通往圣杯的指路明灯。如今这套《美国语文》无论从文章的文学艺术性、选材的宽泛多样性来说，还是从编排的科学合理性上来看，都要遥遥领先。阅读这套书的少年从中可以先领略中世纪灿若星河的文艺复兴，再遇见近现代疾风怒涛般的工业革命；可以先认识一生锋芒毕露最后却功亏一篑的拿破仑，再偶遇始终沉默寡言却在危难之际挽大厦于将倾的华盛顿。从弗吉尼亚的崎岖山岭到欧亚大陆的广袤平原，短短千言却包罗万象、荟萃乾坤，包含了世界历史、地理、博物、人物、传奇、诗歌等领域的精华。

在我看来，如果说《上下五千年》只是星星点点的火苗，那么这套《美国语文》则是那光芒四射的火炬。我想读者尤其是那些处于学习阶段的青少年，必然可以像当年的我那样，从这套书中找到点燃自己心中火种的火焰，照亮通往圣杯的道路。

最后，用我最爱的诗歌《伊萨卡岛》中的一句话来结尾——"当你启程，前往伊萨卡岛时，愿你的道路漫长，充满奇迹，充满发现。"这也是我对所有有幸读到这套丛书的读者的祝福。我想说的就这么多了，希望我无知和浅薄的序言不会让这套书的光芒逊色。

Preface

Good expression in reading is the product of sympathy and understanding, and therefore, the child who likes to read is quite sure to take first rank as a good reader. The controlling purpose of Classics, Old and New is to inspire in children a love for reading, and thus, without their being conscious of the fact, induce in them the reading habit. This is about the best and safest of all habits. If we contrive to teach young people the mechanical art of reading, and fail, at the same time, to breed in them the impulse and desire to continue their education throughout life by reading, we have cheated them out of the best thing to be obtained by going to school.

Good literature is an expression for the best of the world's activity, and the power latent in such literature to lift and enlighten the mind and spirit is greater than any other power, save, perhaps, the influences of home. The formal education of many of the children that will use this series of readers will cease with the elementary schools. This fact makes the preparation of the readers a very serious task, especially to one who knows children well enough to realize how difficult it is to know them at all.

When a child enters the Fourth Reader, he has practically mastered what may be called the mechanics of reading. New words, as words, no longer have any terror for him. He knows how to read, we say. He is, therefore, at a critical moment in his mental life in so far as that life touches literary culture. Let us hope that his imagination is not dulled, and that he has learned, as the earlier readers of this series are planned to teach him, to have a feeling for the good as distinguished from the bad or the commonplace. The selections in this book are the work of three score and ten writers of distinction, writers of the past ages and of the present time-writers of many lands, who were not writing down to children, but uttering their own best thoughts. This book, like the earlier numbers, may, therefore, be appropriately called Classics, Old and New.

No hard and fast culture-epoch theory has determined their selection, though earnest thought has been given. to the interests that appeal to children of this age Constant effort has been made to give variety in subject matter, and yet to maintain a unity of appeal to the understanding and the imagination. The subjects chosen range from nature and myth and adventure to biography and patriotism and ethics.

Our material age is coming more and more to neglect poetry as a thing outside the world of reality. The truth is, that there are no more practical things in the world than poetry and music, for they, even more than bread, bring to life what it needs. Many of us can recall poems that have served us as practically in the day's work as have the multiplication tables. The guiding thought in all the poetry selected has been to acquaint the child with the songs that will always be sung-especially the older poems studied by their fathers and mothers before them, such old and yet ever young treasures as "Lord Ullin's Daughter", Gray's "Elegy", "Annabel Lee".

The author believes that these readers, in the hands of sympathetic teachers, can be so used as to make not only good readers in the technical sense, but also real lovers of fine literature, young people of good taste in letters and of an increasing desire for close friendship with the best that has been thought and said.

The following acknowledgments are made in addition to those already given in the biographies: to Charles Scribner's Sons for the use of "How I Found Livingstone"; to Houghton, Mifflin & Co. for the use of "Playing Theater at River Mouth", and to G.P. Putnam's Sons for the use of "A Tradition of Weatherford".

◈ 译文

前 言

　　优秀的阅读材料能够引起读者共鸣与理解,因此,热爱阅读的孩子也一定希望遇到一流的好读物。这套《美国语文》最主要的目的是为了激发孩子对于阅读的热爱,虽然他们不一定理解书中的道理,但是这套书却能帮助他们养成良好的阅读习惯。而阅读是最有意义的习惯,有百利而无一害。如果我们只是照本宣科地教授年轻学生们关于阅读的技巧,却未能燃起他们对于阅读的热爱与渴望,不能对他们未来一生的学习都有所帮助的话,就是剥夺了他们在学校所能收获的最棒的东西。

　　优秀的文学作品可以诠释世间最美好的事物,作品中隐含的力量足以启迪心智、振奋精神,这种力量远大于一切其他力量,甚至可以弥补来自家庭的不良影响。很多正规教育会将本套图书作为引导孩子们完成小学阶段的学习材料。因此此套读物的准备工作十分艰巨,只有那些非常了解孩子的人们才知道真正了解孩子有多难。

　　当学生开始阅读到第四册时,他应该已经掌握了基本的阅读技巧。面对新单词时,他应该不再感到恐惧。可以说,他懂得了如何阅读。这是他开始接触文学之后,心灵成长的关键时期。我们希望他的想象力还没有变得枯竭,并能有所收获,通过前几册的学习,他能有辨别是非的能力和分辨优秀作品与平庸作品的能力。本书收录的作品均为古今中外德高望重的作者所著。他们不是专门的儿童作家,但依然表达出了最优秀的思想观念。本书和前几册书一样,当得起"古今经典"这个名字。

　　在选录过程中,我们排除了艰涩难懂的理论以及快餐文化,尽管那些文字也是根据现代年轻人的兴趣经过慎重思考之后写出来的。在选题上,我们不断地尝试,试图挖掘多样化的主题,同时兼顾易读性和想象力。我们挑选的主题有自然、神话、探险、传记、爱国主义和伦理道德等。

在这个物质化的时代，人们越来越忽视诗歌的价值，甚至将其视为脱离现实的东西。其实，世间没有任何东西比诗歌与音乐更实用了，因为比起粮食，诗歌与音乐能为生活提供更多的滋养。在日常生活中，诗歌对于我们大多数人来说，就像乘法表一样，具有现实意义。本册书收录诗歌的原则是挑选那些朗朗上口的、孩子们熟悉的歌谣，特别是那些他们的父母也曾学过的经典诗歌，包括《惊涛篇》、格雷的《挽歌》以及《安娜贝尔·李》等，这些诗古老却又充满活力。

作者相信，在老师的帮助下，阅读本书的孩子们不仅能提高阅读技能，还能真正热爱优秀文学作品，成为拥有对文字具有良好品位与鉴赏力、渴望和珍视友谊的一代年轻人。

除了在作者简介中已经致谢过的个人或机构，还要感谢查尔斯·斯克里布纳父子出版公司提供了《寻找利文斯敦》一文，霍夫顿霍顿·米夫林出版公司提供了《河口剧院》一文以及G.P.普特南父子出版公司提供了《韦瑟福德的传统》一文。

目 录

Chapter 1　Stories | 故事 ... 001

The Lord Helpeth Man and Beast | 上帝保佑万物 ... 003

The Stone-Cutter | 切石匠变形记 ... 007

The Minnows with Silver Tails | 银尾鲦鱼 ... 012

The Foolish Little Air-Current(1) | 无知的小气流（1）... 019

The Foolish Little Air-Current(2) | 无知的小气流（2）... 023

The Loyal Knight | 忠实的骑士 ... 026

Chapter 2　Nature Scene | 自然风光 ... 031

The Great Pyramid | 宏伟的金字塔 ... 033

Dog-Sleighing in the North | 北极的狗拉雪橇 ... 037

A Departure from Cairo | 从开罗出发的旅程 ... 043

Tharald's Otter | 哈拉尔德的水獭 ... 049

A Pair of Eagles | 一对秃鹰 ... 054

A Journey in Brazil | 巴西之旅 ... 059

Hunting the Cougar in Mississippi | 在密西西比狩猎美洲豹 ... 064

A Tradition of Weatherford | 韦瑟福德的传说 ... 070

Two Minutes | 两分钟 ... 075

Chapter 3　Miscellaneous Poems ｜ 杂诗 079

Queen Mab ｜ 麦布女王 081

The Flower ｜ 花 084

Lucy ｜ 露西 086

The Eagle ｜ 鹰 088

The Kitten and the Falling Leaves ｜ 小猫与落叶 089

Patriotism ｜ 爱国主义 092

Beauty ｜ 美 094

Incident of the French Camp ｜ 法国军营事件 095

Lochinvar ｜ 洛金伐尔 099

Fame ｜ 名声 103

Chapter 4　History ｜ 历史 105

Elizabeth Zane ｜ 伊丽莎白·赞恩 107

The Capture of Quebec ｜ 魁北克陷落 111

Rescue of the Crew of the Merrimac ｜ 解救梅里麦克号船员 117

At Lucerne ｜ 卢塞恩游记 122

How I Found Livingstone ｜ 寻找利文斯敦 126

How Franklin Learned to Write ｜ 富兰克林是怎么学写作的 134

Longfellow ｜ 朗费罗 138

Saluting Mount Vernon ｜ 致敬弗农山庄 143

Scott and His Home ｜ 司各特和他的家园 146

The Coronation of the Czar and the Czarina | 沙皇和皇后的加冕..150

Chapter 5　Stories of Children　|　孩子们的故事 **157**

A Poet at Home | 一位居于家中的诗人.................................159
A Second Trial | 再试一次的机会......................................169
Playing Theater at River Mouth | 河口剧院.............................177
American Salmon | 美国鲑鱼...182
A New England Boyhood | 在新英格兰度过的少年时代....................189
A War-Time Adventure | 战时历险记...................................196
A Wolf-Hunt | 猎狼记...205
On a Higher Level | 升华 215
"Muskratting" | "逮水耗子"..222
The Perfect Life | 完美的人生..227

《美国语文》译者名录

Chapter 1

Stories ｜ 故事

The Lord Helpeth Man and Beast

预习

concealed /kənˈsiːld/ 隐蔽的
consequently /ˈkɑːnsəkwentli/ 因此；所以
custody /ˈkʌstədi/ 羁押
defendant /dɪˈfendənt/ 被告
edible /ˈedəbl/ 可食用的
hospitably /ˈhɒspɪtəbli/ 善于款待地
perplexed /pərˈplekst/ 困惑的
plaintiff /ˈpleɪntɪf/ 原告

During his march to conquer the world, Alexander the Macedonian came to a strange people in Africa. Dwelling in a remote and secluded corner in peaceful huts, they knew neither war nor conqueror. They led him to the hut of their chief, who received him hospitably, and placed before him golden dates, golden figs, and bread of gold.

"Do you eat gold in this country?" said Alexander.

"I take it for granted," replied the chief, "that thou were able to find edible food in thine own country. For what reason, then, art thou come among us?"

"Your gold has not tempted me hither," said Alexander, "but I would willingly become acquainted with your manners and customs."

"So be it," rejoined the other, "sojourn among us as long as you please."

At the close of this conversation two citizens entered as into their court of justice. The plaintiff said, "I bought of this man a piece of land,

and as I was making a deep drain through it, I found a treasure. This is not mine, for I bargained only for the land, and not for any treasure that might be concealed beneath it; and yet the former owner of the land will not receive it."

The defendant answered, "I hope that I have a conscience as well as my fellow-citizen. I sold him the land with all it's existing advantages, and consequently the treasure was included."

The chief, who was at the same time their supreme judge, repeated their words, in order that the parties might see whether or not he understood them aright. Then, after some reflection, he said, "Thou hast a son, friend, I believe?" "Yes."

"And you," said the judge, turning to the other, "A daughter?" "Yes."

"Well, then, let the son marry the daughter, and bestow the treasure on the young couple for their marriage-portion."

Alexander seemed surprised and perplexed. "Think you my sentence unjust?" the chief asked him. "Oh, no," replied Alexander, "but it astonishes me."

"And how, then," rejoined the chief, "would the case have been decided in your country?" "To confess the truth," said Alexander, "we should have taken both parties into custody, and have seized the treasure for the king's use."

"For the king's use!" exclaimed the chief, now in his turn astonished. "Does the sun shine on that country?" "Oh, yes!" "Does it rain there?" "Assuredly." "Wonderful! But are there in that country tame animals which live on the grass and green herbs?" "Very many, and of many kinds."

"Ay, that must be the cause," said the chief, "for the sake of those innocent animals, the All-gracious being continues to let the sun shine and the rain fall on your country."

(Samuel Taylor Coleridge)

译文

上帝保佑万物

　　在征服世界的进程中，马其顿的亚历山大大帝在非洲遇见过一群奇怪的人。他们在与世隔绝的偏僻角落聚群而居，住在平和宁静的小木屋里，从没有经过战争和征伐。他们把亚历山大领到了首领的木屋，首领非常热情地接待他，在他面前放满了金海枣、金无花果和金面包。

　　亚历山大问道："在你们国家，人们吃金子吗？"

　　首领回答说："如果在自己的国家找不到可以吃的东西，吃金子不是理所当然的事吗？话说回来，你又是因为什么而来到我们这里的呢？"

　　"我并不是被你们的金子引诱到这里来的。"亚历山大说，"但我非常乐意了解你们的风俗习惯。"

　　首领说："既然如此，你愿意在这里待多久就待多久吧。"

　　谈话结束的时候，两位居民走了进来，请首领给他们公正的裁决。原告说："我从这个人手里买了一小块土地，结果在地里挖下水道的时候，挖出了一笔财宝。这不属于我，因为我只买了地，并没有买下藏在地里的财宝。但是，这块地的前主人却不肯要这笔财宝。"

　　被告辩护说："我希望我的良心跟我的同胞一样好。我卖给他土地以及土地里的一切东西，这笔财宝自然也包含在内。"

　　同时作为双方的最高法官，首领复述了他们说过的话，以便让双方确认他是否正确理解了他们的意思。然后，他思考了一会儿，说："我的朋友，我记得你有一个儿子？""是的。"

　　这时法官转向了另一方，接着说："而你有一个女儿？""是的。"

　　"那么，就让你们各自的儿子和女儿结婚，然后把财宝作为结婚礼金赠送给这对年轻的夫妇。"

　　亚历山大看上去又惊讶又困惑。首领问他："你觉得我判决得不公正吗？"亚历山大回答说："哦，不，我只是非常震惊。"

　　"那么，这种情况在你的国家是怎样处理的呢？"首领问道。亚历山大回答说："坦白地说，我们会把双方都抓起来，财宝供国王使用。"

"供国王使用！"首领惊叫起来，现在轮到他感到震惊了，"那个国家有太阳照耀吗？""哦，有的！""那里会下雨吗？""当然会。""太好了！但是你们的国家也有温顺的食草动物吗？""当然，而且有很多不同种类的食草动物呢。"

"啊，那肯定是因为这个。"首领说，"因为这些无辜的动物，上帝继续让太阳照耀着你的国家，让雨水滋润着你的国家。"

（塞缪尔·泰勒·柯勒律治）

（译注：文中亚历山大提到的国王掠夺国民财富的习惯在欧洲各国十分盛行，柯勒律治借这个故事表达了对欧洲各国国王的强烈谴责。）

作者介绍

塞缪尔·泰勒·柯勒律治（1772-1834）是一名英国诗人。他有时也会给杂志写散文。不过，他最为人所知的身份还是诗人。他对美的感知敏锐而纤细，而他的诗歌则极富音乐的韵律美。他最受欢迎的诗歌有《古舟子咏》《夜莺》《白日梦》《成吉思汗》和《克里斯特贝尔》。华兹华斯、柯勒律治和罗伯特·索西常被称为"湖畔诗人"。

The Stone-Cutter

Once upon a time there was in Japan a poor stone-cutter——a simple workman in the quarries. His life was rude; he worked much, gained little, and was not at all contented with his fate.

"Oh, if I could only be rich enough to rest, to sleep on thick matting, wrapped in a robe of soft silk!" Such was the sigh that he breathed to Heaven. An angel heard it.

"It shall be according to thy desire," said the angel.

The stone-cutter at once became rich; and he rested, slept upon thick matting, and wrapped himself in a robe of soft silk.

It happened that the emperor passed by. He was heralds on foot and on horseback, followed by a brilliant escort of cavaliers, and surrounded by persons who held over his head an immense parasol, shining with gold.

"What good does it do to me to be rich," murmured the rich man, "as long as I have not the right to go out with an escort, and have my head protected by a golden parasol? Why am I not the emperor?"

"Thou shalt be," said the angel.

And, indeed, he became the emperor. He had an escort before and behind him, and people who above his head an immense parasol, resplendent with gold.

However, the sun, with his ardent beams, dried up the country, and the dusty road, quivering with his brightness, wearied the eyes.

"It is a great advantage to be emperor," cried the man, "when the heat of the day exhausts you, and the sun never ceases to make you feel his power! But if one could be the sun!"

"Behold! Art thou satisfied?" the angel asked; for the emperor has become the sun, and he darted his beams up and down, right and left, and all around him. And he scorched the herbage of the earth and the faces of the princes upon the earth.

But now a cloud thrust itself between the earth and him; it held back the rays of the sun, and prevented them from falling upon the earth's surface.

"There is strength," cried the sun, "a cloud capable of resisting my power. It would be better if I were a cloud."

"Very well," said the angel.

And the change was at once accomplished. The new cloud placed itself haughtily between the sun and the earth, and it soon saw the earth covered with its shadow. Then it caused big drops of rain, and pouring showers, and waterspouts to fall upon the lands, so that the torrents burst their bounds and the rivers spread over and devastated the fields.

Nothing resisted the force of the flood; only a rock defied it, perfectly motionless. In vain the bellowing waters beat in their fury; the rock yielded not, but the foaming waves died at its foot.

"A rock, then, is my superior," said the cloud. "I would rather be in its place."

"Thou shalt be," said the angel.

And he was transformed into a steep unshaken rock, insensible to the rays of the sun, indifferent to the torrents of rain and the shock of the tumultuous waves.

Nevertheless, he distinguished at his feet a man of poor appearance, hardly clothed, but armed with chisel and hammer; and the man, with the help of these implements, struck off pieces of the rock, which he dressed into stones proper for cutting.

"What is that?" cried the rock. "Has a man the power of rending pieces of stone from my breast? Shall I be weaker than he? Then it is absolutely necessary that I should be that man."

"Have thy will," said the angel.

And he became again what he had been——a poor stone-cutter, a simple workman in the quarries. His life was rude, he worked much, and gained little; but he was contented with his a lot.

(Bayard Taylor)

✎ 译文

切石匠变形记

从前,日本有一位切石匠,是采石场里的一名普通工人。他的生活很窘迫,干得多,赚得少,对命运愤愤不平。

"唉,如果我有钱该多好,我就可以穿上柔软的丝质睡袍,躺在厚厚的床垫上,好好地休息了!"他对着天空叹息道。一位天使刚好听到了他的话。

"应该让你愿望成真。"天使说道。

于是,这位切石匠立刻成了一个有钱人,他真的可以穿上柔软的丝质睡袍,躺在厚厚的床垫上,好好地休息了。

碰巧国王从这里经过。而国王身前有步行和骑马的传令官,身后有庞大的骑士护卫队,身旁还有侍从撑着一把巨大的遮阳伞,遮阳伞是镀金的,发出耀眼的光芒。

"做个有钱人有什么好的,"切石匠低声抱怨道,"我既没有护卫队护送我出门,也没有侍从为我撑镀金的遮阳伞,我为什么不是一个国王呢?"

"你可以成为国王。"天使说道。

之后,他便真的成了国王。外出时,身前身后都有护卫队,身旁还有人为他撑着巨大的遮阳伞,闪闪地发着金光。

然而,太阳光太炽烈了,使整个国家陷入了干旱之中。路上尘土飞扬,掩盖了国王身上的光芒,模糊了他的双眼。

"当国王固然很好,"切石匠喊道,"可是太阳会让你感到精疲力竭,而且无时无刻不让你感受到它强大的存在!要是我能变成太阳就好了!"

"瞧!现在你满足了吗?"天使问道。因为国王变成了太阳,他射出的光芒都环绕着他,时而向上,时而向下,时而向左,时而向右。他不仅烧光了世界上的草坪,还灼伤了一些王子们的脸。

但是,现在出现了一片云,把太阳和地面隔开了;这片云朵控制住太阳的光芒,让阳光没法洒落大地。

"这片云很厉害,"太阳喊道,"云可以限制太阳,如果我能做一朵云就更好了!"

"好的。"天使说道。

于是,太阳一下子就变成了云朵,他沾沾自喜,位于太阳和地球之间。这一片云朵完全遮住了太阳的光芒,很快,地球就变得阴沉沉的,之后便下起了雨,雨越来越大。这场倾盆大雨淹没了土地,湍急水流溢出了河床,摧毁了农田。

没有什么能抵挡住汹涌的洪水;唯独有一块岩石藐视它,完全不动。虽然猛烈的洪水不断地拍打着它,它仍岿然不动。这块岩石让喷着泡沫的浪涛屈服了,而自己却不曾低头。

"一块岩石都比我厉害,"云说道,"那我宁愿成为一块岩石。"

"那你就做一块岩石吧。"天使说道。

于是,云朵变成了一块岩石,身处陡峭的位置,却又不可动摇。这块岩石在炎炎烈日的煎熬里,在大雨瓢泼的冲刷下,在惊涛骇浪的拍打中,仍完好如初。

尽管如此,有一天,他发现脚下站着一个男人,样貌平平,衣衫褴褛,但手上拿有一把凿子和一把锤子;男人用这两个工具凿下了几块石头,打磨好,准备切割。

"那是什么?"岩石喊道,"是不是有个男人可以从我身上敲下几块石头?难道他比我强大吗?那我一定要成为那个男人。"

"那就实现你的愿望。"天使说道。

于是,他又变回了他以前的样子,做一个切石匠,是采石场里一名普普通通的工人,过着贫穷的生活,辛辛苦苦却只挣来很少的钱。但不同的是,他现在很知足。

(贝亚德·泰勒)

♢ 作者介绍

贝亚德·泰勒是美国著名诗人、小说家和旅行作家。他大部分的旅行都是徒步完成的,几乎游历了世界上所有的国家。贝亚德写的许多关于外国的文章都曾在美国的刊物上发表,内容十分精彩。贝亚德出版过一些小说、不少游记和诗集,还完成了歌德的作品《浮士德》的英译。《外国的男孩子》

一书受到男孩子的热烈追捧。1862至1863年，贝亚德担任圣彼德斯堡公使馆的大臣，1873年时被任命为美国的驻德大使，最终于1878年在柏林逝世。

朗读

The night has a thousand eyes,
And the day but one;
Yet the light of the bright world dies
With the dying sun.
The mind has a thousand eyes,
And the heart but one;
Yet the light of a whole life dies
When love is done.

(Francis William Bourdillon)

译文

黑夜的眼睛有一千只，
白昼的眼睛却只有一只。
整个世界都会黯淡无光，
如果太阳不再明亮。
思想的眼睛有一千只，
心灵的眼睛却只有一只。
整个人生都会黯淡无光，
如果爱不在身旁。

（弗朗西斯·威廉姆·鲍迪伦）

The Minnows with Silver Tails

预习

acknowledge /əkˈnɑːlɪdʒ/ 承认

chink /tʃɪŋk/ 叮当声

composedly /kəmˈpoʊzdlɪ/ 镇定地

opportunity /ˌɑːpərˈtuːnəti/ 机会

plague /pleɪɡ/ 瘟疫

troll /troʊl/ 搜索

"I'm sick of being at another man's beck and call," said Tom Turner impatiently. "It's 'Tom do this' and 'Tom do that', and nothing but work, work, work from Monday morning to Saturday night.

"I was thinking as I walked over to Squire Morton's to ask for the turnip seed for master. I was thinking, Sally, that I am nothing but a poor workingman after all. In short, I'm a slave, and my spirit won't stand it."

So saying, Tom flung himself out at the cottage door, and his wife thought that he was going back to his work as usual; but she was mistaken. He walked to the wood, and there, when he came to the border of a little tinkling stream, he sat down and began to brood over his grievances.

"Now, I'll tell you what," said Tom to himself, "it's much pleasanter sitting here in the shade, than broiling over celery trenches, and thinning wall fruit, with a baking sun at one's back, and a hot wall before one's eyes. But I'm a miserable slave. I must either work or see my family starve; a very hard lot it is to be a workingman."

"Ahem," said a voice close to him.

Tom started, and to his great surprise, saw a small man, about the size of his own body, standing composedly at his elbow. The man was dressed in green——green hat, green coat, and green shoes. He had very bright black eyes, which twinkled very much, as he looked at Tom and smiled.

"Servant, sir!" said Tom, edging himself a little farther off.

"Miserable slave," said the small man, "are you so far lost to the noble sense of freedom, that your very salutation acknowledges a mere stranger as your master?"

"Who are you," said Tom, "and how dare you call me a slave?"

"Tom," said the small man, "don't speak roughly. Keep your rough words for your wife, my man; she is bound to hear them. What else is she for, in fact?"

"I'll thank you to let my affairs alone," interrupted Tom, shortly.

"Tom. I'm your friend; I think that I can help you out of your difficulty. Every minnow in this stream——they are very scarce, mind you——has a silver tail."

"You don't say so!" exclaimed Tom, opening his eyes very wide. "Fishing for minnows and being one's own master would be much pleasanter than the sort of life I've been leading this many a day."

"Well, keep the secret as to where you get them, and much good may it do you," said the man in green. "Farewell; I wish you joy in your freedom." So saying, he walked away, leaving Tom on the brink of stream, full of joy and pride.

He went to his master and told him that he had an opportunity for bettering himself, and should not work for him any longer.

The next day, he arose with the dawn, and went in search of minnows. But of all the minnows in the world, never were any others so nimble as those with silver tails. They were very shy, too, and had as many turns and doubles as a hare; what a life they led him!

They made him troll up the stream for miles; then, just as he thought his chase was at an end and he was sure of them. They would leap quite out of the water, and dart down the stream again like silver arrows. Miles and miles he went, tired, wet, and hungry. He came home late in the evening, wearied and footsore, with only three minnows in his pocket, but each had a silver tail.

"But, at any rate," he said to himself, as he lay down in his bed, "though they lead me a pretty life, and I have to work harder than ever. Yet I certainly am free; no man can now order me about."

This went on for a whole week; he worked very hard; but up to Saturday, he had caught only fourteen minnows.

After all, however, his fish were really great curiosities; and when he had exhibited them all over the town, set them out in all lights, praised their perfections, and taken immense pains to conceal his impatience and ill temper, he, at length, contrived for them, to sell them all, and get exactly fourteen shillings for them, and no more.

"Now, I'll tell you, Tom Turner," said he to himself. "I've found out this afternoon, and I don't mind your knowing it——that every one of those customers was your master. Why! you were at the beck of every man, woman, and child who came near you——obliged to be in good temper, too, which was very annoying."

"True, Tom," said the man in green, starting up in his path, "I knew you were a man of sense; look you, you are all workingmen; and you must all please your customers. Your master was your customer; what he bought of you was your work. Well, you must let the work be such as will please the customer."

"All workingmen? How do you make that out?" said Tom, chinking the fourteen shillings in his hand. "Is my master a workingman; and has he a master of his own? Nonsense!"

"No nonsense at all; he works with his head, keeps his books, and manages his great mills. He has many masters; else why was he nearly ruined last year?"

"He was nearly ruined, because he made some new-fangled kinds patterns at his works, and people would not buy them," said Tom. "Well, in a way of speaking, then, he works to please his masters, poor fellow!

He is, as one may say, a fellow-servant, and plagued with very awkward masters. So I should not mind his being my master, and I think that I shall go and tell him so."

"I would, Tom," said the man in green. "Tell him that you have no objection now to digging up the asparagus bed."

So Tom trudged home to his wife, gave her the money that he had earned, and got his old master to take him back. His adventure with the man in green and the fish with the silver tails, however, he kept a profound secret.

(Jean Ingelow)

译文

银尾鲦鱼

"我受够了任人摆布的生活,"汤姆·特纳不耐烦地说道,"满耳尽是'汤姆做这个'和'汤姆做那个',从周一早上到周六晚上除了工作,还是工作。

"我走路去莫顿乡绅家,问他要萝卜种子给老板,一路上我都在想这个问题。莎莉,我只是个穷困潦倒的工人。简单地说,我就是个奴隶。在精神上,我无法再忍受这样的生活。"

说罢,汤姆便摔门而出,他的妻子觉得他只是和往常一样去上班而已。但妻子错了。汤姆走进一片树林,来到一条溪水"叮咚"的小溪旁,他坐了下来,开始思忖这些年受的委屈。

"如今,我想告诉你,"汤姆对自己说道,"比起在烈日之下,奔走于芹菜沟里;比起背上晒得发烫,面对着滚烫的墙收割墙上的果实,此刻能坐在树荫下是多么惬意啊。但我仍是个命运多舛的奴隶。我要么工作挣钱,要么眼睁睁看着我的家人受饿。做一名工人真是命苦啊。"

"呃哼。"一个声音从一旁传来。

汤姆开始四处搜寻,让他惊讶不已的是,一个小人儿出现了,身形娇小,镇定自若地站在他的手肘旁。小人儿全身一套绿色的行头——绿色的帽子，绿色的外套和绿色的鞋子，他还有一双明亮的黑眼睛。小人儿望向汤姆，微微一笑，双眼炯炯有神。

"先生，有何吩咐！"汤姆说道，慢慢地往旁边让开了一点。

"真是个命运悲惨的奴隶，"小人儿说道，"你是失去崇高的自由太久，以至于遇到的一个陌生人都要当成自己的主人看待吗？"

"你是谁？"汤姆问，"你怎么敢叫我奴隶？"

"汤姆，"小人儿说道，"讲话要柔和点。你是个男人，这些粗暴的话你可以对你的老婆说；她有义务听这些牢骚话，要不然，她还能干吗？"

"请你别多管闲事。"汤姆立刻打断他。

"汤姆，我是你的朋友，我想我能帮你渡过难关，这条小溪里的鲦鱼都有一条银色的尾巴，我要提醒你的是，这样的鲦鱼是很罕见的。"

"真的吗？"汤姆喊道，睁大双眼，"和我长期以来过的这种生活相比，能钓钓鱼，当自己的主人，这样的人生幸福得多了。"

"好的，那就保守这个秘密，这样或许对你会更好，"小绿人说道，"再见了，我希望你过得自由，过得开心。"说完这句话，小绿人心情愉悦，得意洋洋地离开了，留汤姆一人坐在水边。

汤姆找到了他的老板，告诉老板他现在有更好的选择，并提出了辞职。

第二天，天刚亮，汤姆就起床了，他要去寻找鲦鱼。但是，在这个世界上，银尾巴的鲦鱼比其他鲦鱼都聪明，也很害羞，还和野兔一样好动。这些鲦鱼改变了汤姆的生活！

汤姆为了找到这些鲦鱼，背着鱼竿，沿着小溪走了数千米路。于是，当他认为寻鱼之路走到尽头时，他对自己十分有信心，因为有鲦鱼蹦出了水面，然后又像一支支银箭一样冲向河里。他走了很远的路，汗流浃背，饥饿不已，疲倦不堪。他晚上很晚才回到家，腿脚酸痛，累极了，袋子里只有三只鲦鱼，但都是银尾巴的。

"但是，无论如何，"当汤姆躺在床上时，他对自己说道，"即使它们让我过上了不一样的生活，我还是要比以前更加努力。我现在过着绝对自由的生活，没有人可以使唤我了。"

就这样持续了一周的时间，他很拼命，但是直到周六，他才抓到十四条鲦鱼。

然而，毕竟这些鲦鱼都是珍品，汤姆在全镇展卖这些鲦鱼，全方位地展示它们，鼓吹它们的完美无瑕，在这过程中，他艰难地控制住自己的不耐烦和坏脾气，最终，在他的努力下，鲦鱼全部卖了出去，得到了十四个先令的收入。

"我说，汤姆·特纳，"汤姆对自己说道，"今天下午我发现了一件事情，我不介意告诉你——其实，那些顾客还是你的主人。为什么！因为你要满足在场每个男人、女人和小孩的需求——也就是说你必须得保持好心情，但这也让你觉得很恼火。"

"确实，"小绿人再次出现在汤姆面前，"我知道你是个有头脑的人。但是，瞧瞧你，完全是个打工者的样子，你必须取悦你的顾客，他们就是你的主人，他们来买你的东西你才能赚钱。你要是选择这份工作，就不得不去取悦你的顾客。"

"我就只能是个打工者？你是怎么知道的？"汤姆说道，弄得手里的十四先令"叮当"响，"我的主人不也是个打工者吗？难道他们能主宰自己的人生？简直太荒唐了！"

"一点不荒谬，他会思考，不断地阅读、规划自己的人生。他也有很多的主人。那为什么他去年差点搞砸了呢？"

"他之所以差点搞砸了，是因为他采用了新的管理方式，但人们都不能接受，"汤姆说，"好吧，从某种意义上说来，他也是在奉承他的主人。多么可怜的家伙啊！正如有些人所说的，他和我们一样，也是仆人，被难应付的主人们折磨。所以，我不该介意他是我的上司，而应该去告诉他这个道理。"

"换作是我，我也会这样做的，汤姆，"小绿人说道，"告诉他，你现在可以任劳任怨地挖地种笋了。"

最后，汤姆走了很久回到家中，把挣来的钱交给妻子，还跑到了原来的老板那儿，继续为老板工作。但是，关于他与小绿人和银尾鲦鱼的故事，汤姆再没提起。

（吉恩·英格娄）

⚘ 作者介绍

吉恩·英格娄出生于英国波士顿的林肯郡，是一位诗人和小说家。她为儿童写了很多的书，她的一些诗歌也广受年轻人青睐，其中《恩德比岛的高潮》和《七首歌》尤为著名。本文《银尾鲦鱼》出自《儿童故事》一书,这本书里还囊括了其他有趣的故事,如《小精灵莫帕斯》《绝佳时机》和《摩尔式黄金》等。

The Foolish Little Air-Current(1)

The cyclone was caused by an area of low pressure which was central, last night at nine o'clock, over the Great Lakes.

———the Morning Papers

This is the story of the foolish little air-current that at one time was part of a big cyclone——a very foolish little air-current!

For days and weeks, and ever since the little air-current could remember, they had been circling round and round——all the big and little air-currents up there together——in long, grateful turns, with the sun shining down through them, and glinting and glistening on the dancing, dazzling water far, far below.

The water was the Gulf of Mexico, but of course the little air-current did not know that. He and his brother were just plain, ignorant little currents, and had never seen land.

But they used to have a great deal of fun floating round and round all the long, lazy day, with the sun glinting through them. The little air-current had a foolish idea that this was what he was going to do all his life, if he thought about it at all, and one day he remarked, in the hearing of one of the bigger currents, "My! We're going pretty fast to-day."

"Do you call this fast?" put in one of the big ones. "Huh, just you wait until we get under way!"

"We'll be starting soon," he heard one say to another. The big ones all have hoarse voices.

"Which direction," asked one of the little air-currents.

"North, of course. Are you crazy?"

"North is the only direction in summer-time," said another still bigger current, kindly.

The little air-current said, "Of course, north." Although he did not know anything about it.

And the next day came the word to move.

"There's an area of low pressure up over the Gulf States," some one said. "That's what starts us. We are to go and fill it up."

"Yes, we must go to fill it up," said the foolish little air-current.

"Come on, we're going now," said all the big air-currents, darting and turning more quickly.

"Come on!" cried the little one, excitedly.

"Get in line there!" shouted one of the big ones. And just then the shot off the big circling volume of air, a little to the east of north, toward the state of Mississippi. It was still revolving round and round, but making rapid forward progress now at the same time, like a spinning top that darts off to one side. And the faster it went ahead, the faster it whirled round.

"Oh, dear!" cried the little air-current, really quite frightened. "Where are we going?"

"Hold on tight!" cried the big air-currents. "If you let go, you will be lost!" They, too, were a little frightened, but pretended that they were not. They were not going half so fast as they would be going by and by.

Soon they came over the land, and now they swooped down lower. "Ugh! what's that ugly rough stuff?" screamed the little air-current.

"Land!" whistled one of the larger currents. "Land! land!" roared the biggest currents. "Land! Land!" they all screamed and whistled and roared together. "We'll tear it up?" Now they began to go faster and faster. The little air-current did not say anything more for a while; he just looked scared and whirled round as the others were doing.

"What do you call this game?" he cried to a big current, once in a lull.

"Game!" replied the other contemptuously. "This is no game. We are a cyclone now!" He hissed the word "cyclone".

"Oh, are we a cyclone?" It is the ambition of an air-current's life to be part of a cyclone. "I'm a cyclone," he repeated to himself. "Just think!" and he dashed down among some trees that were waving and tossing their branches wildly and helplessly.

(Jesse Lynch Williams)

✎ 译文

无知的小气流（1）

昨晚九时许，由于受到低压中心的影响，大湖区范围内出现了飓风。

——《晨报》

这则故事描写的是一股出现在昨晚的飓风中的非常无知的小气流！

在小气流的记忆当中，过去的几周里，都是阳光普照大地，海水深处暗流涌动，五彩缤纷，所有的大气流和小气流们在这里不停地旋转，声势浩大，闪闪发光。

这片深海位于墨西哥湾，但小气流浑然不知，他和其他的气流一样，普普通通，懵懵懂懂，未曾见过陆地。

曾经，这些气流可以四处飘浮，晒晒太阳，就这样愉快地度过慵懒、漫长的一天。小气流曾有过无知的念头，他的一生都将这么度过。有一天，小气流听到比他稍微大点的气流说："哎呀！我们今天有些快呀。"

"这样你就认为过得很快了吗？"大气流说道，"哼！你就等着我们发威吧！"

"我们现在就开始。"大气流对另一个气流说，声音都很嘶哑。

"往哪个方向呢？"有一股小气流问道。

"当然是往北啊，你是疯了吗？"

"夏天的时候，我们只能往北。"另一股更大的气流心平气和地说道。

"当然是往北了，"小气流跟着说道，其实他什么也不懂。

于是，第二天气流们接到了命令，大家便行动起来。

"在海湾各州，有个低压区。"有气流说道，"我们应该从那里开始，挤满那个低压区域。"

"是的，我们必须去把那儿填满。"小气流傻乎乎地说道。

"加油！我们出发吧！"大气流们纷纷喊道。说罢，便快速地冲了出去。

"冲啊！"小气流喊道，兴奋不已。

"大家排好队。"一股大气流大声喊道。于是，巨大的气流涌向偏东北的方向，朝密西西比州袭去。气流在旋转的同时，以飞快的速度前进，如同一个飞速运转的陀螺一般。这些气流前进得越快，也就旋转得越快。

"天啊！"小气流喊叫着，内心十分恐惧，"我们要到哪里去啊？"

"跟紧点！"大气流们告诉他，"如果你跟丢了，就再也找不回我们了。"其实，这些大气流心里也有些害怕，只是他们假装镇定。不一会儿，他们就减慢了速度，连正常速度的一半都不到。

很快，气流就到了陆地上，猛扑向地面。"啊！这块又丑又硬的东西是什么？"小气流喊道。

"陆地！"一股大气流大声说。"这是陆地！陆地！"最大的一股气流咆哮着。于是，他们一齐呐喊："陆地！陆地！""我们把地面卷起来？"说罢，气流便移动得越来越快。小气流再不敢多说一句，看起来很害怕，只是默默地跟着其他气流旋转。

"这个游戏叫什么？"内心平静一些后，小气流问道。

"游戏！"其他气流异口同声地回答，"这不是游戏。我们现在是龙卷风。"小气流嘀咕着："龙卷风！"

"啊，我们现在是龙卷风吗？"气流一生的愿望就是成为龙卷风的一部分。"我现在就是龙卷风。"小气流自言自语地重复着，"真不敢相信！"他冲向在风中摇摆的树丛，将无助的树枝疯狂地折断，抛撒到空中。

（杰西·林奇·威廉姆斯）

The Foolish Little Air-Current(2)

Faster and faster they went, and now they came to a farmhouse, which they picked up, turned round, and put down on the same foundation, only backward. Fields of corn were uprooted. Streams boiled. Here was a town. Now houses began to fall and shatter. Roofs were lifted off, rolled up, and dropped on pitiful trees. Trees were picked up and slapped against church steeples, which broke. Houses were twisted. Factories tottered and tumbled. And it was all so easily done.

But the cyclone did not stop to look. It just tore on and on to the next town, sometimes skipping over one village entirely, only to plunge down and entirely demolish the next.

All this time there was roaring and wild howling, and the little air-current, like all the air-currents, was doing his part with the rest. They forgot to ask questions now. They were no longer frightened. They had caught the wild ecstasy of the storm.

All that night they rushed on madly up the United States, howling and shrieking. It was no longer hard for the little air-current to keep up. He did it from force of habit.

With dawn the storm quieted a little, and they had time to look about.

"Oh, didn't we storm?" said the little air-current. "I tell you I knocked over some big trees!" Just then he let go to turn round and see who listened. It is always foolish to turn round in a cyclone.

"Keep still and come on!" whistled one of the big currents.

"Oh, wait!" cried the little air-current. "Wait——wait——oh, I can't catch up!" he whispered.

He saw now, already quite far off in the distance, the cyclone twisting ahead in its quiet, earnest manner, with his little brothers working hard, as if they all knew just what they meant to do and were doing it, while he was whisked quickly over a hill, across a river, and then right into the street of a great city.

Without having an idea of what he was doing, he darted up between two high buildings, on up the street between other high buildings, across a park, over a wall, and into a street where people lived. They were just getting up. A few were coming out-of-doors.

He was so weak by this time that the best he could do was to take a man's hat off. The man ran after it, while the little air-current went on ahead of the hat until he came to a large house with trees in front. He turned in and ran through the tree-tops with all his might, but he noticed that he could only make the leaves rustle, rather pleasantly.

Then before he knew what he was about, he had darted in through an open window, fluttering the curtains a little, and glided across the room to a bed where lay a baby quietly sleeping. Then the baby sneezed.

"Noise," said a lady, "please go and cover the baby up. He is in a draft."

"And to think," sighed the little air-current, who was once part of a big cyclone, "that I can now only make a baby sneeze."

(Jesse Lynch Williams)

译文

无知的小气流（2）

气流前进的速度越来越快，来到了一间农舍，把它卷走，绕个圈，又扔回地上。这个地方比原来靠后了一点。田里的庄稼被连根拔起，河水泛滥。曾经的一座小镇，如今已是房屋倒塌，碎落一地。房顶被掀起，卷入风中，最后砸在可怜的树上。被风卷起的树木落在教堂的尖顶上，毁了教堂。房子都变形了，厂房也摇摇晃晃，倾斜倒塌。这一切，对于气流而言，都轻而易举。

但是龙卷风没有就此收手，而是继续袭击一个又一个的小镇，也许有时会放过一个村庄，但很快就会继续冲向下一个村庄，并完全将之摧毁。

此时此刻，气流不断地嘶吼和咆哮。小气流和其他气流一样，协助大家前进。他们都忘了提问，内心不再慌乱，体会到了当暴风的无限乐趣。

那一夜，这些气流疯狂地席卷美国，呼啸不止，咆哮不已。对于小气流来说，跟上大部队不再是件难事，他轻轻松松就能做到。

随着黎明的到来，风暴平息了一些，他们有时间四处看看。

"哇，难道我们就是龙卷风？"小气流说道，"我告诉你们，我刚刚碰到了一些大树！"他马上转了转，看看谁在听他说话。在龙卷风里，转圈是件很愚蠢的事情。

"别动，跟紧我们！"一股大气流喊道。

"啊。等等我！"小气流大喊，"等——等——我，我跟不上啦！"

小气流飞快地越过小山，跨过河流，又刚好飞进一座美丽城市的街道，此时他距离其他的气流越来越远，眼望着龙卷风如往常一样，凶猛地进攻，而他的兄弟们也在卖力舞动，仿佛很清楚自己在做什么。

而小气流稀里糊涂的，不知道自己要做什么，于是他盘旋于两栋高楼之间，飞过两旁都是高楼的街道，经过一个公园，越过一堵墙，最后来到了一条有人住着的路上，人们刚刚起床，有些人正要出门。

现在，小气流已经很弱小了，他只能吹飞一顶帽子。小气流把路人的帽子往前吹，路人在后面追，一直追到一间大房子前，门前有几棵树，小气流转了个弯，用尽全身的力气飞过树顶，发现自己只能让树叶发出"沙沙"声，但他依然很高兴。

小气流还没有意识到自己现在是什么，他闯入一扇打开的窗户里，轻轻扇动窗帘，悄悄滑入房间，发现床上有个婴儿，安静地睡着，突然打了个喷嚏。

"有点吵。"一个女人说道，"快去给他盖上被子，风有点大。"

"想想看呐。"曾是龙卷风的一部分的小气流叹息道，"如今，我只能让婴儿打个喷嚏。"

（杰西·林奇·威廉姆斯）

✿ 作者介绍

杰西·林奇·威廉姆斯出生于斯特灵，毕业于普林斯顿大学。他撰写了《新生奇遇记》和普林斯顿大学的历史。他的短篇故事收录在《偷来的故事》一书中。

The Loyal Knight

Some centuries ago two kings were contending for the crown of Castile. We forget their names for the present; but to make easy the telling of my story, we shall call one Alfonso and the other John. Alfonso proclaimed, of course, that John was a usurper and a rebel, and John returned the compliment.

Well, John at last defeated his rival, horse and foot, and carried everything triumphantly before him, with the exception of a single fawn. This town had been intrusted by Alfonso to a stout old knight called Aguilar, and after a long siege, still remained unconquered.

"You have done enough for honor," said King John one day to the knight, "surrender, and you shall have the most liberal terms."

"If you had read the history of your country," answered Aguilar, "you would have known that none of my race ever surrendered."

"I will starve you, proud and obstinate fool."

"Starve an eagle if you can."

"I will put you and the whole garrison to the sword."

"Try," was the laconic reply, and the siege went on.

One morning, as the rising sun was beginning to gild with its rays the highest towers of the city, a parley sounded from the camp of the enemy. The old knight appeared on the wall, and looked down on the king below. "Surrender," said John again. "My rival, Alfonso, is dead, and the whole of Castile recognizes my sway as that of its legitimate sovereign."

"Sire, I believe you, but I must see my dead master."

"Go, then, to Seville, where his body lies. You have my royal word that I shall attempt nothing against you on your way; nor against the city in your absence."

The knight came out with banner flying, and a small escort of grim-visaged warriors. Behind him the gates closed; before him the dense battalions of the enemy opened their ranks. As he passed along, slowly riding his noble war-horse, shouts of admiration burst wide and far from the whole host that had so often witnessed his deeds of valor, and the echoes of the loud and enthusiastic greeting accompanied him until the red plume that waved in his helmet was out of sight.

He arrived at Seville, and went straight to the Cathedral, where he found the tomb of his former sovereign. He had it opened, and gazing awhile with moist eyes at the pale face that met his look, he thus addressed the dead monarch, "Sire, I had sworn never to deliver to anybody but yourself the keys of the town, which you had intrusted to my care. Here they are. I have kept my oath." And he deposited them on the breast of King Alfonso. Then, bestriding his good steed, he galloped back to his post.

As soon as he approached, the ranks of the enemy again opened, and King John confronted him. "Well," said the king, "are you satisfied, and do you now give up the contest?"

"Yes, Sire."

"Where are the keys to the town?"

"On Icing Alfonso's breast. Go and get them. We meet no more."

"We shall never part!" exclaimed the king. "Get the keys back yourself and remain in command of the town in my name." The followers of the king murmured, and complained of his rewarding a rebel. "He is no longer one," said King John, "such rebels, when won, become the best subjects."

(Charles A. Gayarr)

译文

忠实的骑士

几个世纪以前,两位国王正在争夺卡斯提尔的王位。虽然我们早已叫不出他们的名字,但是为了把这个故事讲出来,我们称其中一位国王为阿方索,另一位国王为约翰。当然,在他们眼里,对方都在谋朝篡位,是个叛乱分子。

最终，约翰打败了他的对手，缴获了马匹和士兵，征服了一切，但唯独没有征服阿方索的一位忠臣。他就是阿奎勒，一位英勇的老骑士，曾受命于阿方索国王，统治着这座小镇。尽管小镇长期饱受炮火，但仍然未被攻下。

"你已经维护了自己的荣誉，"一天，约翰王对那位骑士说道，"投降吧！你将获得最自由的生活。"

"如果你了解我们国家的历史，"阿奎勒回答道，"你就知道，我们这个民族没有投降的传统。"

"那我就饿死你，你这个自负、固执的傻瓜。"

"那你就尽管试试能不能饿死一只老鹰吧。"

"我会杀掉你和你的部下。"

"那就试一试吧。"阿奎勒简短有力地回答道。于是，小镇的战火再次燃起。

一天清晨，太阳升起，阳光洒在城市里最高的塔上，从敌方的军营传来会谈的消息。于是老骑士来到塔墙边，低头看着约翰王。"投降吧，"约翰王再次说道，"我的对手阿方索已经死了，而且整个卡斯提尔王国已经接受了我的统治，我才是卡斯提尔的合法君主。"

"陛下，我相信你的话。可是，我一定要见到我们已故的国王。"

"那就去塞维利亚吧，他的遗体在那儿。我向你保证，在你不在的时候，对于你所统治的小镇，我不会打任何歪主意。"

这位骑士就带着飞舞的旗帜出发了，身边还有一个小型护卫队，每个战士都面色冷峻。骑士身后的大门关上了，在他面前，敌人的士兵一字排开，声势浩大。骑士骑着高贵的战马，缓缓地从中间经过，四面八方传来鼓舞士气的呐喊，这些士兵见证了他的丰功伟绩，在他走出人们的视线之前，人们一直热情地问候他，回音缭绕。

他来到了塞维利亚，直奔大教堂，国王的坟墓就在那儿。他打开门，面色苍白，眼里泛着泪光，注视着坟墓，开始致悼念词："陛下，除了你，我从未向别人发过誓。我曾发誓，会保住你托付给我的小镇，现在我守住了，履行了我的承诺。"他把城门的钥匙放在了阿方索王的胸上，快速地跨上他的爱马，一路赶回小镇。

阿奎勒抵达小镇的时候，敌人再次罗兵布阵，约翰王出现在他面前，说道："那么，你现在满足了吗？你投降吗？"

"我投降，陛下。"

"城门的钥匙在哪儿？"

"在阿方索王的胸膛上。去拿回来吧。我们以后别再见面了。"

"你以后就留在我这儿吧！"约翰王喊道，"你自己去拿回钥匙，但这座城以后就归我所有了。"国王的手下开始窃窃私语，为约翰王嘉奖了一个叛徒而愤愤不平。"他不再是这样一个反叛者，"约翰王说，"一旦我们赢得了这样的叛徒，他们就会成为最好的帮手。"

（查尔斯·加亚雷）

✐ 作者介绍

查尔斯·加亚雷出生于美国路易斯安那州，是一位诗人。查尔斯曾在费城的法院工作，他25岁时成了一名律师，在新奥尔良工作。查尔斯曾担任过许多公职，还撰写了路易斯安那州的历史。

Chapter 2
Nature Scene | 自然风光

The Great Pyramid

The first glimpse that most travelers now get of the Pyramids is from the window of the railway carriage as they come from Alexandria; and it is not impressive. (It does not take one's breath away.) The well-known triangular forms look small and shadowy, and are too familiar to be in any way startling. It is only in approaching them, and observing how they grow with every foot of the road, that one begins to feel that they are not so familiar after all.

When at last the edge of the desert is reached, and the long sand-slope climbed, and the rocky platform gained, and the Great Pyramid in all its unexpected bulk and majesty towers close above one's head, the effect is as sudden as it is overwhelming. It shuts out the sky and the horizon. It shuts out all the other pyramids. It shuts out everything but the sense of awe and wonder.

Now, too, one discovers that it was with the forms of the Pyramids, and only their forms, that one had been acquainted all these years past. Of their surface, their color, their relative position, their number, one had hitherto no definite idea.

Even the Great Pyramid puzzles us with an unexpected sense of unlikeness. We all know that it was stripped of its outer blocks some five hundred years ago to build Arab mosques and palaces. Nevertheless, the rugged, rock-like aspect of that giant stair-case takes us by surprise. Nor does it look like a partial ruin. It looks as though it had been left unfinished, and the workmen might be coming back tomorrow.

The color again is a surprise. Few persons can be aware beforehand of the rich tawny hue that Egyptian limestone assumes after ages of exposure to the blaze of an Egyptian sky. Seen in certain lights, the Pyramids look like piles of massy gold.

It is no easy task to realize, however imperfectly, the duration of six or seven thousand years. The Great Pyramid, which is supposed to have been some four thousand two hundred and odd years old at the time of the birth of Christ, is now in its seventh millennium. Suddenly the writer became aware, that these remote dates had never presented themselves to her mind until this moment as anything but abstract numerals.

Now, for the first time, they were no longer figures, but years with their changes of season, their high and low Niles, their seed-times and harvests. More impressive by far than any array of figures or comparisons, was the shadow cast by the Great Pyramid as the sun went down.

The mighty shadow, sharp and distinct, stretched across the stony platform of the desert and over full three-quarters of a mile of the green plain below. It divided the sunlight in the upper air; and it darkened the space that it covered like an eclipse.

It was not without a thrill of something approaching to awe, that one remembered how this self-same shadow had gone on registering, not only the height of the most stupendous gnomon over set up by human hands, but the slow passage, day by day, of more than sixty centuries of the world's history.

It was still lengthening over the landscape as we went down the long sand-slope and gained the carriage. Some six or eight Arabs in fluttering white garments ran on ahead to bid us a last good-by. "You come again!" said they. "Good Arab show you everything. You see nothing this time."

(Amelia B. Edwards)

译文

宏伟的金字塔

大多数游客看到金字塔的第一眼，都是透过从埃及的亚历山大港开来的客车的车厢窗户，而且第一眼也并不令人印象深刻（没有那种令人窒息的震撼）。这个著名的四棱锥其实看起来很小，而且很暗淡，人们对它实在是太熟悉了，熟悉到无论何种方式出现都无法给人以惊喜。只有在靠近这些建筑物，仔细观察它们是如何靠支脚拔地而起时，人们才会开始觉得它们并不是如此的熟悉。

当抵达沙漠的边缘，爬过长长的沙丘，登上岩石做的平台，我们也就终于来到一座大金字塔下了。在我们上方，金字塔大得出人意料，雄伟得让人惊叹。一种奇妙的感觉油然而生，势不可挡地将我们浸没。它的身躯遮天蔽日，地平线被它遮挡在外，其他所有的金字塔也被它遮挡在外，天地间的一切都被它遮挡在外，唯留下敬畏和惊叹之情。

即使是在现在，一个人要是想了解金字塔的外形，都要花费很多年的时间。与金字塔的表面、金字塔的颜色、金字塔的相对位置以及数量有关的问题，至今仍未有定论。

哪怕金字塔以一种意想不到的异样感觉困扰着我们，我们都知道它的外层部分曾在五百年前被剥下来，拿去做成阿拉伯的清真寺和宫殿。然而，巨大的台阶上崎岖而状若磐石的那面仍使我们感到意外；它看上去一点也不残缺，它看起来更像是尚未完工，工人们可能明天就会回来。

它的颜色也十分惊艳。几乎无人能事先知晓，在埃及烈焰般的天空下，被炙烤数年后的埃及石灰石会呈现出如此丰富的黄褐色调。在某种光线的照耀下，这些金字塔看上去就像成堆的巨大的黄金。

虽然金字塔并不是十全十美，但持续存在六七千年并不是件容易事。大金字塔，在耶稣降世之时，就已经有四千两百多岁了，而现在它已经有七千个年头了。笔者也才突然意识到，这些久远的年代从未在自己的脑海中展现过，直到这一刻才真切感受到那些抽象的数字之外的含义。

此刻，它们第一次不再是些数字，而是年月里它们季节的变换，是它们的伟岸和尼罗河的暗涌，是它们的发展和成熟。比数据的排列和对比更加令人印象深刻的，是日落时大金字塔投下的阴影。

那巨大的阴影，锋利而清晰，延展出去，穿过沙漠满是石头的平台，遮盖住底下整整一千二百米的绿色平原。它将高空的阳光切开，然后如同日食一般，把它所覆盖到的那片空间投入黑暗之中。

当一个人想到正是这个阴影，不仅以人类所建造的最庞大的日晷高度，还以超过六十个世纪的日复一日的漫长经历载入世界的史册时，人们不会没有一种接近敬畏的兴奋感。

当我们走下长长的沙坡坐上客车时，阴影还在景色里延伸。大概六或八个阿拉伯人衣着翻飞振抖的白色长袍，跑在前面向我们致以最后的告别。

"你们还要再来啊！"他们说，"好让阿拉伯人带你们见识一番。你们这次根本没看到什么东西。"

（阿梅莉亚·B. 爱德华兹）

✍ 作者介绍

阿梅莉亚·B. 爱德华兹是一位英国作家和旅行家。她写过很多小说，还写过一些历史故事和儿童类畅销书。她的书《逆尼罗河1000公里》被认为是一部极为显著的讲述埃及的书籍，本文就是节选自此书。

Dog-Sleighing in the North

Winter-travel in Kamchatka is done entirely upon dog-sledges. In no other pursuit do the people of that country spend more time or show their native skill to better advantage.

There is probably no more hardy animal in the world than their dog. You may compel him to sleep out on the snow in the coldest weather; you may drive him with heavy loads until his feet crack open and print the snow with blood; you may starve him until he eats up his harness; but his strength and spirit alike seem unbroken.

I have driven a team of nine dogs more than a hundred miles in a day and a night. I have often worked them hard for forty-eight hours without being able to give them a bite of food. They are generally fed, once a day, a single dried fish, weighing a pound and a half or two pounds. This is given to them at night.

The sledge to which they are harnessed is about ten feet in length and two in width. It is made with seasoned birch timber, and combines strength and lightness.

The frame work of the sledge is fastened together with lashings of dried seal-skin, and is mounted on broad curved runners. No iron is used in making it, and it does not weigh more than twenty pounds; yet it will carry a load of four hundred pounds.

Under favorable circumstances eleven dogs will make from forty to fifty miles a day with a man and a load of four hundred pounds. They are harnessed to the sledge in couples by a long central thong of seal-skin. To this thong each dog is fastened by a collar and a short trace. They are guided and controlled entirely by the voice and by a dog called a leader, which is especially trained for the purpose.

The driver carries no whip. Instead, he has a stick about four feet in length and two inches in thickness. This is armed at one end with a long iron spike, and is used to check the speed of the sledge in going down hills. The stick may also be used to stop the dogs when they leave the road, as they frequently do to run after reindeer and foxes.

The art of driving a dog-team is one of the most deceptive in the world. The traveler imagines at first sight that driving a dog-sledge is just as easy as driving a horse-car. At the very first favorable chance he tries it.

After being run away with the first ten minutes, capsized into a snow-drift, and having his sledge dragged bottom upward a quarter of a mile from the road, the rash experimenter begins to see that the task is not quite so easy as he had supposed. In less than one day he is generally convinced, by hard experience, that a dog-driver, like a Poet, is born, not made.

I had watched every motion of my Korak driver. I thought that I had learned the manner of thrusting the spiked stick between the upright of the runners into the snow, to act as a brake. I had also committed to memory and practiced the hoarse cries that meant, in dog-language, "right" and "left", as well as many others that meant something else. I soon believed that I could drive as well as a Korak, if not better.

Seating myself firmly astride of the sledge back of the arch, I shouted to the dogs. My voice failed to produce the startling effect that I had hoped for. Then I hurled my spiked stick like a harpoon at the leader, intending to have it fall so that I could pick it up as the sledge passed. The dog, however, dodged it cleverly, and it rolled away ten feet from the road.

Just at that moment three or four wild reindeer bounded out from behind a little rise of ground three or four hundred yards away. They galloped across the plain toward a deep ravine, through which ran a branch of the river. The dogs, true to their wolfish nature, started in pursuit with fierce excited howls. I made a grasp at my spiked stick as we rushed past, but failed to reach it.

Away we went over the snow toward the ravine. Half the time the sledge was on one runner, and was rebounding from the hard drifts with a force that shook me terribly.

Without the spiked stick we were helpless, and in a moment we were left on the edge of the ravine. I shut my eyes, clung tightly to the arch, and took the plunge. The slope became suddenly steeper, and the leader swung to one side, bringing the sledge around like the lash of a whip, and shooting me through the air into a deep drift of snow at the bottom.

I must have fallen at least eighteen feet. I was entirely buried with the exception of my legs, which, above the snow, kicked a faint signal for rescue. Weighed down with heavy furs, I had hard work to pull myself out. As I at last crept out of the drift with three pints of snow down my neck, I saw the round face of my driver smiling at me through the bushes on the edge of the bluff.

"Oona," he hailed.

"Well," replied the snowy figure standing waist-high in the drift.

"Amerikanski nyett dobra kiour, eh?" (American no good driver).

"Nyett sofsem dobra (Not very good)," was the sorrowful reply as I waded out.

The sledge had become tangled in the bushes near me, and the dogs were all howling in chorus, nearly wild because they were stopped. I was so far satisfied with my experiment, that I did not desire to repeat it for a time. I, therefore, made no objection to the Korak's going back to his old position.

(George Kennan)

◇ 译文

北极的狗拉雪橇

堪察加冬季的交通完全靠狗拉雪橇来维持。那个国家的人不会在其他交通方式上花更多的时间，他们与生俱来的驾驭技巧全都用在这个方面了。

世界上可能没有什么动物比他们的狗更吃苦耐劳了。最冷的天气它也可以睡在外面的雪地里；它可以拉着负载沉重的雪橇，直到脚掌裂开，血染雪面；它还可以挨饿直到把身上的系带都吃光。它的力量和勇气都坚不可摧。

我曾经驾驶一辆九条狗拉的雪橇跑了一天一夜，路程超过一百六十千米。它们经常要连着艰苦工作四十八个小时，期间连一口食物都吃不到。通常来说，它们一天要在晚上进食一次，吃一条重六百克以上的干鱼。

它们拉着的雪橇大约三十多米长、六米多宽，由干燥的桦木木料制成，组装得既强韧又轻便。

雪橇的框架紧紧地用绳子——干燥的海豹皮制成的——系在一起，安装在宽阔的弧形转轮上面。雪橇的制造材料中并没有铁，因此非常轻，重量不超过九千克，却可以承担两百千克的重量。

在有利的环境条件下，十一条狗能一天拉着负重两百千克、载有一个成年男人的雪橇跑上六七十千米。一根长长的海豹皮皮带从中央将它们一对对系在雪橇上。每只狗都戴有一个通过短链条系在这条皮带上的项圈。领头狗一声令下，它们就俯首听命。人们会专门为此训练一条领头狗。

驾驶雪橇的人不用鞭子，而是用一根大约一米多长、五厘米粗的棍子，棍子的一端安装着一根长长的铁钉。这根棍子可以防止雪橇下山时滑得过快，也可以用来阻止拉雪橇的狗离开道路，因为它们经常会跑去追驯鹿和狐狸。

驾驭雪橇犬队是世界上最容易让人误解的一门技术。大凡第一眼看见驾驶雪橇的旅行者，总会把它想象得和驾驶一辆马车一样容易，一旦有机会，就想去尝试一番。

很可能刚刚跑了十分钟，他就会翻倒在一个大雪堆里，而他的雪橇则在四百米开外，翻了个底朝天。这时候，这个鲁莽的尝试者才明白，驾驶雪橇这个苦差事并不像他想的那么容易。通过这些艰辛的体验，不出一天他就会确信，驾驶雪橇就和写诗一样，是需要与生俱来的本事的，硬学可不行。

我曾经观察过我那位科里亚克（堪察加的土著人口）雪橇驾者的做法。我以为自己已经学会了怎样把装着长钉的棍子猛然插进轮子的立柱中间，让它起到刹车的作用。我还记住了表示"右边""左边"以及许多表示其他意思的嘶哑犬吠声，并不断进行练习。不久后，我就相信，就算我驾驶雪橇的功夫比不过一名科里亚克人，也起码可以和他们差不多了。

我两腿分开，稳稳跨坐在雪橇后部的拱形座位上，朝着拉雪橇的狗大叫了一声。可惜我的声音并没有产生预期的惊人效果，于是我只好把我的长钉棍子像一根鱼叉一样扔向那只领头的狗。本来我想让棍子摔在雪里，然后在雪橇经过的时候再把它捡起来。谁知那狗灵巧地避开了棍子，棍子也滚到了道路的两米开外。

就在这时，三四只野生驯鹿从两三百米以外的一小块高地后面跳了出来。

它们飞奔过平地，冲向一个深深的河沟，那里是一条河的支流。出于豺狼般的天性，雪橇狗开始追逐这些驯鹿，凶猛、兴奋的咆哮声响彻了整个雪原。这些狗拉着雪橇猛冲而过的时候，我试图去抓我的长钉棍子，但没能抓到。

我们越过雪地朝着沟壑进发。有一半时间，雪橇都只有一个轮子着地，雪橇在坚硬的雪地上不停颠簸，让我剧烈地摇晃起来。

失去了长钉棍子之后，我完全没法让雪橇的速度慢下来。很快，我们就冲到了沟壑的边缘。我闭上眼，紧紧扒住拱形座位，然后冲了下去。斜坡突然变得陡峭起来，领头狗转了个弯，奔向另一边。于是，雪橇像鞭子似的急速甩动起来，把我从空中甩进了谷底的一个雪堆里。

我至少是从五米多高的半空里摔下来的，整个人被埋进了雪里。除了两条腿还露在外面，挣扎着踢动着求救。我身上穿着厚重的皮衣，很难从雪里爬出来。等我最终带着脖子里灌满的三十多升的雪从雪堆里爬出来的时候，我看到陡坡边上的灌木丛里一张笑眯眯的圆脸，那是曾经帮我拉雪橇的人。

"嘿。"他打招呼说。

我站在齐腰深的雪堆里，身上到处是雪，回答说："嘿。"

"美国人不会拉雪橇。"

我一边艰难地走出雪堆，一边悲哀地回答："确实不怎样。"

雪橇在我旁边的灌木丛里乱成一团。雪橇狗们追不成驯鹿了，正在齐刷刷地吼叫，叫声堪称狂野。我对这次尝试非常满意，所以我一点都不想再重试一次了。于是，那位科里亚克的雪橇驾驶人提出由他来重操旧业，我一口就答应了。

（乔治·凯南）

✍ 作者介绍

乔治·凯南美国作家，演讲家。他曾经在俄罗斯帝国和东方游历，并创作了《西伯利亚和流放体制》和《在西伯利亚的帐篷生活和在堪察加的冒险》。本文选自后一本书，由世纪出版公司授权。

✎ 练习

写一写你学习做某事的经历，如滑冰、放风筝、骑马或驾马、烤蛋糕、做晚饭、划船。

为你的故事制订一个大纲。

比如，学习滑冰的大纲是这样的：
我家不靠水。
冬季去拜访住在湖边的朋友。
和滑冰滑得好的男生或是女生见面。
滑冰看起来能带来的愉悦。
我的学习计划。
开始的经历：a 幸运；b 不幸。
后来的经历。
学会滑冰的好处。

A Departure from Cairo

"The camels are ready——"

"Yes, commander, and so are the Howadji."

The sun was nearing the pyramids, and doubly beautiful in the afternoon, "the delight of the imagination" lay silent before, compelling our admiration. I lingered and lingered upon the little balcony. "Ha-ha", said the donkey-boys beneath, and I leaned over and saw a company trotting along.

The camels lay under the trees, and a turbaned group, like the wise men at the manger, in old picture, awaited our departure with languid curiosity. The Pasha descended the stairs, and I followed him, just as the commander announced for the twelfth time——

"The camels are ready."

The camels lay patiently under the trees before the door, quietly ruminating. Our caravan consisted of seven, four of which had been loaded and sent forward with their drivers, and were to halt at a village beyond the city; the other three awaited the pleasure of the Howadji and the commander. It was time to mount, and the farewells must be spoken.

Addio! With the word trembling upon my tongue, and half looking back and muttering last words, I laid my left hand carelessly upon the back of the recumbent camel to throw myself leisurely into the seat.

I had seen camels constantly for two months, and had condemned them as the slowest and most conceited of brutes. I had supposed an elephantine languor in every motion, and had anticipated a luxurious cradling over the desert in their rocking gait, for to the outward eye their movement is imaged by the lazy swell of summer waves.

The saddle is a wooden frame, with a small upright stake, both in front and behind. Between these stakes, and upon the frame, are laid the blankets, carpets, and other woolen conveniences for riding. Over all is thrown the brilliant Persian rug.

The true method of mounting is to grasp the stakes in each hand,

and to swing yourself rapidly and suddenly into the seat, while the camel driver——if you are luxurious and timid——holds his foot upon the bent fore-knee of the camel. Once in the seat you must cling closely, through the three convulsive spasms of rising and righting, two of which jerk you violently forward and one backward.

This is a very simple mystery. But I was ignorant, and did not observe that no camel driver was at the head of my beast. In fact, I observed only that the great blue cotton umbrella, covered with white cloth, and the two water jugs dangling from the rear stake of my saddle, were an amusing combination of luxury and necessity.

Ready to mount, I laid my hand as carelessly and leisurely upon the front stake as if my camel had been a cow. But scarcely had my right foot left the earth on its meditative way to the other side of the saddle, when the camel snorted, threw back his head, and sprang up nimbly as a colt.

I, meanwhile, was left dangling with the blue cotton umbrella, and the water jugs at the side, several feet from the ground. I made a grasp at the rear stake, but I clutched only the luxuries, and down we fell, Howadji, pocket-pistols, umbrella, and water jugs in a confused heap. The good commander arrived at the scene, and swore fiercely at the Arabs. Then very blandly, he instructed me in the mystery of camel-climbing, and in a few minutes we were on the way to Jerusalem.

With the first swing of the camel, Egypt and the Nile began to recede. With this shuttle the desert was to be woven into the web of my life. We passed through the outskirts of the city. The streets were narrow and dirty as we approached the gate, although they wound under beautiful lattices, and palms drooped over the roofs.

Superior to the scene, we rode upon our lofty camels. They swayed gently along, and occasionally swung their heads and long necks awkwardly aside to peer through the lattices. The odd silence and sadness, whose spell I had constantly felt in Cairo, brooded over "the superb town, the holy city" to the last. As we passed out of the gate into the desert, no hope called after us.

As we advanced, we saw more plainly the blank sand that overspread the earth, from us to the eastern horizon. Out of its illimitable reaches paced strings of camels, with swarthy Arabs. Single horsemen, and parties upon donkeys ambled quietly by. Our path lay northward along the line where the greenness of the Nile-valley blends with the desert. There was a little scant shrubbery upon the sides of the way——groves of mimosa, through which stretched the light sand, almost like a road.

As the sun set, I turned upon my camel, and saw Grand Cairo for the last time. The evening darkened, and we paced along in perfect silence. The stars shone with the crisp brilliancy of our January nights, but the air was balmy, veined occasionally with a streak of strange warmth, which I knew was the breath of the desert.

The Arabs that had gone forward with the pack camels were to encamp just beyond a little town which we entered after dark. It was a collection of mud hovels, and we reflected with satisfaction upon the accommodation of our new tent, and the refreshing repose it promised. A few steps beyond the town brought us to the white-domed tomb of a sheik, just on the edge of the desert, and there the camping-ground was chosen.

In a few minutes our desert palace was built. The riding camels were then led up, and made to kneel while the carpets, blankets, and matting were removed from the saddle. We laid the matting on the sand, spread over it a coarse, thick carpeting, and covered the whole with two Persian rugs. The traveling-bags were then thrown in, and we commenced Arabian housekeeping.

(George William Curtis)

译文

从开罗出发的旅程

"骆驼已经准备好了——"
"是，长官。夏瓦吉也已准备就绪。"

太阳已下落到金字塔旁,为这下午增添了一份双重的美丽,让我们不由得赞美那静静躺在眼前的"如同想象般的美好"。我在小露台上踱来踱去,听到下面有个赶驴人叫一声"哈,哈",靠过去一看,发现有一群骆驼正快步走来。

骆驼们在树下躺下了,有一队戴着头巾的人看上去就跟那古老的图画中所画的马槽旁的智者一样。他们满脸倦意又心怀好奇地等待着我们出发。我跟着帕夏走下楼去,此时长官第十二次喊道:

"骆驼已经准备好了。"

骆驼们在门前的大树下耐心地躺着,安静地咀嚼食物。我们的队伍由七头骆驼组成,其中四头已经装载完毕和赶驼人一起出发了,他们将在城市外的一个乡村等候着。其余三头则等待着夏瓦吉和长官觉得合适时起程。出发的时刻到了,必须说再见了。

"再见了!"我颤悠悠地喊出了这个词,说到一半时回头看了一眼,然后低声喃喃完余下的话。我左手不经意地搭在躺着的骆驼的背上,打算轻松地坐进椅子中。

我已经看了两个月的骆驼,我觉得它们是世界上最慢而且最自大的动物。我觉得那每一个动作都显得笨重沉闷,并期待着在它们摇摆的步伐中进行一次奢侈的跨越沙漠的摇篮之旅。在外人的眼里,他们的行进就像那夏日中慵懒的浪潮。

鞍子是一个木制的框架,它的前后各有一个直立的小木桩。这俩木桩间的架子上面铺着被毯、地毯和其他便于骑乘的羊毛制品。最上面还放了一块很棒的波斯毛毯。

如果你出身高贵且胆小如鼠,骑上骆驼的要诀是:当赶驼人把脚踩在骆驼那弯曲的前膝时,你要两手各抓住一根木桩,然后迅速摆动,一下子坐进座位。一旦你坐上了座位就必须抓紧了,在接下来骆驼起身站直的过程中,会有三次剧烈的抖动,其中两次会猛烈地把你推向前方,另一次向后。

诀窍其实很简单,但我对此一无所知,也没有注意到我骆驼的前头并没有赶驼人。实际上,我只看到了那盖有白布的、巨大的蓝棉布伞,还有荡在鞍子后柱上的两个水壶,它们真是奢侈品和必需品的奇妙组合。

准备骑上骆驼时,我悠然地一手搭在前立柱上,把骆驼当成了一头奶牛。当我的右脚刚离开地面,还迟疑着没有来得及跨到鞍子另一边去时,骆驼"哼"了一声转过头去，像一匹小马驹那样敏捷地站起身来。

此时，我便同蓝布伞和水罐一样被悬在了骆驼身体的一边，离地有几米高。我设法抓上了鞍子的后桩，但只够到了奢侈品而已。随后，夏瓦吉、小手枪、伞和水壶便一起乱糟糟地掉了一地。好心的长官赶了过来，狠狠地骂了那群阿拉伯人一顿。然后非常和善地教会我爬上骆驼的诀窍，几分钟后我们就踏上了去耶路撒冷的旅途了。

随着骆驼摇摆的步伐，埃及和尼罗河随之渐渐向后退去，这片沙漠也随着这"梭子"织入了我的生活之网。我们穿过了城市的市郊，一路走向大门。棕榈叶从路边的屋顶垂落下来，大街在漂亮的格子窗间蜿蜒伸向前方，但还是显得又窄又脏。

我们骑着高大的骆驼，凌驾于这景象之上。骆驼们轻柔地摇摆前行，偶尔会笨拙地把头和长脖子转向一边，凝视着格子窗的那一头。我在开罗经常感受到的那种独特的寂静与忧伤一直到最后都弥漫在这个"华美圣城"之中。一旦我们穿过大门进入沙漠，就没有什么可期盼的了。

随着不断前行，我们可以明显地看到土地上铺满了漫漫黄沙，从我们所在之地一直延伸到东方的地平线。除了那无边无际的沙土就是一条条穿行其间的骆驼长队，还有那黑黝黝的阿拉伯人。单个的骑马人，以及一伙骑着驴子的旅人安静地走过。尼罗河谷的绿意同沙漠渐渐融合起来，我们正沿着这一线向北行进。路边有些许的灌木，那是小丛的含羞草，轻沙随着它们延展开来，几乎成了一条路。

太阳落山了，我在骆驼上转过身来最后看了一眼那伟大的开罗。天色暗了下来，我们悄无声息地向前走着。星星在一月的夜空中清亮地闪烁着，但空气还很温暖，偶尔会有一丝奇怪的暖意穿过，我明白这就是沙漠的气息。

我们在天黑后来到了一个小镇，和驮着行李的骆驼一起走在前头的阿拉伯人正在那里准备安营。这是一些小泥屋，我们对于新帐篷内的住处表示满意，期待着此处的休息能让我们恢复体力。在小镇上走不多远处有一个白色半球形的酋长坟墓，它正好处在沙漠的边缘，而露营的地点也选在了这里。

几分钟内我们在沙漠中的官殿就完成了，骑乘的骆驼被带过来跪坐下来，地毯、被毯和垫子从鞍子上被拿了下来。我们把垫子放在沙土上，铺上一块粗糙的厚地毯，然后在最上面放了两块波斯毛毯。把旅行包扔在上面后，我们便开始了阿拉伯式的家务劳作。

作者介绍

乔治·威廉·柯蒂斯出生于罗得岛州的普罗维登斯。他曾经作为一名社论作者为纽约《论坛报》工作过,后来成了《哈珀杂志》的一名编辑。他关于外国旅行的作品不但有趣,还很有教育意义。这里的故事选自他的书籍《夏瓦吉在叙利亚》。他还写了《夏瓦吉的尼罗河记》(夏瓦吉这个词被阿拉伯人用来称呼欧洲游客)。他的作品《我与普鲁》也很有名,深受大家喜爱。

练习

1. 重新阅读《西伯利亚的狗拉雪橇》,相比之下谁的任务更艰难?是试图驾驭一群狗的凯南先生,还是打算爬上骆驼的柯蒂斯先生?

2. 对下列动物之一进行描述:骆驼、大象、水獭、熊、狼、鲸鱼、鲨鱼、海豹、鲑鱼、河狸、短吻鳄、虎。
1)在哪里可以找到这种动物?
2)它有着怎样的高度、长度、重量、形状和颜色?
3)它的习惯是怎样的?住在什么样的地方?它吃什么?如何捕食?怕什么动物?
4)它有什么用?能训练它干活吗?如何捕获它?

3. 讲一个关于上述动物的小故事。
描述一种熟悉的动物,比如马、奶牛、绵羊、松鼠、山羊、猪、兔子、猫、狗。

Tharald's Otter

♢ 预习

amazing /əˈmeɪzɪŋ/ 令人惊异的
desperate /ˈdespərət/ 绝望的
inquisitive /ɪnˈkwɪzətɪv/ 好奇的
nimble /ˈnɪmbl/ 机敏的
peer /pɪr/ 同等的人
supple /ˈsʌpl/ 易于弯曲的
trait /treɪt/ 特殊的品质
vainly /ˈveɪnli/ 徒劳地
wake /weɪk/ 醒来

  You would scarcely think that an otter could be a pleasant companion. Strange as it may seem, this one, whose name was Mons, improved greatly as soon as he got into civilized society.

  He was scarcely six inches long when Tharald caught him. But he was so sleek and nimble and glossy, that it was a delight to handle him. His fur was of a dark brown, and when it was wet, it looked black. It was so thick that you could not, even by pulling the hair apart, get the slightest glimpse of the skin.

  But the most remarkable things about Mons were the webs he had between his toes, and his long glossy whiskers. Of the latter he was proud, and would allow no one to touch them.

  As the strongest trait of character, this otter was very inquisitive.

Again and again he explored the flour barrel, and came out as white as a miller. Once he put his nose into an inkstand, and in drawing it out, poured the contents over his head.

In the part of Norway where Tharald's father lived, the people earned some of their money by salmon-fishing. Some who had no land made their living by fishing and shooting.

Every spring the salmon came from the sea into the rivers to lay their eggs. You could see their young darting over the pebbles in the stream, followed by big fish that wanted to eat them. The perch and the trout grew fat, and the pike and the pickerel made royal meals out of the perch and trout.

It was during this season that Tharald one day walked down to the lake to try his luck with a fly. Mons, who was now a year old, was sitting on Tharald's shoulder. The otter was so fond of his master that he followed him like a dog.

"Mons," said Tharald, after having vainly thrown the fly dozen times into the river, "I think that this is a poor day for fishing. What do you think?"

At that very instant a big six-pound salmon-trout leaped for the fly. The line flew with a hum from the reel, and Tharald braced himself to "play" the fish, until he could land it. The trout sprang out of the water, and his beautiful spotted sides gleamed in the sun.

That was a sight for Mons! Before his master could prevent him, he plunged from his shoulder into the lake, and shot through the clear tide like a black arrow. The trout saw him coming, and made a desperate leap! The line snapped; the trout was free!

Free! It was delightful to see Mons' supple body as it glided through the water, bending upward, downward, sideward, with amazing swiftness and ease. His two big eyes, so near the tip of his nose that he could see in every direction with scarcely a turn of his head, peered through the tide, keeping ever in the wake of the fleeing fish.

Finally, by a brisk turn, the otter plunged his teeth into the trout's neck, and brought him to land. You need not be told that Tharald made a hero of Mons. He hugged him and patted him and called him pet names, until Mons grew quite bashful. But this event gave Tharald an idea. He determined to train the otter as a salmon-fisher.

When Mons was two years old, he landed his first salmon. Soon he had a second and a third. Tharald felt like a rich man that day, as he carried home in his basket three silvery beauties, worth a dollar and a half apiece. He made haste to dispose of them to an English yachtsman, and went home, dreaming of "gold and forests green," as the Norwegians say.

"Now, Mons," he said to his friend, "if we do as well every day as we have done to-day, we shall soon be rich enough to go to school. What do you think of that Mons?"

(Boyesen H. Hjalmar)

译文

哈拉尔德的水獭

你不会想到一只海獭能成为令人愉快的伙伴。虽然这有点不可思议，但这只名字叫作蒙斯的海獭在人类文明社会里进步得很快。

哈拉尔德抓住他的时候，他只有十五厘米长。他长得圆头圆脑，身形敏捷，皮毛光滑，摸起来很舒服。他有一身深棕色皮毛，但被水湿透后看起来像是黑色的。他的皮毛非常厚，即使你拨开毛发也看不见底下的皮肤。

但蒙斯最引人注目的地方，还是他脚趾间的蹼和那充满光泽的长长细须。他很为自己的细须感到自豪，不让任何人碰他们一下。

这只海獭最突出的性格就是好奇。他一而再、再而三地钻到面粉桶中探险，出来的时候裹了一身白面粉，像个磨坊主。还有一次，他把鼻子伸进了墨水瓶，出来的时候把整瓶墨水都倒在了自己头上。

哈拉尔德的父亲生活在挪威，那里的人们依靠捕捉鲑鱼补贴家用。一些没有土地的人则完全依靠捕鱼和打猎为生。

每年春天，三文鱼从海洋里游到河里产卵。你会看见小三文鱼在小溪的卵石间横冲直撞，大鱼在后面追着，想要吃掉他们。鲈鱼和鳟鱼长肥时，狗鱼和梭子鱼就有豪华大餐可吃了。

在这个季节，有一天，哈拉尔德步行到了湖边，打算用一只苍蝇碰碰运气，看能不能钓到鱼。一岁大的蒙斯坐在哈拉尔德的肩膀上，他非常喜爱他的主人，像一只小狗一样到哪儿都跟着他。

投了十几次苍蝇之后，哈拉尔德一无所获。他说："蒙斯，我想今天不适合钓鱼。你觉得呢？"

就在此时，一条三千克重的大三文鱼跃出水面咬住了苍蝇。随着一声绕线轮的"嗡嗡"声，钓线飞舞了起来。哈拉尔德已经做好准备，他打算把鱼钓到手之前，好好玩一玩。鲑鱼跳出了水面，布满斑点的美丽侧身在阳光下闪着光芒。

蒙斯看到了这种景象！他的主人还没来得及阻止，他就从他的肩膀上一个猛子扎进了湖里，像一支黑色的箭般穿过清澈的水流。鲑鱼看见了他，孤注一掷地跳了起来。钓线断了，鱼儿逃走了！

自由自在！蒙斯灵活的身体在水里滑行，上下左右摆动着，敏捷又轻松，让人看着倍感愉悦。他的两只大眼睛紧靠着鼻子尖，几乎不用转头就能看见每一个方向。蒙斯紧盯着水流，追踪着那条消失的鱼，等待他再度出现。

最终，蒙斯轻快地转了个身，用牙齿咬住鲑鱼，把他叼上了陆地。显而易见，哈拉尔德给予蒙斯英雄般的待遇。他拥抱他，爱抚他，叫他的昵称，把蒙斯搞得害羞起来。这件事让哈拉尔德想到了一个主意，他决定训练海獭成为一个鲑鱼捕手。

蒙斯两岁的时候，他逮到了第一条鲑鱼，接着很快逮到了第二条和第三条。那天，哈拉尔德的篮子里装着三条银白的漂亮的鱼儿，每一条都值一美元五十美分。在回家的路上，他感觉自己就像个有钱人。他急匆匆地把这些鱼儿卖给了一个驾着游艇的英国人，然后带着挪威人那种"金子满地绿树成荫"的梦想回家了。

他对他的朋友说："蒙斯，如果我们每天都干得像今天一样好，我们很快就能有钱去上学了。你觉得怎么样？"

（博伊森·H. 哈尔马）

✍ 作者介绍

博伊森·H. 哈尔马出生于挪威，年仅二十一岁时来到美国。他在康奈尔大学担任了六年德文教授，之后成了哥伦比亚大学的教师。他创作小说、诗歌、散文和论文。他最有名的作品是《北欧生命的传说：贡纳》《一个北欧人的朝圣之旅》和《挪威的田园诗》。本文选自《现代维京人》，由查尔斯·斯克里布纳出版公司授权。

A Pair of Eagles

In a thick damp wood near a lake in Levy County, Florida, stands a tall pine tree, which for fifteen years has held a nest of the bald eagle. For ninety-one feet the great pine raises its slender trunk without a branch. Thirty feet higher is the nest in the main fork of the tree, which here sends out three limbs.

The nest is a large one. Year after year it has been used, and the birds each season, in repairing it, have added material until it has become more than four feet in thickness. In width it is likewise about four feet. Some of the sticks used extend outward at the sides, making the diameter of the nest fully six feet.

The materials of the nest are largely dead twigs and small pine branches. Some are only a few inches in length, while others are two feet long. The structure is slightly basin-shaped on top, and the depression in the center is about four inches deep. This is lined with dry moss.

These shrewd old eagles have long been a terror to the wild ducks that gather in winter on the neighboring lake, and a source of continual annoyance to the sheep raisers of the surrounding country. Their careers would long ago have been cut short if the plans of any of the numerous hunting expeditions against them had been successfully carried out.

Poison has been repeatedly set, and scores of rifle balls have sung their way through the forest, or across the lake, to strike out the lives of these troublesome enemies. But the bald eagles have lived on unharmed.

Exasperated at the number of lambs carried out of his pasture one year by these birds, the owner vowed that he would never know happiness again until he had killed at least one of the robbers. No opportunity came to him that summer for carrying out his threat.

Desiring to examine the nest more closely than could be done with an opera glass, I determined to climb the tree. This I accomplished on January twentieth. Taking a narrow board three feet long, I nailed it crosswise to the tree about five feet from the ground.

Clambering up this board by the aid of climbing irons strapped to my feet, I stood and nailed another cleat in like manner five feet above the first. A rope thrown over one shoulder and tied around the tree aided me in holding my position as I nailed.

The strips of wood were drawn up with a cord as they were used, my companion on the ground setting the nails in each beforehand. By this slow method I reached the nest at the end of an hour and a half.

Above my head was a cart load of sticks and rotting twigs which had yet to be passed. In order to climb up one of the large limbs against which the nest rested, I was obliged to tear away several armfuls of the materials.

At length I raised my head above the level of the nest and beheld two eaglets lying flat upon their breasts. They were about the size of half-grown chickens, and had bodies covered with whitish down. They offered no resistance to my handling, and uttered only a low whistling cry.

Soon after I began the ascent the old birds appeared. As long as I remained in the tree, they continued to soar anxiously about, at a safe distance, uttering occasionally a high-pitched scream.

Only once was there any appearance of an attack from them. The larger one, which I thus judged to be the female, while flying at a distance of perhaps one hundred yards, and at an equal elevation with myself, suddenly changed her course, and came at me straight as an arrow. With raised hatchet I awaited the assault, but when within thirty feet her courage failed, and she turned sharply to one side and passed on.

I had hoped to find eggs, and determined to be at the nest on time for this another season. The next year the weather was stormy, and I was delayed until the fourteenth of the same month. The nest was again found to contain young. This time they were larger than those of the previous year. From tip to tip of wings they measured three and on half feet.

The feathers of the adult bird are dark brown, except the head, neck, and tail, which are white. On account of the white appearance of the head, so different from the back and wings, the bird might be thought at a distance not to have any head feathers. Hence, possibly, came the name by which it is usually known——the bald eagle. This white part of the plumage does not come until the bird is over two years old.

An eagle's foot is especially adapted to seizing and holding its prey. The muscles of the legs are so arranged that when the weight of the body is thrown on the foot, the long sharp claws are driven deep, and once they close on a victim there is no escape.

In mountainous regions bald eagles often build their nests on cliffs. In many places they are more or less destructive to lambs and young pigs.

Where the supply of fish, grouse, squirrels, or other natural prey is plentiful, domestic animals are seldom disturbed. Only once have I witnessed such a capture. An eagle carried off before my eyes a grown hen from a neighbor's barnyard.

They are especially fond of fish. These they usually procure by swooping down and snatching them from the water in their talons. It is also well known that they sometimes rob the ospreys of the fish which they have caught. There is, therefore, little neighborly love between the eagles and fish hawks of a community.

(T. Gilbert Pearson)

译文

一对秃鹰

佛罗里达州的来维县里有一座湖，湖旁边是幽深而潮湿的森林，这里矗立着一棵高大的松树。秃鹰在树上筑了一个巢，已经有十四年了。这棵高大的松树，笔直的主干长达二三十米，没有一点多余的枝丫。再往上十几米，是秃鹰巢的所在，也就是在这里，主干开始分叉，长出了三根粗壮的枝干。

秃鹰的巢十分巨大。它们年复一年地在这里居住，每个季节都要加点材料，将它修补一番。久而久之，巢就厚达一米多，宽度几乎也有一米多。巢里的一些树枝从侧面伸了出来，这么一来，巢的直径简直就快有一米半了。

大量的枯枝和小根的松枝构成了秃鹰的巢,有的只有两厘米长,有的却能长达半米多。巢的顶部略呈盆形,中央约有一米多深,里面垫着干燥的苔藓。

每年冬天,野鸭会在森林旁的湖里聚集。狡猾的秃鹰们一直是它们可怕的天敌,周围地区的牧羊人也同样不堪其扰。从很久以前开始,就有不少人捕猎秃鹰,他们一旦得手,秃鹰的寿命就会戛然而止。

为了对付秃鹰这样棘手的宿敌,人们四处布下毒药;来福枪声时而在秃鹰飞过的森林里回响,时而在湖泊的上空飘荡。但是,秃鹰们始终安然无恙。

这一年里,秃鹰多次抓走了牧场里饲养的羊羔,这些损失让牧场主火冒三丈。他发誓一定要宰掉至少一只像秃鹰这样的抢劫犯,否则他会一直快快不乐。然而,一整个夏天过去了,他都没有机会下手。

我不再满足于用望远镜观察秃鹰的巢了,我渴望近距离接触这只秃鹰,于是我决定爬上那棵松树。一月二十日,我做到了。那天,我拿着一块半米多长的窄木板,在距离地面大约一米多高的地方,把这块木板横着楔入了松树的躯干里。

我在脚上捆上了攀爬用的鞋钉,借此爬上那块板子站着。又在往上一米多的地方,用同样的办法,把另一块木板楔了进去。我在肩膀上绕了一根绳子,把它套在树上,如此一来,我就能在楔板子的时候稳住身体。

我们会用绳子固定好木板。在我每次开始钉板子之前,树下的同伴也会准备好钉子。这种办法速度缓慢,一个半小时以后,鸟巢终于触手可及了。

那一大团枯枝败叶筑成的巢穴,就在我的头顶上方。我得先把身上和树套在一起的辅助工具拆掉,才能爬到鸟巢所在的巨大枝干上。

最后,我把头抬高,在巢穴上方俯瞰两只平躺在巢里的小鹰。它们大概有半成年的鸡那么大,身上披着白色的绒毛。它们毫无抵抗之力,任我抚摸,只能发出类似哨音的低鸣。

在我开始攀爬之后不久,成年的秃鹰就现身了。只要我还在树上,它们就保持着安全的距离一直在附近焦急地盘旋,偶尔还发出尖利的啸叫。

它们只有一次想要攻击我。那一只身形较大的鸟,估计是雌鸟,飞到和我齐平的高度,在距离我大概一百米的地方,突然就改变路线,像利箭一般径直朝我冲了过来。我举起手里的小斧头,等待着它的攻击。它却在离我三十多米之外泄了气，猛地转向飞走了。

　　我想找到秃鹰的蛋，下决心在明年这个季节再按时到巢里来。一年以后，还是在一月份，因常常有暴风雨，我就把计划推迟到了十四号。我发现，巢里的小鹰还在，个头比去年大了不少。它们张开翅膀的话，从左翼尖丈量到右翼尖，大概有三米多那么长。

　　成年秃鹰除了头部、颈部和尾部是白色之外，身上的羽毛都是深棕色的。小鹰要到两岁以后，头部、颈部和尾部的毛才会变成白色。秃鹰身子上和背上的毛色与头部的颜色相差太大，远远看去，可能会产生秃鹰的头部没有羽毛的错觉，"秃鹰"一名为大家熟知，大概就是这个原因吧。

　　秃鹰的脚特别适合抓捕猎物，当它把全身重量都压到脚上，腿上的肌肉就会收缩，这样它才能把又长又锋利的爪子深深地刺进猎物的肉里。一旦被它抓住，没有猎物可以逃出生天。

　　在深山里，秃鹰常常把巢筑在峭壁上。在其他地方，它们或多或少会对家养的仔猪和羔羊构成威胁。

　　但在鱼、松鸡、松鼠和其他野外猎物充足的地方，秃鹰很少会去捕食家养动物。我只亲眼看到过一次，一只鹰从我邻居的谷仓里抓走了一只母鸡。

　　秃鹰尤其喜欢捕食鱼类。捕鱼时，秃鹰向着水面俯冲下去，爪子随即紧紧地把鱼抓住。众所周知，它们还经常抢食鱼鹰的渔获。秃鹰和鱼鹰在同一片区域栖息，邻里之间大概会因此产生一点爱恨情仇吧。

（托马斯·吉尔伯特·皮尔森）

♪ 作者介绍

　　托马斯·吉尔伯·皮尔森，是一位生物学和地质学教授，任教于美国北卡罗来纳州格林斯博罗的州立师范和工业大学。他热爱户外生活，常常近距离观察大自然。本文选自一本有趣的书《鸟的生活》，皮尔森教授在这本书里说："对于这些居住在野外和森林里的鸟类邻居，要是读者能因为本书中的故事对它们产生一点亲密感，我的目的就达到了。"

A Journey in Brazil

December 29th, 1865, Pedreira.

I have said little about the insects and reptiles which play so large a part in most Brazilian travels, and, indeed, I have had much less annoyance from this source than I had expected. But I must confess that the creature which greeted my waking sight this morning was not a pleasant object to contemplate. It was an enormous centipede close by my side. He was nearly a foot in length. His innumerable legs looked just ready for a start, and his two horns or feelers were protruded with a most venomous expression.

These animals are very hideous to look upon, and their bite is painful, though it is not dangerous. I crept softly away from my sofa without disturbing my ugly neighbor, who presently fell a victim to science; being very adroitly caught under a large tumbler, and consigned to a glass jar filled with alcohol.

Captain Faria says that centipedes are often brought on board with wood, among which they usually lie concealed, seldom making their appearance, unless disturbed and driven out of their hiding places.

To less noxious visitors of this kind, one soon gets accustomed. As I shake out my dress, I hear a cold flop on the floor, and a pretty little house-lizard, which has found a warm retreat in its folds, makes his escape with all celerity. Cockroaches swarm everywhere, and it would be a vigilant housekeeper that could keep her closets free from them.

Ants are the greatest nuisance of all, and the bite of the fire-ant is really terrible. I remember once having hung some towels to dry on the cord of my hammock; I was about remove them when suddenly my hand and arm seemed plunged into fire. I dropped the towels as though they had been hot coals, and then I saw that my arm was covered with little brown ants.

Brushing them off in all haste, I called the servant. Who found an army of them passing over the hammock, and out of the window near which it hung. He said that they were on their way somewhere, and if left undisturbed, would be gone in an hour or two. And so it proved to be. We saw no more of them.

Yesterday we arrived at Pedreira, a little village consisting of some fifteen or twenty houses hemmed in by forest. The place certainly deserves its name of the "place of stones". For the shore is fringed with rocks and boulders. We landed at once, and Mr. Coutinho and Mr. Agassiz spent the morning in geologizing and botanizing.

In the course of our ramble we came upon an exceedingly picturesque Indian camp. The river is now so high that the water runs far up into the forest. In such an overflowed wood, a number of Indian Boats were moored; while on a nearby tract of land, the Indians had cleared a little grove, cutting down the inner trees, and leaving only the outer ones standing, so as to make a circular arbor. Within this arbor the hammocks were slung; while outside were the kettles and water-jugs, and utensils of one sort and another.

In this little camp were several Indian families, who had left their mandioca plantations in the forest, to pass the Christmas festa in the village. We asked the women what they did, they and their babies, when it rained.

They laughed and pointing to their canoes, said that they crept under the arched roof of palm-thatch, which always encloses the stern of an Indian boat, and were safe. Even this in the open river, would not be a protection; but, moored as the boats are in the midst of a thick wood, they do not receive the full force of the showers.

After we returned to the village and rested at the priest's house half an hour, he proposed to send us to his little man-dioca plantation at a short distance in the forest, where a particular kind of palm, which Mr. Agassiz greatly coveted, was to be obtained. In this country of inundated surfaces, land journeys are often made by water. So we started in a boat, and after keeping along the water for some time, we turned into the woods and began to navigate the forest.

The water was still and clear as grass: the trunks of trees stood up from it, their branches dipped into it. As we wound in and out among them, putting aside a bough here and there, or stooping to float under a green arbor. The reflection of every leaf was so perfect that wood and water seemed to melt into each other, and it was difficult to say where one began and the other ended. Silence and shade so profound brooded over the whole scene, that the mere ripple of our paddles seemed a disturbance.

After half an hour's row we came to dry land, where we went on shore, taking our boatmen with us. The wood soon resounded with their hatchets as the palms fell under their blows. We returned with a boatload of palms, besides a number of plants of various kinds that we had not seen elsewhere. We reached the boat just in time; for scarcely, were well on board and in snug quarters again when the heavens opened and the floods came down.

(Louis Agassiz)

译文

巴西之旅

1865年12月29日 写于佩德里拉

正如我之前所说，在巴西之行中，昆虫爬虫随处可见，然而这并没有像我想象中那样困扰我。但我必须承认，我今早醒来映入眼帘的生物的确令人烦躁。那是一条巨大的蜈蚣，足足有我的脚那么长，我醒来时发现它就在我身旁。它密密麻麻的脚似乎正准备要开始爬行，两只触角来回摆动，令人生厌。

这类动物样子很恶心，咬人也很疼，尽管被咬了没什么危险。我轻轻地离开沙发，生怕惊扰到我丑陋的"邻居"。这位"邻居"已经成了科学的受害者。我快速地拿起一个大玻璃杯，把它盖住，然后迅速地把这个小东西丢到一个装满酒精的玻璃瓶里去了。

法里亚船长告诉我，蜈蚣常隐藏在木头里，所以经常跟着木头被误带到了船上。不过一般它们不会出来，除非它被侵扰了或是被赶出了"隐居地"。

因为这类动物对乘客并没有害，所以人们也就渐渐习惯了。我抖了抖我的上衣，一只小壁虎便敏捷地逃走了，它准是把我的口袋当温暖的住所了。蟑螂随处可见，得多么细心的管家才能把她的衣橱收拾得一只蟑螂都没有啊。

蚂蚁这种小东西是最讨人厌的。要是被火蚁咬上一口，那是非常疼的。我记得有一次，我准备拿些干毛巾去擦擦我的吊床，我的手刚碰到毛巾便感受了一阵火烧般的疼痛，我赶紧像丢烫手山芋一样甩开了毛巾，但我的胳膊上还是爬满了棕色的蚂蚁。

我连忙把胳膊上的蚂蚁抹掉，喊服务员进来。服务员发现一个蚂蚁"军团"正从我的吊床爬到吊床悬挂的窗外。服务员解释说这些蚂蚁正在搬家，我们不要管它们，一两个小时它们就走光了。果然，一两个小时后，它们真的走光了。

昨天我们到达了佩德里拉，一个仅有十五或者二十家人家的小村庄，靠近森林。这个被称作"石头之地"的地方果然名不虚传，海岸线满是岩石和卵石。我们登陆后，顾汀博先生和阿加西先生一早上都在进行质地研究和植物调查。

漫步时，我们偶然发现了一个棒极了的印第安营地。河流地处高地，水流湍急，向森林奔去。在这样一个茂密的丛林中，停泊着许多印第安船只。在旁边的一片土地上，印第安人将内部的树砍倒，只留着外部的树木，这样就形成了一个圆形的"凉亭"。凉亭中悬挂着些吊床，凉亭外则是一个个水壶、器皿。

在这个小营地中，住着几家印第安人，他们在森林里开垦了一些木薯种植园，现在正在村子里庆祝圣诞节呢！我们问当地的妇女们，要是下雨了她们和孩子们怎么过河？

妇女们开怀大笑，指着她们的木船，说她们可以在棕榈叶和茅草做的拱形屋顶下匍匐前行，很安全。尽管如此，要是在开阔的河面就没有这样的保护了；但是船只要是划到浓密的丛林中，他们也可以免受淋雨之苦。

我们回到村子后，在牧师家休息了半小时，他答应可以送我们去他的木薯种植园，里面有阿加西先生一直梦寐以求的一种特种的棕榈叶，不远，在森林中走一小段路可以到达。于是我们乘船出发，在水面上前进了一段时间后，我们进入丛林，开始在森林中探寻了。

水面平静，青翠如草。树干在水边林立，树枝轻拂水面，随着我们在树木之间穿行，树枝左右摇摆，溅起晶莹的水花，翠绿色的藤架和绿叶相互映衬，水和树仿佛融为一体，分不清开头和结尾。整个世界静悄悄的，在绿荫的笼罩下，只听见桨与水的缠绵。

经过一个半小时的路程，我们来到了陆地，在岸边登陆后，我们邀请船夫一同前行。不久后，森林就回响着树叶摩擦的簌簌声，那是我们在摘采棕榈叶呢。我们满载着一船的棕榈叶而归，还有一些我们从未见过的植物。之后，我们及时地上船了，要不然我们可就在这如天堂般舒适的地方忘而不归啦。

（路易斯·阿加西）

♪ 作者介绍

路易斯·阿加西，著名自然学家。出生于瑞士，在德国接受教育。他在冰川及岩石研究领域做出了极大贡献。四十岁时他访问美国，受哈佛大学邀请成为哈佛大学教职工的一员。之后，他转入美国籍，并为这个他所热爱的国家在给民众普及自然科学知识方面做出了巨大贡献。1865年他前往巴西考察亚马逊下游。据说他在此流域发现了超过一千五百种新品种的鱼。他与他的妻子随后出版了一部关于巴西的书。此选段经米夫林出版公司授权。

Hunting the Cougar in Mississippi

预习

alter /ˈɔːltər/ 改变
dangle /ˈdæŋgl/ 松散地挂着
elated /iˈleɪtɪd/ 愉快的，狂喜的
equipped /ɪkˈwɪpt/ 安装，装备
fatigued /fəˈtiːgd/ 劳累的
interior /ɪnˈtɪriər/ 在内部的，里面的
procure /prəˈkjʊr/ 取得
terminating /ˈtɜːmɪneɪtɪŋ/ 终结
vehemently /ˈviːəmənt li/ 狂怒地；大声地

  The morning after my arrival at the squatter's cabin, I joined him while he threw a few ears of corn to his pigs. As he counted the animals, he told me that for some weeks their number had been greatly diminished by the ravages committed upon them by a large panther.

  By this name the cougar is designated in America. The ravenous animal now and then carried off one of his calves, and On several occasions had robbed him of a deer. Delighted by his description of the "painter" as he sometimes called it, I offered to assist him in destroying the enemy.

  He was highly pleased, but assured me that unless some of his neighbors would join us with their dogs, the attempt would prove fruitless. Soon afterward, mounting a horse, he went off to his neighbors, several of whom lived at a distance of some miles, and appointed a day of meeting.

  The hunters, accordingly, one fine morning made their appearance at the door of the cabin. They were five in number, and fully equipped for the chase. Few words were uttered by the party until we had reached the edge of the swamp: There it was agreed that all should scatter and seek for the fresh track of the "painter", it being previously settled that the discoverer should blow his horn, and remain on the spot until the rest should join him.

In less than an hour, the sound of the horn was clearly heard, and, sticking close to the squatter, off we went through thick woods, guided only by the now and then repeated call of the distant huntsmen. We soon reached the spot, and in a short time the rest of the party came up.

The best dog was sent forward to track the cougar, and in a few moments the whole pack were observed diligently trailing, and bearing in their course for the interior of the swamp. The rifles were immediately put in trim, and the party followed the dogs, at separate distances, but in sight of each other, determined to shoot at no game but the panther.

The dogs soon began to mouth, and suddenly quickened their pace. Putting our horses to a gentle gallop, we followed them, guided by their voices. All of a sudden, the mode of barking became altered, and the squatter urging me to push on, told me that the beast was treed. By this he meant that it had got upon some low branch of a large tree to rest a few moments. Should we not succeed in shooting him when thus situated, we might expect a long chase of it. As we approached the spot, we all united in a body, but on seeing the dogs at the foot of a large tree, separated again, and galloped off to surround it.

Each hunter now moved with caution, holding his gun ready, and allowing the bridle to dangle on the neck of his horse, as it advanced slowly towards the dogs. A shot from one of the party was heard, on which the panther was seen to leap to the ground, and bound off. The dogs set off in pursuit with great eagerness and a deafening cry.

The hunter that had fired came up and said that his ball had hit the monster, and had probably broken one of his fore-legs near the shoulder, the only place at which he could aim. The dogs proceeded at such a rate that we now put spurs to our horses and galloped towards the center of the swamp.

These determined hunters knew that the cougar being wounded, would shortly ascend another tree, where in all probability he would remain for a considerable time, and that it would be easy to follow the track of the dogs. We dismounted, took off the saddles and bridles, set the bells attached to the horses' necks at liberty to jingle, hoppled the animals, and left them to shift for themselves.

After marching for a couple of hours, we again heard the dogs. Each of us pressed forward, elated at the thought of terminating the career of the cougar. Some of the dogs were heard whining, although the greater number barked vehemently. We felt assured that the cougar was treed, and that he would rest for some time to recover from his fatigue.

As we came up to the dogs, we discovered the ferocious animal lying across a large branch, close to the trunk of a cotton-wood tree. His broad breast lay toward us; his eyes were at one time bent on us and again on the dogs beneath and around him. One of his fore-legs hung loosely by his side, and he lay crouched, with his ears lowered close to his head, as if he thought that he might remain undiscovered.

Three balls were fired at him, at a given signal, on which he sprang a few feet from the branch, and tumbled headlong to the ground. Attacked on all sides by the enraged dogs, the infuriated cougar fought with desperate valor; but the squatter, advancing in front of the party, and almost in the midst of the dogs, shot him immediately behind and beneath the left shoulder. In another moment the cougar lay dead.

The sun was now sinking in the west. Two of the hunters separated from the rest to procure venison, whilst the squatter's sons went home to be ready to feed the pigs in the morning. The rest of the party agreed to camp on the spot. The cougar was despoiled of its skin, and its body left to the hungry dogs.

Whilst engaged in preparing our camp, we heard the report of a gun, and soon after one of our hunters returned with a small deer. A fire was lighted, and each hunter brought out his pone of bread. The deer was skinned in a trice, and slices placed on sticks before the fire. These materials afforded us an excellent meal, and as the night grew dark, stories and songs went round, until fatigued, we lay down, close under the smoke of the fire, and soon fell asleep.

At daybreak we left our camp, the squatter bearing on his shoulder the skin of the late destroyer of his stock, and retraced our steps until we found our horses, which had not strayed far from the place where we had left them. These we saddled, and jogging along in a direct course, we soon arrived at my host's cabin.

(John James Audubon)

↬ 译文

在密西西比狩猎美洲豹

在到达寮屋居民小屋的那天早晨，我帮他一起撒些玉米穗给他养的猪吃。他数了一下牲口的数量，告诉我说，这几个星期以来，一只大型豹子来这肆虐破坏，导致牲口的数量急剧减少。

在美国，"豹子"就是指美洲豹。这只贪得无厌的野兽时不时就掳走一只他养的小牛犊，还屡次掠去了他的鹿。而被他所描述的"包子"（他有时候这么叫它）给逗乐的我，决定帮助他一起消灭敌人。

他对此非常高兴，但又很肯定的对我说，除非他的邻居们愿意带上猎狗和我们一起去，否则就是"竹篮打水一场空"。很快，他就攀上马背，出发去找一些住在几千米外的邻居们，并和他们约定见面的日子。

于是，在一个美好的清晨，猎人们出现在了木屋门口。他们一共有五个人，为捕猎做好了充分的准备。路上这一伙人几乎一言不发，直到我们到达湿地边缘。大伙达成一致，要把杂草都清理开来，方便寻找"包子"刚留下的痕迹。根据之前的约定，发现猎物的人应当吹响号角，直到其他人来到之前都要待在原地。

不到一小时，号角的声音清晰地传了过来。然后，靠不时反复传来的远处猎人们的喊声，我紧跟寮屋居民的步伐，穿过茂密的森林。我们马上就赶到了指定点，没多久其他人也来了。

他们派出最好的猎狗前去追捕美洲豹，之后的几分钟整队人马就万分留心的尾随着，朝着它们追捕的方向进入湿地了。一伙人将步枪上膛，跟着猎狗们，保持在不同的距离但能互相看见的位置，决心真枪实弹地对付豹子而不是当成游戏。

很快，猎狗们开始吠叫起来，然后猛然加速。我们循着声音，跟在后面，并让马放缓驰骋。突然，狗吠的声音变了。寮屋居民催促我上前，还告诉我说那只野兽被赶到了树上。他的意思是，那豹子已经跑到一棵大树较矮点的树干上去休息了。在这种情况下，要是我们不能成功将它击毙，那之后会是一场漫长的追捕。在我们向目标接近时，我们聚在一起，但是等看到猎狗们已经在大树脚下时，就再次分散开，快速地把它包围起来

每个猎人现在都小心翼翼地移动着，手里端着枪、做好准备了。他们的马慢慢地向猎狗们走近，摇晃的缰绳就悬挂在马脖子上。人群中响起了一声枪响，有人看到豹子跳到地面上后迅速逃走了。猎狗们热切地追击，并发出震耳欲聋的狂吠。

那个开火的猎人走过来，告诉我们他的子弹已经打中了那只野兽，还很可能打断了它靠近肩膀的一只前腿，那里是他唯一能瞄准的地方。猎狗们继续保持原速追踪，而我们则策马奔去湿地中心。

这些果决的猎人们很清楚，一旦美洲豹受了伤，就会立刻再找一棵树爬上去，然后极可能在那儿待上相当长的一段时间，这样，我们也能很容易就跟上猎狗的踪迹了。我们下了马，取下马鞍和马辔，把铃铛随意的挂在马脖子上，让其发出"叮铃"声，然后把马脚拴在一起，让它们自主活动。

前进了两三个小时后，我们重新听到了狗的声音。每个人都奋力向前逼近，对终结美洲豹生命的想法感到得意洋洋。有些狗的声音听起来有些闷闷不乐，然而绝大多数都在激烈的全力吠叫着。我们确信那只美洲豹已经被赶到了树上，它需要休息一段时间从疲惫中恢复过来。

当走到猎狗身边时，我们发现那凶猛的动物就横卧在一根大树枝上，靠近一棵棉木树的树干。它宽厚的胸部正对着我们；它的眼睛一会儿盯着我们，一会儿又盯着下面围着它的猎狗。它的一条前腿松垮地垂落在身体一侧，身子作蜷伏状，耳朵压低贴在脑袋上，好像是以为自己还没被发现。

三颗子弹向它射去，如同一个发出的信号，使它从树干上跃出几米，一

头跌向地面。暴怒的猎狗从各个方向袭来，愤怒的美洲豹勇猛而绝望的回击；这时，寮屋居民从大伙中走上前来，几乎走到猎狗们中间后，开枪射中它左肩的后下方。下一刻，美洲豹就躺在那儿死掉了。

太阳缓缓沉入西边。两个猎人从队伍中离开去找野味，与此同时，寮屋居民的儿子们也回到了家中准备明早喂猪。队伍中剩下的人决定在原地扎营。那只美洲豹被剥了皮，它的尸体被留给饥饿的猎狗。

忙着准备扎营时，我们听到一声枪响，不久之后，一个猎人就带着一只小鹿回来了。点着火后，每个猎人都拿出自己的玉米饼。转眼间，鹿就被剥去了皮切成片，然后串起来放到火上烤。这些食材给我们提供了一顿丰盛的晚餐，而当夜色渐晚之时，四周便有了歌声和讲故事的声音，直到困意袭来，我们才将火苗熄灭，纷纷睡下进入梦乡。

破晓时分，我们便离开了营地，寮屋居民背上背着已死的那畜养破坏者的皮，踩着来时的脚印返回找我们的马，它们并没有从我们离开时的地方跑远。就这样，我们上好马鞍，朝着既定的方向缓慢的稳步前行，很快就到达了那房主人的小木屋。

（约翰·詹姆斯·奥杜邦）

⟡ 作者介绍

约翰·詹姆斯·奥杜邦，美国著名的鸟类爱好者，出生于新奥尔良路易斯安那州。他曾在法国接受教育，并在伟大的画家大卫的教导下学习。回国后，他住在美国几个不同的地方。他喜欢把他的大部分时间花在森林和田野间流浪，研习鸟类的习性。不久之后，他就以有关鸟类的画作和文章闻名于世。他不仅在绘画他那些带羽毛的朋友上有着特殊的技巧，在用有趣的语言描述它们上也有着令人钦佩的才华。他的主要著作《美洲鸟类》每套价格为一千美元。以上的这篇文章授权自查尔斯·斯克里布纳父子出版公司。

⟡ 练习

1. 写一篇有关你熟悉的鸟类的文章，描述它有多大？是什么颜色？栖息地在哪儿？

2. 描述一下它的鸟巢和鸟蛋。

A Tradition of Weatherford

Just below the junction of the Alabama and Tombigbee rivers, on the east side of the stream, you will find the little town of Tensaw. Near this Fort Mims once stood. Not far away were Fort Sinquefield and Fort White, and farther south was Fort Glass. On the 30th of August, 1813, the Indians attacked Fort Mims, and after a desperate battle, destroyed it, killing all but seventeen of the five hundred and fifty people who living in it.

The news of this terrible slaughter quickly spread over the country, and everybody knew now that a general war had begun, in which the Indians meant to destroy the whites utterly, not sparing even the youngest children. The fiercest and most conspicuous leader of the Indians in this war was Weatherford, or the Red Eagle. He planned and led the assault upon Fort Mims, and was everywhere foremost in all the fighting.

As rapidly as possible people gathered into the forts for safety, but by one accident and another many were cut off. Among the latter was Sam Hardwicke, a boy of sixteen. Mounted on a good horse Sam tried to make his way to safety.

With a party of about twenty-five Indians, Weatherford bivouacked one night in the edge of the woods, and when Sam mounted his horse the next morning the Indians were lying asleep immediately in his path.

The first intimation that he had of their presence was a grunt from a big savage lying almost under his horse's feet. Coming to himself, Sam took in the whole situation at a glance. He saw before him the savages, rising from the ground at sight of him. He saw their horses browsing at some little distance from them. He saw a rifle, on which hung a powder-horn and a bullet-pouch, standing against a bush. He saw that he had already aroused the foe, and that he must stand a chase.

His first impulse was to turn around and ride back, in the direction whence he had come. But in that direction lay the thicket through which he could not ride rapidly. Just beyond the group of Indian he saw the open fields. He made up his mind at once that he would push his horse into a run, dash right through the camp of the savages, pick up the convenient rifle if possible, and reaching the open country, make all the speed he could.

Without pausing or turning, he pushed his horse at a full run through the group of savages, receiving a glancing blow from a war club and dodging several others as he went. He succeeded in getting possession of the rifle, and reached the field before a gun could be aimed at him. Infuriated by his boldness, the Indians immediately mounted their horses and gave chase.

The question had now resolved itself, Sam thought, into one of endurance. How long the Indians would continue a pursuit in which he had the advantage of half a mile the start, he had no way of determining, but he had every reason to hope.

Just as he had comforted himself with his thought, a new danger assailed him. One of the Indians, with a minute knowledge of the country, had saved a considerable distance by riding through a strip of woods and cutting off an angle. When Sam first caught sight of him, coming out of the woods, the savage was within a dozen yards of him, and evidently gaining upon him at every step.

Sam's horse was a fleet one, but that of the Indian was apparently a thoroughbred, whose speed remained nearly as great after a mile's run as at the start. Finding at last that he must shortly be overtaken, Sam resolved upon a bold maneuvre, by which to kill his foremost pursuer. Seizing his hatchet, he suddenly stopped his horse, and, as the Indian came alongside, Sam aimed a savage blow at his head.

"Don't you know me, Sam?" said the Indian in good English, dodging the blow. "I'm Weatherford. If I had wanted to kill you, I might have done so a dozen times in the last five minutes. You know that I don't want to kill you, though you're the only white man on earth I'd let go. But the others will make an end of you if they catch you.

"Ride on, and I'll chase you. Turn to the left there, and ride to the bluff. I'll follow you. There's a gully through the top. Ride down it as far as you can and jump your horse over the cliff. It is nearly fifty feet high, and may kill you, but it is the only way. The other warriors are coming up, and they will kill you if you don't jump. Jump, and I'll tell them I chased you."

San knew Weatherford well, and he knew why the chief wished to spare him if he could. Sam had rescued Weatherford once from an imminent peril at great risk to himself. So the two rode on, Sam going down the gully furiously, that his horse might not be able to refuse the frightful leap.

Coming to the edge of the precipice with headlong speed, the animal could not draw back, but plunged over with Sam sitting bolt upright on his back. He had no saddle or stirrups in which to become entangled, and as the horse struck the water fairly, the blow was not so severe a shock to the boy as he had expected.

Both went under the water, but rising again in a moment. Sam slid off the animal's back, to give the poor horse a better chance to escape by swimming. Striking out boldly the boy reached the bank, and, crawling up, looked for his horse. For a time he drifted while Sam ran along the bank, calling and encouraging him. He struck the shore at last, and Sam, examining him, found that while his was stunned and bruised no serious damage had been done.

(George Cary Eggleston)

译文

韦瑟福德的传说

小镇滕索坐落在阿拉巴马州边界和汤比格比河的相交处，它位于河流的东岸。在这附近曾经有个闵士堡，不远处还有辛克费尔德堡和怀特堡，而格拉斯堡则在更南边的地方。1813年8月30日印第安人袭击了闵士堡，并在激烈的战斗后摧毁了这座堡垒，杀害在那里生活的人民，整个小镇上的五百五十人中只有十七人幸存。

这场可怕的大屠杀的消息飞速传遍了整个国家，人人都意识到一场全面战争已经开始：印第安人打算把白人全数消灭，连最年幼的孩子都不放过。在这场战争中，印第安人最勇猛、最引人注目的领袖是韦瑟福德，也就是"红鹰"。他策划并领导了袭击冈士堡的行动，在各地的所有战斗中都起着重要作用。

　　人们尽可能快地向各个堡垒集中以确保安全，但由于各种意外不断发生，很多人被落下了。这些人当中有一个人叫山姆·哈德威克。他是一个十六岁的男孩，骑着一匹良马，向安全地区赶去。

　　一天夜里，韦瑟福德带领着一队大约二十五名印第安人在树林边露营。当第二天早晨山姆骑马经过时，印第安人正躺在他前行的道路上打瞌睡。

　　直到马脚边传来一个躺着的原始人大汉的呼噜声时，他才意识到这群人的存在。山姆醒悟过来后审视了整个局势。眼前是那群看到他以后正站起身来的原始人，而他们的马则在一段距离以外吃着草。他看到有杆来复枪靠着灌木丛，上面还挂有一个装火药的牛角和一个弹药袋。他意识到自己已经惊动了敌人，接下来肯定要经历一次大追捕了。

　　他的第一反应是转身沿着来时的路逃走，但那个方向有着茂密的草丛，骑马跑不快。他看到越过印第安人群更远处是广阔的平原，便立刻决定以最快的速度赶着马笔直地冲向原始人的营地，可能的话拿走用得上的来复枪，然后跑到开阔的田地上去。

　　山姆没有停顿，也没有转向，骑着马全速穿过了原始人。他被一根棍子稍微扫了一下，但躲开了其余几次攻击。他成功地拿到了来复枪，并在敌人举枪瞄准之前到达了田野。印第安人被他那大胆的行为激怒了，立即跨上马开始追赶。

　　山姆认为，谁胜谁败就要看谁更持久。他从一开始就有领先八百米的优势，这种情况下印第安人会坚持追赶多远呢？他无从判断，但有理由相信结果会好的。

　　正当他自我安慰地这样想着，一个新的威胁向他袭来。一个印第安人对这片土地了如指掌，他骑马穿过了一片树林，由于绕过了拐角而省去了很大一段追赶距离。当山姆发现他从树丛中跑出来时，这个原始人离他只有十几米远了，并且很明显地正在赶上来。

　　山姆的马跑得很快，但印第安人的明显是纯种良马，它们跑了一千六百米后速度和刚开始一样快。山姆最后发现自己过不了多久肯定会被抓获，就决定采取一个大胆的策略，杀了那个冲在最前面的追捕者。那个印第安人手握战斧，突然停下了马，当他走到身边时，山姆瞄准这个原始人的头开了枪。

"山姆，你不认识我了吗？"印第安人一边躲开了枪击，一边以流利的英语说道，"我是韦瑟福德，如果我想杀你，在前面五分钟我有十几次机会可以下手。你知道我不想杀你，你是这个世界上我唯一会放过的白人。但其他人如果逮住你，肯定会结果你的性命。

"骑着马继续向前跑，我会追赶你。在那里向左转骑到悬崖边，我会一直跟着你。顶上有一条峡谷穿过，朝着峡谷尽可能多跑点，然后让你的马跳过山崖。落差约有四米五。或许你会摔死，但这是唯一逃脱的方法。其他的战士们正在追上来，如果你不跳，他们就会杀了你。跳吧，我会告诉他们我在追赶你。"

山姆很了解韦瑟福德，他明白这个首领为什么会尽可能地放他走，他曾经冒着巨大的危险在一场迫在眉睫的危机中救了韦瑟福德。因此，两人继续策马向前。山姆疯狂地冲下山谷，让他的马无法拒绝进行那可怕的一跃。

马以极快的速度跑到了悬崖边缘，无法退缩而只能载着直挺挺地坐在它背上的主人一起向下跳去。山姆没有被马鞍和马镫所束缚，当马完全跳入水中时，他并没有受到想象中那么强烈的冲击。

他们朝水下沉去，但过了一会儿便浮了上来。山姆从马背上下来，让这可怜的家伙游泳逃生的机会大一些。他自己勇敢地拍打着水面游到了岸边，爬起身来寻找他的马。马儿漂在水面上那会儿，他沿着河岸奔跑着，大声叫着鼓励它。等马终于上岸后，山姆便去检查伤势，发现它没有因为撞晕和碰擦受到严重的伤害。

（乔治·卡里·埃格尔斯顿）

Two Minutes

He was a third lieutenant in the engineers. It was after the great mine explosion at Petersburg, and the engineers were at that time busily engaged in using all their devices for the discovery of other mines. They had found one in process of construction in front of General Gracie's lines.

They had proceeded at once to run a deeper tunnel under this one. They had loaded the end of it, just underneath the enemy's works, with an incredible amount of gunpowder, and on that morning it was to be fired. A slow-match had been brought from the powder to the mouth of the mine. It was lighted, and a period of waiting ensued.

The match had evidently gone out. Where, nobody knew or could guess. The general in command of that part of the line turned to the captain of engineers and said, "The mine must be blown up at once; will you go in and light the match again?"

The captain hesitated, saying, "I don't know; it may go off at any moment."

Thereupon the third lieutenant stepped forward, touched his cap to the general, and said, "With your permission, I will go in and fire it."

"Thank you," said the general. "Go."

The man picked up the torch and started into the mine. It seems that the slow-match had gone out, within a very short distance of the powder magazine. But disregarding that, he touched the torch to it, set it off again, and ran with all his might for the mouth of the opening.

It was two minutes' work. The mine went off just before he reached the outlet, and the air pressure literally blew him out of it. He fell sprawling on his face. He was considerably bruised and scratched in his contact with the gravelly ground, but he was not in any serious way injured.

Picking himself up, grimed as he was, he took off his cap, and dusting himself like a school-boy that had fallen in the street, he approached the commanding officer and said, "General I have the honor to report that I have fired the mine, and that it has gone off."

The general touched his cap and replied, "I had observed that fact, and I thank you very much. I beg to say that I will make an official report of the circumstance."

Two days later we all touched our caps to a freshly made brigadier-general of the engineers. The captain that had hesitated remained a captain.

(George Cary Eggleston)

译文

两分钟

他是工程队里的第三中尉。彼得堡矿井大爆炸前，工程队所有的设备都用来开采其他矿井了。在格雷斯将军的阵地前方，他们发现有一座正在建设的矿井。

他们立刻赶到这口矿井的更深处，用大量火药填满了这条通道，它位于敌人工事的正下方，打算当天早晨引爆火药。一根导火索从矿井口伸出来。人们点燃了这根引线，要过一段时间才会爆炸。

导火线突然熄灭了，没人知道是怎么回事。军队将军对工程队上尉说："这口矿井必须如期引爆；你能进去把引线再次点燃吗？"

上尉犹豫片刻，说："我不知道；爆炸随时可能发生。"

这时，工程队第三中尉出列，向将军脱帽致敬，说道："请批准我进入矿井，点燃引线。"

"谢谢，"将军说道，"去吧。"

第三中尉拿起火把，向矿井走去。他瞧了一眼，引火线已经烧得快到火药包了，十分危险。但他仍然坚定地用火把点燃了导火线，然后立刻全速跑开。

这前后不过两分钟的工夫。他刚刚跑到出口，矿井就爆炸了。他被空气流炸了出去。他甚至能感受到脸部肌肉的扭曲。他重重地摔在满是碎石的地面，皮肤擦伤严重。但幸好他没有负什么重伤。

他强忍着痛苦，挣扎着爬起来，拿下他的帽子。他的身上满是灰尘，就像一个摔倒在街上的小学童。他回到了司令部，说："将军，我很荣幸地向您汇报，我点燃了引线，矿井已爆炸。"

　　接着，将军向他脱帽致敬，说："我已了解情况，十分感谢你。我将会正式通报此事。"

　　两天后，我们全体脱帽，向新上任的工程队准将致敬。而那位在危险任务面前犹豫的上尉再也没有被提拔。

（乔治·卡里·艾格雷斯顿）

✎ 练习

　　1.这篇文章的作者是谁？作者笔下，将军问的第一句话是什么？上尉是怎样回答将军的？中尉又是怎样说的?

　　2.作者是用什么词引出人物的言语的？哪种单词可以引导直接引语？直接引语用什么标点结束？

　　3.直接引语被分段时，怎样结束直接引语？用什么标点符号？

　　4.抄写并注意发音：

1）"如你所愿。"天使说道。

2）"你将这个国家的金子纳入囊中了吗？"亚历山大问道。

3）"哦，不。"亚历山大说，"这太烦人了。"

4）"而你，"法官对另一个人说，"有一个女儿？"

5）气流说道："当然，北方。"然而他并不知道。

Chapter 3
Miscellaneous Poems | 杂诗

Queen Mab

A little fairy comes at night,
Her eyes are blue, her hair is brown,
With silver spots upon her wings,
And from the moon she flutters down.
She has a little silver wand,
And when a good child goes to bed,
She waves her hand from right to left,
And makes a circle round its head.
And then it dreams of pleasant things,
Of fountains filled with fairy fish,
And trees that bear delicious fruit,
And bow their branches at a wish:
Of arbors filled with dainty scents
From lovely flowers that never fade;
Bright flies that glitter in the sun,
And glowworms shining in the shade.
And talking birds with gifted tongues,
For singing songs and telling tales,
And pretty dwarfs to show the way
Through fairy hills and fairy dales.
But when a bad child goes to bed,
From left to right she waves her rings,
And then it dreams all through the night
Of only ugly, horrid things!
Then lions come with glaring eyes,
And tigers growl, a dreadful noise,
And ogres draw their cruel knives,
To shed the blood of girls and boys.
The stormy waves rush on to drown,
Or raging flames come scorching round,

Fierce dragons hover in the air,
And serpents crawl along the ground.
Then wicked children wake and weep,
And wish the long black gloom away;
But good ones love the dark, and find
The night as pleasant as the day.

(Thomas Hood)

译文

麦布女王

小仙女随着夜幕降临了,
她的眼睛是蓝色的,她的头发是棕色的,
她的翅膀上闪着银斑,
她从月亮上飞下来。
她有一支小小的仙女棒,
当一个好孩子上床睡觉,
她就从右向左挥手,
再在他的头上绕一圈。
接着他就会梦见美好的事物,
喷泉中游动着仙鱼,
树梢上结满了硕果,
将树枝打结许下愿望:
愿花儿永不凋谢,
藤蔓满是馨香;
晶亮的飞蝇在日光下闪光,
萤火虫在暗处发亮。
叽喳的鸟儿既会唱歌,又能讲故事,
真是天赐的好嗓子,

可爱的侏儒来领路,
穿过仙女岭与仙女谷。
可是当一个坏孩子上床睡觉,
她就将铃铛从左向右挥舞,
而他只会整夜整夜
梦见既丑陋,又可怕的东西!
狮子瞪着炯炯的眼睛在逼近,
老虎咆哮,声音可怖,
食人怪拖着他们无情的大刀,
专取男孩与女孩的鲜血。
忽而惊涛骇浪似要把人淹没,
忽而熊熊大火要将土地全部烧焦,
猛龙在天上盘旋,
巨蛇在地下伏行。
于是顽童惊醒了,
哭着祈祷这长长的黑暗阴霾散去;
可是好孩子喜爱黑夜,并且发现
夜晚与白天一样可爱。

(托马斯·胡德)

The Flower

Once in a golden hour
I cast to earth a seed.
Up there came a flower,
The people said a weed.

Then it grew so tall
It wore a crown of light,
But thieves from o'er the wall,
Stole the seed by night.
Sowed it far and wide
By every town and tower,
Till all the people cried,
"Splendid is the flower."

(Alfred Tennyson)

译文

花

曾有一个黄金时间
我埋下一粒种子。
那里长出一朵花,
人们说这是杂草。

它却长得如此高大
戴着光之冠冕,
然而墙那边的小偷,
夜里来偷了这种子。

在遥远的地方四处散播
散播到每一个城镇和高楼，
直到所有的人们都大叫：
"这花真美丽！"

（阿尔弗雷德·丁尼生）

Lucy

She dwelt among the untrodden ways
Beside the springs of Dove;
A maid whom there were none to praise,
And very few to love.

A violet by a mossy stone
Half-hidden from the eye!
Fair as a star, when only one
Is shining in the sky.

She lived unknown, and few could know
When Lucy ceased to be;
But she is in her grave, and, O!
The difference to me!

(William Wordsworth)

译文

露西

她住在人迹罕至的路边,
达夫河源头旁,
没有谁赞赏这姑娘,
也没有几个人爱上她。

像长满青苔的岩石边上
若隐若现的紫罗兰;
像夜间独一无二的星光

在天上荧荧闪闪。

露西啊,她活着时无人留意,
死去也无人知晓;
但是如今她已躺进坟墓里,
而我却恍如隔世!

(威廉·华兹华斯)

The Eagle

He clasps the crag with crooked hands;
Close to the sun in lonely lands,
Ring'd with the azure world, he stands.

The wrinkled sea beneath him crawls;
He watches from his mountain walls,
And like a thunderbolt he falls.

(Alfred Tennyson)

译文

鹰

铁钩般的铁爪紧扣峭壁,
于孤绝之地与太阳比邻,
在蓝天的环抱中,屹立。

脚下如皱的海浪缓缓流逝,
他于他的高山岩壁守望凝视,
恍若雷霆般俯冲下去。

(阿尔弗雷德·丁尼生)

The Kitten and the Falling Leaves

See the kitten on the wall,
sporting with the leaves that fall.
Withered leaves —— one, two and three
from the lofty elder tree.
Though the calm and frosty air,
of this morning bright and fair.
Eddying round and round they sink,
softly, slowly; one might think.
From the motions that are made,
every little leaf conveyed
Sylph or Faery hither tending,
to this lower world descending.
Each invisible and mute,
in his wavering parachute.

But the Kitten, how she starts,
crouches, stretches, paws, and darts!
First at one, and then its fellow,
just as light and just as yellow.
There are many now, now one,
Now the stop, and there are none.
What intenseness of desire,
in her upward eye of fire!
With a tiger-leap half-way,
now she meets the coming prey.
lets it go as fast, and then;
Has it in her power again.
Now she works with three or four,
like an Indian conjuror;
quick as he in feats of art,

far beyond in joy of heart.

(William Wordsworth)

译文

小猫与落叶

看墙上那只小猫，
正与落叶嬉笑玩闹。
枯黄叶子——
一片，两片，三片
自那高耸的老树干落下。
飘过静谧又寒冷的空气，
今晨明亮而美丽。
转呀，转呀，轻柔舒缓，
随你能想象的那般。
看它们飘落的姿态，
一片片树叶在飞舞，
温柔的风神与精灵，
下凡到大地来巡行。
每一位都无声无息地，
驾驭这升起的降落伞。

但是这小猫，她如何行动？
躬身，伸腰，张爪，扑跳！
先抓一片，再抓更多，
一样的轻盈，一样的黄灿灿。
忽而纷纷，忽而一片，
忽而停止降落，一片也不见；
那种渴望多么热切，

她火焰般的眼神向上!
虎跃似地一跳,
现在她把到来的猎物拥抱。
放手,让它尽快逃走,
捉回,再玩弄于股掌之间:
此刻她捕捉三四遍,
就像印度的杂耍者;
他的技艺虽娴熟,
也远不如小猫挥洒快乐。

(威廉·华兹华斯)

Patriotism

Breathes there the man with soul so dead,
Who never to himself hath said,
"This is my own, my native land!"
Whose heart hath ne'er within him burned,
As home his footsteps he hath turned;
If such there breathe, go, mark him well;
For him no minstrel raptures swell;
High though his titles, proud his name,
Boundless his wealth as wish can claim:
Despite those titles, power, and pelf,
The wretch, concentred all in self,
Living, shall forfeit fair renown,
And, doubly dying, shall go down
To the vile dust, from whence he sprung,
Unwept, unhonoured, and unsung.

(Walter Scott)

译文

爱国主义

那里有个人在低语，
他的灵魂如此死气沉沉，
从没对自己说过：
"这是属于我自己的，天赋的土地！"
他的心一刻也没有燃烧过，
即使他的足迹回到祖国；
即使他在那里能自在呼吸、行走、被人们记得。

没有诗人能因他诗兴大发；
他头衔再高，名字再响亮，
财富再多，再源源不断：
就算有那些头衔、权利、钱财，
这可怜人只专注于自己的事。
他活着就应让他失去名誉，
他临死就应让他永远倒下，
从他来的地方，到低微的尘土去，
无人悲泣，无人尊敬，无人歌唱。

（沃尔特·司各特）

Beauty

A thing of beauty is a joy forever:
Its loveliness increases; it will never,
Pass into nothingness, but still will keep,
A bower quiet for us, and a sleep,
Full of sweet dreams, and health, and quiet breathing.

(John Keats)

译文

美

美丽的事物是永恒的喜悦:
它的美妙与日俱增;它绝不会
化为乌有;而会使我们永远拥有
一座幽静的花亭,一个充满美梦、
健康和匀静呼吸的睡眠。

(约翰·济慈)

Incident of the French Camp

You know, we French stormed Ratisbon:
A mile or so away
On a little mound, Napoleon
Stood on our storming-day;
With neck out-thrust, you fancy how,
Legs wide, arms locked behind,
As if to balance the prone brow
Oppressive with its mind.

Just as perhaps he mused "My plans
That soar, to earth may fall,
Let once my army-leader Lannes
Waver at yonder wall"——
Out 'twixt the battery-smokes there flew
A rider, bound on bound
Full-galloping; nor bridle drew
Until he reached the mound,

Then off there flung in smiling joy,
And held himself erect
By just his horse's mane, a boy:
hardly could suspect——
(So tight he kept his lips compressed.
Scarce any blood came through)
You looked twice ere you saw his breast
Was all but shot in two.

"Well," cried he, "Emperor, by God's grace
We've got you Ratisbon!
The Marshal's in the market-place,

And you'll be there anon
To see your flag-bird flap his vans
Where I, to heart's desire,
Perched him!" The chief's eye flashed; his plans
Soared up again like fire.

The chief's eye flashed; but presently
Softened itself, as sheathes
A film the mother-eagle's eye
When her bruised eaglet breathes.
"You're wounded!" "Nay!" the soldier's pride
Touched to the quick, he said,
"I'm killed, Sire!" And his chief beside,
Smiling, the boy fell dead.

(Robert Browning)

译文

法国军营事件

你知道的，我们法国风暴般突袭了雷根斯堡：
差不多一千六百米远的地方
在一个小土墩上，拿破仑
在我们攻击这一日站立着，
伸长着脖子，你猜如何？
他双腿张开，手臂背在背后，
好像是为了展平
被头脑压弯的眉毛。

也许他正在沉思，
"我凌云壮志的计划，

可能会跌落在地,
让我的军队领袖兰斯威尔
在那边的城墙也指挥一次"——
在炮台的硝烟之间
一位骑兵,猛扑而行
一路飞奔;也没拉缰绳
直到他到达了土丘。

然后在那里下马,在微笑的欢乐中,
他挺直了身体
只到马鬃那么高,这只是一个小男孩:
你几乎不用怀疑 ——
(他的嘴唇抿得如此紧,
以致缺血)
你来回检视会发现他的胸膛
已经被射中两处。

"好吧,"他喊道,"陛下啊,靠着神的恩典,
我们为你攻占了雷根斯堡!
元帅在指挥所,
你不久就会在那
看到鸟儿拍打着翅膀。
我打从心底希望,
让他休息一下!"长官的眼睛闪着光;他的计划
再次像火焰般腾飞。

长官的眼睛闪着光;
然而暂时缓和了下来,
如同鹰妈妈的眼睛
看着她受伤的小鹰喘气。
"你受伤了!""不!"

士兵的骄傲令他迅速做出反应,他说:
"我是战死了,长官!"而他的长官站在旁边
微笑着,男孩倒地而死。

(罗伯特·勃朗宁)

Lochinvar

O, young Lochinvar is come out of the west,
Through all the wide Border his steed was the best;
And save his good broadsword he weapons had none,
He rode all unarmed, and he rode all alone.
So faithful in love, and so dauntless in war,
There never was knight like the young Lochinvar.

He staid not for brake, and he stopped not for stone,
He swam the Eske river where ford there was none;
But ere he alighted at Netherby gate,
The bride had consented, the gallant came late:
For a laggard in love, and a dastard in war,
Was to wed the fair Ellen of brave Lochinvar.

So boldly he entered the Netherby Hall,
Among bride's-men, and kinsmen, and brothers and all.
Then spoke the bride's father, his hand on his sword,
(For the poor craven bridegroom said never a word)
"O come ye in peace here, or come ye in war,
Or to dance at our bridal, young Lord Lochinvar?"

"I long wooed your daughter, my suit you denied;——
Love swells like the Solway, but ebbs like its tide——
And now I am come, with this lost love of mine,
To lead but one measure, drink one cup of wine.
There are maidens in Scotland more lovely by far,
That would gladly be bride to the young Lochinvar."

The bride kissed the goblet: the knight took it up,
He quaffed off the wine, and he threw down the cup.

She looked down to blush, and she looked up to sigh,
With a smile on her lips and a tear in her eye.
He took her soft hand, ere her mother could bar,——
"Now tread we a measure!" said young Lochinvar.

So stately his form, and so lovely her face,
That never a hall such a galliard did grace;
While her mother did fret, and her father did fume,
And the bridegroom stood dangling his bonnet and plume;
And the bride-maidens whispered, "Better by far
To have matched our fair cousin with young Lochinvar."

One touch to her hand, and one word in her ear,
When they reached the hall-door, and the charger stood near;
So light to the croupe the fair lady he swung,
So light to the saddle before her he sprung!
"She is won! we are gone, over bank, bush, and scar;
They'll have fleet steeds that follow," quoth young Lochinvar.

There was mounting among Graemes of the Netherby clan;
Forsters, Fenwicks, and Musgraves, they rode and they ran:
There was racing and chasing on Cannobie Lee,
But the lost bride of Netherby never did they see.
So daring in love, and so dauntless in war,
Have ye ever heard of gallant like young Lochinvar?

(Walter Scott)

◈ 译文

洛金伐尔

噢，年轻的洛金伐尔从西边出来了，
在整个战线上他的战马是最好的；
他得留下刀，什么武器都没带，
他骑着马，手无寸铁，独自一人。
对爱情如此忠诚，对战斗如此无畏，
从来就没有骑士像年轻的洛金伐尔一样。

他不因阻碍减缓步伐，不被石头绊住脚步，
他游过艾斯克河，那里完全没有浅滩；
但他在内瑟比的大门停下，
新娘已经许下承诺，英雄却来晚了：
爱情中的落后者，战争中的怯懦者，
将要与勇士洛金伐尔的美丽的艾伦结婚。

他大胆地走进内瑟比的厅堂，
站在新娘的追求者、亲戚、兄弟和所有其他朋友中间。
然后新娘的父亲手上握着剑，对他说：
（可怜的新郎从来没有说过一句话）
"噢，你是为和平而来，还是为战争来，
或者年轻的洛金伐尔先生，你要在我们的婚礼上跳舞吗？"

"我一直追求你的女儿，我的恳求被你拒绝；——
爱像索尔韦河一样，潮起潮落——
现在我来了，带着我失去的爱，
只想做一件事，喝一杯葡萄酒。
苏格兰有更可爱的女孩，

愿意成为洛金伐尔的新娘。"

新娘吻了高脚杯：勇士拿了起来，
他喝下了酒，然后扔下杯子。
她脸红着低头，然后抬头叹息，
她唇边在微笑，眼中却有泪水。
他握住她柔软的手，在她母亲面前，
"现在我们做一件事吧！"年轻的洛金伐尔说。

他的身影如此庄严，她的脸蛋如此可爱，
从来没有一个厅堂里有如此优美活泼的舞蹈；
而她的母亲烦恼，她的父亲不安，
新郎站在那儿摆动他的帽子和羽毛；
新娘的伴娘窃窃私语："那里才是更好的新郎，
洛金伐尔才配得上我们年轻美丽的表妹。"

他握住她的手，在她耳边低语，
当他们跳到大厅的门，战马就等在附近；
他拉着美丽的少女如此轻盈地舞动着，
他在她面前如此轻盈地跳跃着！
"她说对了！我们逃走，穿过河岸、灌木和巉崖；
他们将派战马追击。"年轻的洛金伐尔说。

内瑟比的格雷姆斯家族很有势力；
福斯特、芬威柯斯和马斯格雷姆斯宗族，他们骑马，他们奔跑：
他们一刻不停地追，
但他们再没见过内瑟比走失的新娘。
爱情中如此勇敢，战场上如此无畏，
你听说过其他如年轻的洛金伐尔一样的勇士吗？

（沃尔特·司各特）

Fame

Her house is all of echo made
Where never dies the sound;
And as her brows the clouds invade,
Her feet do strike the ground.

(Ben Jonson)

译文

名声

她的房子回音缭绕,
各种声音不绝于耳;
一皱眉,便是乌云密布,
一跺脚,便是地动山摇。

（本·琼森）

作者介绍

　　本·琼森是一位英国戏剧作家。因为家境贫寒,他不得不从大学辍学,去帮助他做瓦工的继父。但是他对这种生活感到厌烦,于是加入了英国军队,对抗佛兰德斯。因为在战场上的英勇事迹,他名声大噪,当他回到英国时,"除了勇敢的名声和一知半解的荷兰语,他一无所长"。二十五岁时,他创作了一部戏剧《脾气人各不同》,因此广为人知。自此,他创作了大量优秀的戏剧。莎士比亚也曾演过其中一部戏剧。一位批论家说过,尽管莎士比亚更加幽默风趣,但本·琼森更像一个诗人,他说道,"我敬佩琼森,但我更爱莎士比亚"。

Chapter 4
History ｜ 历史

Elizabeth Zane

In the autumn of 1777 the British commander of the West, Colonel Hamilton, resolved to attack Wheeling. For this purpose he employed a man named Simon Girty. When a boy, Girty had been captured by the Indians. and had joined their tribes, and become one of them.

Collecting about five hundred Indians, he marched south-ward from the Great Lakes toward Kentucky. Then turning to the left, he hurried up the Ohio River to surprise Fort Henry [Wheeling].

At first the white men were very unfortunate, and many of them were killed outside the fort. The few who were left to protect the women and children in the fort determined to fight to the last.

Soon they found to their dismay that there was hardly any gunpowder in the fort. They had forgotten the keg of powder in one of the houses. It was only about sixty yards away from the gate of the fort, but how were they to get it?

Colonel Shepherd, the commander of the fort, told his men exactly how the matter was. He would not order any man to go and get the powder, he said, as the Indians were almost sure to kill him, but if any one chose to volunteer, he would accept the offer.

Three or four young men and boys stepped forward, and said that they would be willing to go. One would do, and they must agree among themselves which one it was to be. One said that he would go, but another said that he would. So they disputed and lost time, until there was danger that the Indians would renew the attack before the white men came to any agreement.

At this moment a young lady came forward and said that she was ready to go. Her name was Elizabeth Zane, and she had just come home from boarding-school in Philadelphia. This made her brave offer all the more remarkable as she had not been trained up in the fearless life of the frontier.

Of course the men would not hear of such a thing. It was their place, they said, to expose their lives, not the place of women and girls.

Elizabeth urged, on her part, that they could not spare a man, as they had so few, but that the loss of a girl would not amount to much. At length, they reluctantly agreed that she should go for the keg of powder.

When Elizabeth Zane ran out from the fort, a few straggling Indians were dodging about three or four hundred yards east of Fort Henry. The rest of the savages were withdrawn a little in the woods. They all saw the girl for the people in the stockade observed them looking at her; but for some reason they did not fire at her.

They may have supposed that she was running to the house merely for the purpose of getting her clothes, or a hair-brush, or some other article that girls like to have. It is quite as likely, however, that they thought it, would only be throwing away a load of gunpowder to fire at a girl, who was of no use to anybody. easily kill her afterward with a tomahawk. So they quietly looked at her. and not a shot was fired.

As they were so anxious to capture Fort Henry, it would have been better for them to kill that girl, for she was destined to have it. She hastened into the house, found the keg of gun-powder, which was probably small, and holding her precious load close to her breast with both arms, darted out again, and ran with it in the direction of the fort.

As she ran the Indians saw her, and now understood what she had come for. Uttering a wild yell, they leveled their guns, and sent a shower of bullets at her, but all Hew wide the mark. They whistled to the right and left, but did not strike her. With the keg still hugged close to her bosom, she reached the fort, and the gate closed as the bullets of the Indians buried themselves in the thick panels behind her.

A weak girl had thus saved a dozen men and their wives and children. It was a brave act and Americans should never forget to honor the name of Elizabeth Zane.

(John Esten Cooke)

译文

伊丽莎白·赞恩

  1777年秋天，英国西部指挥官哈密尔顿上校决定攻打威尔灵市。为此他雇佣了一个叫西蒙·格蒂的男人。当格蒂还是个孩子时，他就被印第安人俘虏了，加入了当地的部落并成了他们的人。

  格蒂带领着五百个印第安人从五大湖南下，向肯塔基州行军。再左转，加紧赶到俄亥俄河，突袭亨利堡［威尔灵］。

  起初，白人处于劣势，他们中许多人在城堡的外围就被杀死了。少部分留在城墙内保护妇女和儿童的白人，也决定战斗至死。

  不久，他们沮丧地发现，城堡里的火药所剩无几。他们把一桶火药忘在了一栋离城堡城墙只有五十五米的房子里，问题是他们怎么去那里呢？

  城堡指挥官谢波德上校，把情况原原本本地告诉了手下。他没有命令任何人去取回火药，因为无论是谁，都必然会死在印第安人手下，但是如果有人自愿去，他会同意这一义举。

  三四个年轻的男性走上前去，表示他们自愿去取回火药。他们中只能选出一个人执行这个任务，可每个人都争着要去。他们争论起来，时间白白浪费，而此时大家面临着巨大危险，可能在印第安人发动新一轮攻击之前，他们也争不出什么结果来。

  这时，一位年轻的女士站了出来，说她自愿前去。她的名字叫伊丽莎白·赞恩，刚从费城的一所寄宿学校回来。她这样做要付出比其他人更大的勇气，毕竟她接受的教育可不是为前线这种无畏的生活准备的。

  毫无疑问男人们当然不会同意。献出自己的生命，这是男人们的事，可不能让女人来干。

  伊丽莎白解释道，现在城堡里的男人太少了，我们不能再损失男人了，相比而言，失去一个女人不算什么。最终，他们同意让她去取回那桶火药。

  当伊丽莎白·赞恩跑出城堡时，几个印第安的散兵游勇正在离亨利堡东边三四百米的地方巡视。其他的野蛮人躲在树丛中。他们都看到了伊丽莎白，栅栏里的人也注意到了她；但不知什么原因，他们没有朝她开火。

他们或许以为这个女孩跑到房子里就是去拿她的衣服、梳子，或者其他的一些女孩子用的东西。更可能的是，他们认为浪费火药去杀死一个没有任何用处的姑娘，实在是不值得。他们确信自己可以攻下城堡，之后他们用斧头也能杀了她。所以他们只是看着她，没有射击。

他们想要占领亨利堡的心情十分迫切，然而他们不知道的是，杀了这个注定要拯救亨利堡的姑娘，他们就能达到目的。伊丽莎白快步跑进房子，找到了那桶或许很小的火药桶，用双臂紧紧地环绕在胸前，然后飞奔而出，向城堡跑去。

印第安人再次看见了她，现在他们明白她是冲着什么来的了。他们怒吼着，举起他们的枪，疯狂地冲她射击。她仍然紧紧地抱这火药桶，她到达城堡了！在她跑进去之后，城堡大门就紧紧地关上了，印第安人雨林一般的子弹最后成了他们自己的陪葬。

这位柔弱的姑娘，拯救了十二个男人和他们的妻儿。这是一个壮举，美国人民将永远铭记伊丽莎白·赞恩的英名。

（约翰·埃斯腾·库克）

✏ 作者介绍

约翰·埃斯腾·库克，弗吉尼亚州作家，写过许多发生在弗吉尼亚州的历史故事。著有《皮袜和丝绸》《鹰巢马车》《尔法克斯》和《绅士亨利·圣约翰》。他还为斯通威尔·杰克逊和R.E.李写过传记。

✏ 练习

In the autumn of 1777, the British commander of the West, Colonel Hamilton, resolved to attack Wheeling.

哈密尔顿上校是英国指挥官。哈密尔顿上校是英国指挥官的解释，这样的解释叫作同位语。

同位语及其修饰语应用什么符号修饰？

The Capture of Quebec

The sun rose, and from the ramparts of Quebec, the astonished people saw the plains of Abraham glittering with arms, and the dark-red lines of the English forming in array of battle. Breathless messengers had borne the evil tidings to Montcalm, and far and near his wide extended camp resounded with the rolling of alarm drums and the din of startled preparation.

In spite of all difficulties he had trusted to hold out till the winter frosts should drive the invaders from before the town; when, on that disastrous morning, the news of their successful temerity fell like a cannon shot upon his ear. Still he assumed a tone of confidence. "They have got to the weak side of us at last," he is reported to have said, "and we must crush them with our numbers."

With headlong haste, his troops were pouring over the bridge of St. Charles, and gathering in heavy masses under the western ramparts of the town. Could numbers give assurance of success, their triumph would have been secure; for five French battalions and the armed colonial peasantry amounted in all to more than seven thousand five hundred men.

Full in sight before them stretched the long thin lines of the British forces,——the half-wild Highlanders, the steady soldiery of England, and the hardy levies of the provinces,——less than five thousand in number, but all inured to battle, and strong in the full assurance of success.

Yet, could the chiefs of that gallant army have pierced the secrets of the future, could they have foreseen that the victory which they burned to achieve would have robbed England of her proudest boast, and that the conquest of Canada would pave the way for the independence of America, their swords would have dropped from their hands, and the heroic fire have gone out within their hearts.

At a little before ten o'clock, the British could see that Montcalm was preparing to advance, and in a few moments, all his troops appeared in rapid motion. They came on in three divisions, shouting after the manner of their nation, and firing heavily as soon as they came within range. In the British ranks, not a trigger was pulled, not a soldier stirred; and their ominous composure seemed to damp the spirit of the assailants.

It was not until the French were within forty yards that the fatal word was given, and the British muskets blazed forth at once in one crashing explosion. Like a ship at full career, arrested with sudden ruin on a sunken rock, the ranks of Montcalm staggered, shivered, and broke before that wasting storm of lead. The smoke, rolling along the field, for a moment shut out the view.

When the white wreaths were scattered on the wind, a wretched spectacle was disclosed; men and officers tumbled in heaps, battalions resolved into a mob, order and obedience gone; and when the British muskets were leveled for a second volley, the masses of the militia were seen to cower and shrink with an uncontrollable panic. For a few minutes, the French regulars stood their ground, returning a sharp and not ineffectual fire. But now, echoing cheer on cheer, redoubling volley on volley, the British troops advanced and swept the field before them.

In the short action and pursuit, the French lost fifteen hundred men, killed, wounded, and taken. Of the remainder, some escaped within the city, and others fled across the St.Charles to rejoin their comrades who had been left to guard the camp. The pursuers were recalled by sound of trumpet; the broken ranks were formed afresh, and the English troops withdrawn beyond reach of the cannon of Quebec.

Yet the triumph of the victors was mingled with sadness, as the tidings went from rank to rank that Wolfe had fallen. In the heat of the action, as he advanced at the head of the grenadiers of Louisburg, a bullet shattered his wrist; but he wrapped his handkerchief about the wound, and showed no sign of pain.

A moment more, and a ball pierced his side. Still he pressed forward, waving his sword and cheering his soldiers to the attack, when a third shot lodged deep within his breast. He paused, reeled, and staggering to one side, fell to the earth. He was borne to the rear and laid softly on the grass. They asked if he would have a surgeon; but he shook his head and answered that all was over with him. His eyes closed with the torpor of approaching death, and those around him sustained his fainting form.

Yet they could not withhold their gaze from the wild turmoil before them, and the charging ranks of their companions rushing through fire and smoke. "See how they run," one of the officers exclaimed, as the French fled in confusion before the leveled bayonets.

"Who run?" demanded Wolfe, opening his eyes like a man aroused from sleep. "The enemy, sir!" was the reply, "they give way everywhere." "Then," said the dying general, "tell Colonel Burton to march Webb's regiment down to St. Charles River, to cut off their retreat from the bridge. Now, God be praised, I will die in peace," he muttered; and turning on his side, he calmly breathed his last.

Almost at the same moment fell his great adversary, Montcalm, as he strove, with vain bravery, to rally his shattered ranks. Struck down with a mortal wound, he was placed upon a litter and borne to the General Hospital on the banks of the St. Charles. The surgeons told him that he could not recover. "I am glad of it," was his calm reply. He then asked how long he might survive, and was told that he had not many hours remaining. "So much the better," he said, "I am happy that I shall not live to see the surrender of Quebec."

Officers from the garrison came to his bedside to ask his orders and instructions. "I will give no more orders," replied the defeated soldier. "I have much business that must be attended to, of greater moment than your ruined garrison and this wretched country. My time is very short; therefore, pray leave me."

The officers withdrew, and none remained in the chamber but his confessor and the Bishop of Quebec. To the last he expressed his contempt for his own mutinous and half-famished troops, and his admiration for the disciplined valor of his opponents. He died before midnight, and was buried at his own desire in a cavity of the earth formed by the bursting of a bombshell.

(Francis Parkman, selected)

译文

魁北克陷落

太阳从魁北克的城墙上缓缓升起，惊恐的人们看见了亚伯拉罕平原上暗红色的英国军队方阵，远远看去金光闪闪。气喘吁吁的通信兵把这个坏消息带给了德蒙卡尔姆。无论远方还是近处的营地，都回响着报警的鼓声，以及慌忙准备的喧嚣声。

尽管困难重重，他还是相信能够坚持到冬季，因为那时霜冻就会把侵略者们逼出小镇。但是这个悲惨的早晨，敌人成功突袭的消息像一枚炸弹在耳边爆炸一般。可他还是装出一种自信的口吻。"他们最终还是找到了我们的弱点。"他听说是这样的，"我们必须用数量来碾压他们。"

仓促之间，他的军队已经蜂拥至圣查尔斯桥，全部都聚集到了西边的城墙下。如果这场战役单从人数来算的话，他胜券在握。因为五个营地的法国士兵以及武装的殖民地农民加起来有七千五百多人。

远远望去，前方的英军呈一条细细的线——那些都是半开化的苏格兰高地人，他们是英军稳定的军力，同时那里也是个征兵艰难的地方——一共不足五千人，但他们战斗经验丰富，也是成功的保障。

如果这些英勇的军队将领们能够窥视未来秘密的话，他们会发现，他们誓死追求的胜利粉碎了大英帝国最引以为豪的扬言，这次征服加拿大的战争为美国独立铺平了道路，他们手中之剑就此掉落，心中燃烧的英雄之火也随之熄灭。

十点还没到，英军们看见蒙特卡姆正准备拔营前进，几分钟后，他的军队快速向前移动，呈三队前进，喊着自己国家的口号。他们在刚步入射程范围内，便火力全开。反观英军，没有一个人拔枪，也没有一个士兵行动，这份预料中的冷静似乎削弱了敌军的气势。

法国军队逐渐逼近至三十七米以内，英军才收到开火的命令，一时间，英军那里火光四射，响声四起。就像一艘全速前进的船触上暗礁，德蒙卡尔姆军队的队列也在这场铅弹的风暴中被打乱、打散，然后被分开。地面立刻升起滚滚浓烟，一时间连眼前的景色都难以分辨。

当白烟随风而逝，望远镜也逐渐能够看清远方的时候，士兵和军官们都四下分散成团，整个营都分散开来，丝毫看不出任何的纪律，当英国军队经过调整后准备进行第二次截击，民兵们看起来更加畏缩，在陷入难以控制的恐慌后人数减少了许多。不一会儿，法国军队便到达了他们的阵地，并进行了一场猛烈有效的反击。此时，欢呼声和枪声此起彼伏，英军向前进军，扫荡了前面的阵地。

在这次短暂的交火中，法军死伤和被俘人数在一千五百左右。其余的人，有的逃进城里，其他的跨过圣查尔斯桥混入留下守营的士兵中。追捕的人被喇叭声召回，剩下的人重新整队，英军们撤回至魁北克城墙上大炮的射程范围之外。

胜利的喇叭声掺杂着一丝丝伤感，因为，沃尔夫已经受伤的小道消息已经在各个营之间传开了。在激烈的战斗中，身在路易斯堡近卫步兵队伍最前端的他被一颗子弹打中手腕，但他用手帕捂住了伤口，并丝毫没有表现出疼痛的样子。

又一会儿，子弹穿过了他的身体，但是他仍然向前行进着，挥舞着手中的剑，鼓励着他的士兵们向前进攻。第三颗子弹深深地射进了他的胸膛。他顿住了，感觉晕晕乎乎的，摇摇晃晃地倒在了地上。紧接着，他被运往后方，轻轻地放在草坪上。人们问他需不需要外科医生，他回道，"不需要了，已经太迟了"。他闭上眼睛，忍受着死亡来临前的麻木，周围的人也不再打扰他。

但是他们的眼神无法从眼前的混乱中挪开，己方的冲锋兵们在浓烟和炮火向前冲着。"看他们，都逃跑了。"其中一个军官说道，此时的法军正趁着英军再次调整军力前的混乱逃走。

"谁逃跑了？"沃尔夫问道，他像一个刚醒的人一样睁开双眼。"是敌人，长官。"有人回复说，"他们在四处溃逃。""去，"奄奄一息的长官说道，"告诉伯顿上校，联合韦伯的人马，快去圣查尔斯河，从桥上切断他们的退路，上帝保佑，让我死得瞑目。"

几乎同时，他伟大的敌人，德蒙卡尔姆，虽然勇敢无畏地召集残余的军队，但是也受了致命伤，被放在担架上，运往位于圣查尔斯银行的综合医院。当医生宣布他没有救了的时候，他回复道："我其实很开心。"他又问医生自己还能活多久，医生回复他活不了几个小时了，"这样更好，"他说，

"很高兴,我不用眼睁睁看着魁北克宣布投降。"

　　守卫军军官们来到他的身边来询问他的指令。"我没什么命令可下达,"这个战败的军人说道,"我还有很多事情要亲自处理,这些都比这个失败的驻军和这个悲惨的国家更重要,我时间不多了,所以,别找我吧。"

　　军官们退下了,除了魁北克的主教大人和他的信徒,没有人再留在忏悔室。在最后,他对自己的反抗和半农兵化的军队进行了自嘲,同时对对手的纪律严明和勇敢表示钦佩。最后,根据他的遗愿,他被埋葬在一颗炸弹爆炸留下的弹坑中。

(弗兰西斯·帕克曼,有删改)

❧ 作者介绍

　　弗兰西斯·帕克曼,美国历史学家,生于波士顿。他的历史著作包括《庞蒂亚克阴谋》(本文便节选自此书)《法国开拓者的新词汇》《西部大开发》以及《德蒙卡尔姆和沃尔夫》。他是一个有趣的作家,在美国文学界有着很高的地位。

Rescue of the Crew of the Merrimac

A great rush of water came up the gangway, settling and gurgling out of the deck. The mass was whirling from right to left "against the sun"; it seized us and threw us against the bulwarks, then over the rail. Two were swept forward as if by a momentary recession, and one was carried down into a coal-bunker. In a moment, however, with increased force, the water shot him up out of the same hole and swept him among us.

The bulwarks disappeared. We charged about with casks, cans, and spars. The life-preservers stood us in good stead, preventing chests from being crushed, as well as buoying us up on the surface. When we looked for the life-boat we found that it had been carried away. The catamaran was the largest piece of floating debris; we assembled about it.

The firing had ceased. It was evident that the enemy had not seen us in the general mass of moving objects; but soon the tide began to drift these away, and we were being left alone with the catamaran. The men were directed to cling close in, bodies below and only heads out, close under the edges.

We mustered; all were present, and direction was given to remain as we were till further orders, for I was sure that in due time after daylight a responsible officer would come out to reconnoiter. It was evident that we could not swim against the tide to reach the entrance. Moreover, the shores were lined with troops, and the small boats were looking for victims that might escape from the vessel.

The only chance lay in remaining undiscovered until the coming of the reconnoitering boat, to which, perhaps, we might surrender without being fired on. The moon was now low. The sunken Merrimac was bubbling up her last lingering breath. The boat's crew looking for refugees pulled closer, peering with lanterns. Again the discipline of the men was put to severe test, for time and again it seemed that the boats would come up, and the impulse to swim away was strong.

The air was chilly and the water positively cold. In less than five minutes our teeth were chattering; so loud, indeed, did they chatter, that it seemed the destroyer or the boats would hear. In spite of their efforts, two of the men soon began to cough, and it seemed that we should surely be discovered. I worked my legs and body under the raft for exercise, but in spite of all, the shivers would come and the teeth would chatter.

We remained there probably an hour. Frogs croaked up the bight, and as dawn broke, the birds began to twitter and chirp in the bushes and trees near at hand along the wooded slopes. Day came bright and beautiful. It seemed that nature disregarded man and went on the same, serene, peaceful, and unmoved. Man's strife appeared a discord, and his tragedy received no sympathy.

About daybreak a beautiful strain went up from a bugle at Punta Gorda battery. It was pitched at a high key, and rose and lingered, long drawn out, gentle and tremulous; it seemed as though an angel might be playing while looking down in tender pity. Could this be a Spanish bugle?

Broad daylight came. The destroyer got up anchor, and drew back again up the bight. We were still undiscovered. Then some one announced, "A steam-launch is heading for us, sir." I looked around, and found that a launch of large size, with the curtains aft drawn down, was coming from the bight around Smith Cay and heading straight for us. That must be the reconnoitering party.

It swerved a little to the left as if to pass around us, giving no sighs of having seen us. No one was visible on board, everybody apparently being below the rail. When it was about thirty yards off I hailed. The launch stopped as if frightened, and backed furiously. A squad of riflemen filed out, and formed in a semicircle on the forecastle, and came to "load, ready, aim".

A murmur passed about among my men, "They are going to shoot us." A bitter thought flashed through my mind, "The miserable cowards! A brave nation will learn of this and call for an account." But the volley did not follow. The aim must have been merely for caution, and it was apparent that there must be an officer on board in control.

I called out in a strong voice to know if there was not an officer in the boat; if so, an American officer wished to speak with him with a view to surrendering himself and seamen as prisoners of war. The curtain was raised; an officer leaned out and waved his hand, and the rifles came down.

I struck out for the launch, and climbed on board aft with the assistance of the officer, who, hours afterward, we learned was Admiral Cervera himself. With him were two other officers, his juniors. To him I surrendered myself and the men, taking off my revolver-belt, glasses, canteen, and life-preserver.

The officers looked astonished at first, perhaps at the singular uniforms and the begrimed condition of us all, due to the fine coal and oil that came to the surface. Then a current of kindness seemed to pass over them, and they exclaimed, "Valiente!" The launch then steamed up to the catamaran, and then men climbed on board, the two that had been coughing being in the last stages of exhaustion and requiring to be lifted. We were prisoners in Spanish hands.

(Richmond Pearson Hobson)

译文

解救梅里麦克号船员

一大片水漫上了舷梯,"哗哗"地流到了甲板上。这个大家伙沿着逆时针从右向左打着转;它抓起我们抛向舷墙,扔过围栏。两名船员如同遇上了瞬间的退潮那样向前滑去,另一个则被往下带入了煤仓。然而不一会儿,随着增大的压力,他又被水流从原来的入口射了出来,跌落在我们中间。

船的舷墙已经没了,我们带着木桶、罐子和桅杆向前直冲。救生衣很好地保护了我们的胸膛,还支撑着我们浮在水面上。我们寻找着救生艇,但它已不知去向。筏子成了一片残骸中最大的漂浮物,我们便集中到了它的周围。

大火已经被扑灭了。很明显,敌人在大片漂动着的物体中并没有发现我们，但海潮不久就会将它们吹开，只剩下我们和那筏子。船员们听从了指示紧贴着船体将身体埋了下去，只让脑袋贴着边缘伸出来。

我们集中在一起，所有人都在场。我下令在下一个指令下达前，大家守候在原地，因为我确信黎明过后某个时刻一定会有一名负责的军官出来勘查战场。我们很明显不能逆着潮汐游到这片水域的入口处，而且岸边都驻扎着部队，小船也正在搜寻着从船上逃出来的幸存者。

唯一的机会就是直到侦察船开过来以前一直待着不被发现，或许我们能够向它投降而不遭到敌军射击。月亮已经落得很低了，沉没的"梅里麦克号"正冒着泡吐出最后残存的气息。那些在灯光下仔细搜捕难民的船员们越来越近，大家的纪律性再次受到了严峻的考验。一次又一次，那些船眼看着就要靠上来了，我们想要跳入水中游走的冲动非常强烈。

空气冰凉冰凉，水也相当的冷。五分钟不到我们的牙齿就开始打颤了，那打颤的声音实在是太响了，似乎驱逐舰或小船上的人都能听到。有两个人虽然努力克制着，但还是咳嗽了起来，看样子我们肯定会被发现了。我在筏子底下活动着我的腿脚和身子，但无论怎么做，身体还是瑟瑟发抖，牙齿依旧打着颤。

我们在那里待了大约一个小时。破晓时分青蛙在港湾里"呱呱"地叫了起来，在那树木繁茂的斜坡上，鸟儿们在离我们近在咫尺的树丛与灌木丛中叽叽喳喳地叫着。美丽灿烂的一天来到了，似乎大自然根本不去理会人类，依旧如初地不为所动，那样宁静，那样平和。人类的冲突只是世间一个不和谐的音调，而他们的悲剧也得不到一丝的同情。

黎明时分，从蓬塔戈尔达炮兵连的军号中传来了一首美丽的曲子。它的音调很高，随后继续升高并稍作逗留，然后又拖起了柔和而又颤抖的长音。它如同一位怀着怜悯之意下视凡间的天使所奏响的乐章。这是一首西班牙军曲吗？

天已大亮，只见一艘驱逐舰起锚航行，但随即又转回港湾里去了。我们还是没有被发现。有人说道："先生，一艘蒸汽船正朝着我们过来。"我看了看四周，发现一艘巨大的汽船正从史密斯礁笔直地往我们的方向驶来，船尾还挂着帐幕。那一定是侦察部队。

看样子它没有发现我们，稍微往左转了向打算从旁边驶过。甲板上看不到一个人，很明显他们的人都在围栏底下。当它离我们大约二十七米时，我大声招呼起来。汽船像受到了惊吓一般停下了，然后急速往后退去。一队步枪手鱼贯而出，在前甲板排成了半圆形队伍，接着就是"装弹，准备，瞄准"。

我方船员们窃窃私语起来："他们打算要开枪射杀我们了。"一个痛苦的念头闪过了我的脑海，"这些可悲的懦夫！一个勇敢的国家是会记录下这一刻，并从中获得教益的"。但随之而来的不是枪的齐射，看来瞄准只是为了警戒而已。很明显，船上有一位军官指挥着他们的行动。

我高声大喊，想知道对方船上是否有军官；如果有，一名美国军官想当面和他谈话，他自己以及水兵们都会作为战俘投降。帐幕拉了起来，一个军官探出身来挥了挥手，士兵们便放下了步枪。

我前往那艘汽船，在那位军官的帮助下爬上了船尾，几小时后我们才知道那就是塞尔韦拉海军上将本人。和他在一起的还有两位军官，那是他的下属。我代表自己和船员们向他投降，并摘下了佩枪带、眼镜、水壶和救生衣。

那位军官一开始看上去很震惊，可能是瞧见了我单薄的制服，以及被漂在水面的细粉煤和油弄得浑身脏兮兮的样子。然后，似乎有一股善意在他们之间传开，他们呼喊着："真是勇敢！"然后汽船便靠向小筏子，水员们爬上了甲板，那两个咳嗽着的极度衰弱的人已经需要别人抬上去了。我们落入了西班牙人手中，成了俘虏。

（里士满·皮尔逊·霍布森）

✍ 作者介绍

里士满·皮尔逊·霍布森出生于阿拉巴马州，并在1898年同西班牙的战争中一举成名。他为了封锁航道，把煤船"梅里麦克号"沉在了圣地亚哥港，将西班牙的战舰困在了港口中。他被西班牙人俘虏后在古巴的要塞中关了大约六周，但在美国击败西班牙后被释放了。他写下了让煤船沉没的全过程，而《解救"梅里麦克号"船员》正是节选自此书。他也写了几本内容关于他本职工作的书。

At Lucerne

Photographs, casts, and carvings of the Lucerne Lion, all, even the best of them, fall short of expressing the simple grandeur of Thorwaldsen's boldest work. The face of a perpendicular sand-stone cliff was hewn roughly,——not smoothed or polished in any part. Half-way up was quarried a niche, and in this, as in a lair, is a lion nearly thirty feet long.

The splintered shank of a lance projects from his side. The head——broken or bitten off in his mortal throe, lies by the shield of France, which is embossed with the fleur-de-lis. One huge paw protects the sacred emblem. He has dragged himself, with a final rally of strength, to die upon, while caressing it. He will never move again. The limbs are relaxed, the mighty frame stretched by the convulsion that wrenched away his life.

He is dead,——not daunted; conquered,——not subdued. The blended grief and ferocity in his face are human and heroic, not brutal. In the rock above and below the den are cut a Latin epitaph, and the names of twenty-six men. "Helvetiorum fidei ac virtuti. Die X Aug. II et III Sept. 1792," begins the inscription.

Who has not read, oft and again, how the Swiss Guard of twenty-six officers and seven hundred and fifty privates were cut to pieces to a man in defence of the royal prisoner of the Tuileries against the mob thirsting for her blood? In the shop near the monument they show a facsimile of the king's order to the Guards to be at the palace upon the fatal day.

Trailing vines have crept downward from the top and fissures of the cliff. Tall trees clothe the summit. A pool lies at the base, a slender fountain in the middle. There are always travelers seated upon the benches in front of the railing, guarding the water's brink, contemplating the dead monarch. It is the pride of Lucerne.

Around Lake Lucerne, otherwise known as the Lake of the Four Cantons, every rood of ground is memorable in the history of the gallant little Republic. Near it, Arnold Winkelried gathered into his breast the red sheaf of spears upon the battle-field of Sempach, July 9th, 1386.

The Confederate Brethren of Uri, Schwyz and Unter-walden met at Rütli upon the very border of the lake, on the night of November 7th, 1307, and swore to give no rest to mind or body until Switzerland should be free.

William Tell was born at Bürglen, a few miles above Flülen. By the time we had re-read Schiller's "William Tely," and visited, with it in hand, Altorf, Küssnacht, and Tell's Platte, we credited the tales of his being and daring almost as devoutly as do the native Switzers.

Küssnacht is but a few miles back from the lake in the midst of a smiling country lying between water and the mountains. A crumbling wall on a hill-side to the left of the road was pointed out to us as the remains of Gessler's Castle. The Hollow Way in which Tell shot him is a romantic lane between steep, grassy banks and overhanging trees.

The exact place of the Tyrant's death is marked by a little chapel. A fresco in the porch depicts the scene described by Schiller. The purple Alpine heather blossoms up to the church-door, and maiden-hair ferns fringe the foundation walls.

Tell's Platte——or Leap——is marked by a tiny chapel upon the extremest water's edge near Rütli. Its foundations are built into the rock upon which the patriot sprang from Gessler's boat. A great Thanksgiving Mass for Swiss liberty is performed here once in the year, attended by a vast concourse of people in gayly-decorated boats. There is not room on the shelving shore for a congregation.

Altorf is a clean Swiss village where the window curtains are all white, and where the children, clean, too, but generally bare-legged and bare-headed, turn out in a body to gather around the strangers that stop to look at the monument. A very undignified memorial it is of the valiant Liberator. "With which I meant to kill you had I hurt my son!" says the inscription on the pedestal. The lime-tree to which the boy Albert was tied to be shot at was one hundred forty-seven measured paces away. That spot is now marked by a fountain.

(Mary Virginia Terhune)

译文

卢塞恩游记

卢塞恩狮子像是托瓦尔森最大胆的作品。即使是最好的照片、铸像和雕塑都无法表达出它那由简练的线条营造出的宏大感。垂直的砂砾岩在悬崖表面粗粗砍过——没有在任何部位进行润滑和打磨。悬崖中间开凿出一个壁龛,在里面一只近九米长的狮子好似卧在巢穴中。

一根长矛的柄部从它身体的侧面捅出,而长矛的尖端则落在饰有鸢尾花浮雕的法兰西盾徽旁。也许是狮子在致命的剧痛之下打断了它或是咬断了它。一只巨大的爪子保护着这神圣的徽章。在死亡的那一刻,狮子集聚了最后一丝力量去拥抱它,从此再也没有动过。它的四肢松弛,巨大的身体因夺去它生命的剧痛而瘫软。

它已死亡,但并没有丧失斗志;它被征服,但并没有向敌人屈服。它脸上凶猛与悲哀混杂的表情并不残忍,反而展现出人性化和英雄主义的一面。巢穴上方和下方的岩石上刻着一段拉丁文墓志铭和二十六个男人的名字。碑文的开端是这样的:"献给1792年8月10日、9月2日及9月3日牺牲的英勇而忠诚的赫尔维西亚人。"

谁没有一遍又一遍读过瑞士近卫队的故事呢?当暴民们渴求玛丽王后的鲜血时,是这二十六名军官和七百五十名士兵为捍卫杜伊勒里宫而粉身碎骨,他们最终凝聚成一个勇士的象征。纪念碑附近的办事处陈列着在卫士们殉难那天,国王下达给近卫队守卫官殿的命令的副本。

蜿蜒的藤蔓从悬崖的顶部和裂缝里攀援而下。崖顶上空覆盖着参天大树的树冠,中间流出一道细小的泉水,轻轻滴落在底部的池塘里。水边设置了保护性的栏杆,而旅行者们总会坐在它前方的凳子上,凝视着这死去的狮子君王。它是卢塞恩的骄傲。

在卢塞恩湖——或者说"四州森林湖"四周,每一寸地面都印刻着这个小小的共和国家在历史上的英勇表现。1386年7月9日,在这附近的森帕赫战场,阿诺德·温克尔里德被一束红色的长矛刺穿了胸膛。

1307年11月7日晚,结成联盟的乌里、施维茨和下瓦尔登代表在位于卢塞恩湖边界的吕特利会面，并宣誓只要瑞士一天不解放，他们就一天不会停止为此奉献他们的身体和灵魂。

威廉·特尔出生于离博伦几千米远的博格林。如果我们重读过席勒的《威廉·特尔》，然后再带着它参观阿尔特多夫、屈斯纳赫特和退尔斯普拉特，我们几乎会像天真的瑞士当地人一样相信那些关于他的存在和英勇的传说。

屈斯纳赫特坐落在这个风景明媚的国家的中部，依山傍水，离卢森湖仅有几千米远。道路左边的山坡上有一道破碎的墙，向我们表明这里就是盖斯乐城堡的残迹。特尔射杀盖斯乐的霍洛路是一个浪漫的小巷，两边有耸立的峭壁、青草依依的堤岸和伸出枝丫的树木。

人们在暴君盖斯乐死亡的确切地点建了一所小教堂作为标志。门廊上的一幅壁画展示了席勒描写的场景。教堂的门边盛开着紫色的高山石楠花，铁线蕨则围绕着墙基爬行。

特尔斯普拉特——也就是利普，位于靠近吕特利水边极其边缘的地带，也有一座小教堂作为标志，它的地基建在一块岩石里。当时特尔这位爱国者就是从盖斯乐的船上纵身跃上了这块岩石。这里每年都会举办一场庆祝瑞士解放的盛大感恩弥撒，不过一大群人只能挤在装饰华美的船里，因为逐渐倾斜的河滨无法为人群提供足够的空间。

阿尔特多夫是一个干净整洁的瑞士村庄，窗帘全都是白色的。孩子们也是整洁，但通常光着腿、不戴帽子。他们总是一块儿出现，围着停下来看纪念碑的陌生人。那是一块有损英勇解放战士尊严的纪念碑，其基座的题词上写着："我打算杀了你，结果却伤害了我的儿子！"男孩艾伯特被绑着射杀的那棵菩提树离这里一百四十七步远。那里现在建起了一座喷泉。

（玛丽·弗吉尼亚·特休恩）

✍ 作者介绍

玛丽·弗吉尼亚·特休恩1831年出生于弗吉尼亚州。从14岁起，她就以玛丽恩·哈兰德为笔名给大众出版物写作。她也在杂志《其间》《圣尼古拉斯》和《完全清醒》等部门任职。她创作了种类繁多的作品，在其众多魅力十足的青少年读物中，有一本叫《祖母当年十四岁》。本文选自一本讲述旅行的书《闲晃于愉悦之地》，由查尔斯·斯克里布纳父子出版公司授权。

How I Found Livingstone

预习

animated /ˈænɪmeɪtɪd/ 生气勃勃的
deliberately /dɪˈlɪbərətli/ 故意地
fervid /ˈfɜːrvɪd/ 炽热的；热情的
gigantic /dʒaɪˈɡæntɪk/ 巨大的
mutually /ˈmjuːtʃuəli/ 互相地
oblivious /əˈblɪviəs/ 不注意的
realize /ˈriːəlaɪz/ 实现

We push on rapidly, lest the news of our coming may reach the people of Bunder Ujiji before we come in sight, and are ready for them. We halt at a little brook, then ascend the long slope of a naked ridge, the very last of the myriads we have crossed. This alone prevents us from seeing the lake in all its vastness. We arrive at the summit, travel across and arrive at its western rim, and——the port of Ujiji is below us.

At this grand moment we do not think of the hundreds of miles we have marched, of the hundreds of hills we have ascended and descended, of the many forests we have traversed, of the jungles and thickets that annoyed us, of the fervid salt plains that blistered our feet, of the hot suns that scorched us, nor of the dangers and difficulties, now happily surmounted. At last the sublime hour has arrived! Our dreams, our hopes, and our anticipations are now about to be realized!

"Unfurl the flags, and load your guns!"

"One, two, three——fire!"

A volley from nearly fifty guns roars like a salute from a battery of artillery: we shall note its effect presently on the peaceful-looking village below. Before we had gone a hundred yards our repeated volleys had the effect desired. We had awakened Ujiji to the knowledge that a caravan was coming, and the people were witnessed rushing up in hundreds to meet us.

The mere sight of the flags informed every one that we were a caravan; but the American flag borne aloft by gigantic Asmani, whose face was one vast smile on this day, rather staggered them at first. However, many of the people that now approached us remembered the flag. They had seen it float above the American consulate, and from the masthead of many a ship in the harbor of Zanzibar, and they were soon welcoming the beautiful flag with "Bindera Kisungu!"——a white man's flag! "Bindera Merikani!"——the American flag!

Then we were surrounded by them, and almost deafened by the shouts of "Yambo, yambo, bana! Yambo, bana! Yambo bana!" To all and each of my men the welcome was given. We are now about three hundred yards from the village of Ujiji, and the crowds are dense about me. Suddenly I hear a voice on my right say, "Good morning, sir!"

Startled at hearing this greeting in the midst of such a crowd of black people, I turn sharply around in search of the man, and see him at my side with the blackest of faces, but animated and joyous.

"Who are you?" I ask.

"I am Susi, the servant of Dr. Livingstone," said he, smiling.

"What! Is Dr. Livingstone here?"

"Yes, sir."

"Good morning, sir," said another voice.

"Hallo," said I. "What is your name?"

"My name is Chumah, sir."

"What! Are you Chumah, the friend of Wekotani?"

"Yes, sir."

"And is the Doctor well?"

"Not very well, sir."

"Where has he been so long?"

"In Manyuema."

"Now, you, Susi, run, and tell the Doctor that I am coming."

"Yes, sir," and he darted off like a madman.

By this time we were within two hundred yards of the village, and the multitude was getting denser, and almost preventing our march. Flags and streamers were out; Arabs and Wangwana were pushing their way through the natives in order to greet us, for, according to their account, we belonged to them.

Soon Susi came running back, and asked me my name. He had told the Doctor that I was coming, but the Doctor was too surprised to believe him, and when the Doctor asked him my name, Susi was rather staggered.

But during Susi's absence the news had been conveyed to the Doctor that it was surely a white man who was coming, whose guns were firing, and whose flag could be seen. The great Arab magnates of Ujiji had gathered together before the Doctor's house, and the Doctor had come out from his veranda to discuss the matter and await my arrival.

In the meantime the head of the Expedition had halted, and the kirangozi was out of the ranks, holding his flag aloft. Selim said to me, "I see the Doctor, sir. Oh, what an old man! He has a white beard."

Pushing back the crowds, and passing from the rear, I walked down a living avenue of people until I came in front of the semicircle of Arabs, in the front of which stood the white man with the gray beard. As I advanced slowly toward him I noticed that he was pale, looked wearied, wore a bluish cap with a faded gold band round it, had on a waistcoat and a pair of gray tweed trousers.

I would have run to him, only I was a coward in the presence of such a mob——would have embraced him, only, he being an Englishman, I did not know how he would receive me; so I did what cowardice and false pride suggested——walked deliberately to him, took off my hat, and said, "Dr. Livingstone, I presume?"

"Yes," said he, with a kind smile, lifting his cap slightly.

I replace my hat, and he puts on his cap, and we both grasp hands, and then I say aloud, "I thank God, Doctor, I have been permitted to see you."

He answered, "I feel thankful that I am here to welcome you. "

I turn to the Arabs, take off my hat to them in response to the saluting chorus of "Yambo" I receive, and the Doctor introduces them to me by name. Then oblivious of the crowds, oblivious of the men who shared with me my dangers, we——Livingstone and I——turn our faces toward his cottage.

He points to the veranda, or rather, mud platform, under the broad overhanging eaves; he points to his own particular seat, which I see that his age and experience in Africa have suggested, namely, a straw mat, with a goatskin over it, and another skin nailed against the wall to protect his back from contact with the cold mud. I protest against taking this seat, but the Doctor will not yield: I must take it.

We are seated——the Doctor and I——with our backs to the wall. The Arabs take seats on our left. More than a thousand natives are in our front, filling the whole square densely, indulging their curiosity, and discussing the fact of two white men meeting at Ujiji——one just come from Manyuema, in the west, the other from Unyanyembe in the east.

Conversation began. What about? I declare I have forgotten. Oh! We mutually asked questions of each other, such as:

"How did you come here?" and "Where have you been all this long time?——the world has believed you to be dead." Yes, that was the way it began; but whatever the Doctor informed me, and that which I communicated to him, I cannot correctly report, for I found myself gazing at him, conning the wonderful man at whose side I now sat in Central Africa.

Every hair of his head and beard, every wrinkle of his face, the manners of his features, and the slightly wearied look he wore, were all imparting intelligence to me——the knowledge that I craved for so much ever since I heard the words, "Take what you want, but find Livingstone." What I saw was deeply interesting intelligence to me, and unvarnished truth. I was listening and reading at the same time. What did these dumb witnesses relate to me?

(Henry M. Stanley)

译文

寻找利文斯敦

我们加快速度前进，以免乌吉吉港的人们在我们现身并准备好之前就得知我们到来的消息。我们停在一条小溪边休整了一下，然后沿着一道光秃秃的山脊的长坡向上攀爬。这是我们需要攀越的无数山脊中的最后一道，单单这一座山脊，就足以阻碍我们看到湖泊了。最后我们爬上了山脊的最高点，横穿过去，到达了它的西部边缘。看，乌吉吉港就在我们下面！

在这重要一刻，沿途曾遭遇的危机四伏和艰难困苦早已在我们的脑海中远去。我们跋涉了几百千米长途，攀越了几百座山峰，横穿了许许多多森林。丛林和灌木曾困扰过我们，炎热的太阳曾炙烤我们，灼热的盐原曾令我们的脚起泡。而现在，这激动人心的时刻终于来临。我们的梦想、希望和期待即将实现。

"张开旗帜，装填子弹！"

"一二三——开火！"

近五十支枪齐射的声音呼啸而过，像炮兵部队用炮台发射的礼炮般轰然作响；我们即刻就能发现它对底下这个和平村庄的影响。走了不到九十米后，五十支枪再次齐发，这次我们得到了想要的效果。我们成功让乌吉吉觉察到一支商队的到来，数百名村民冲上前来与我们相见。

本来只要一看见旗帜，大家就会知道我们是一支商队。但扛着美国国旗的阿玛尼人高马大，于是美国国旗高高飘扬在半空，刚开始的时候让人们有些犹豫不决，虽然阿玛尼的脸上洋溢着一朵大大的笑容。不过，朝我们迎来的大多数人都记起来了这旗帜，他们曾经在美国大使馆的上空和桑给巴尔港船只的桅顶看见它随风飘扬。不久，他们就纷纷嚷着"一面白人的旗帜"和"美国国旗"来表示他们对这面旗帜的欢迎。

人们围绕在我们周围，"Yambo, yambo, bana! Yambo, bana! Yambo bana"的呼声震耳欲聋，热情表达着对我们每一个人的欢迎。我们现在离乌吉吉村还有二百七十四米远，而我几乎要被密集的人群淹没了。突然，我听见左边有个声音说："先生，早上好！"

在这样一群黑皮肤的人当中听见这样一句问候，我惊讶地立刻转身四处寻找声音的主人。他就在我旁边，是所有人中最黑的一个，但脸上却洋溢着愉悦与快乐。

我问："你是谁？"

他笑着回答："我是利文斯敦医生的仆人苏西。"

"什么！利文斯敦医生就在这里吗？"

"没错。"

这时，另外一个声音说："先生，早上好！"

"你好！"我说，"你叫什么名字？"

"我的名字叫朱曼。"

"什么！你是沃克坦的朋友朱曼？"

"是的。"

"那么医生一切都好吗？"

"不太好。"

"这么长时间他去哪儿了？"

"他去了曼越马。"

"苏西，现在就请你跑去告诉医生我来了。"

"好的。"他答应着，疯了一般飞奔而去。

此时我们离村庄不到一百八十三米，围上来的人群越来越密，几乎挡住了我们前进的道路。旗帜早被抛到脑后。阿拉伯人和万瓦那把我们视作自己人，从当地人中挤到我们面前问好。

苏西很快跑回来问我的名字。他告诉医生我来了，但医生十分讶异，对此不相信。当医生问起我名字的时候，苏西有些迟疑。

但是在苏西跑回来的这段时间，确认有一个白人到来的消息已经传到了医生的耳朵里。人们听见了他的枪声，也看见了他的旗帜。乌吉吉重要的阿拉伯首领聚集在医生的房子前，医生也从长廊里走出来，边和他们讨论着整件事，边等待我的到来。

同一时间，我们这支探险队的先头部队停下了脚步，向导扛着飘扬的旗帜离开了队伍。塞利姆对我说："先生，我看见医生了。他年纪真老，胡子都是雪白的！"

我从后面挤过去，穿过夹道的人群，来到阿拉伯人围成的半圆前。那里站着的正是一名白胡子的白人。我缓慢朝着他靠近，留意到他脸色苍白，看上去疲惫不堪。他身上穿着马甲和粗花呢裤子，头上戴着蓝色帽子，帽子四周镶着的金缎带已经褪了颜色。

我本该向他跑去，但在如此多的民众面前我感到怯懦；我本该拥抱他，但他是英国人，我不知道他是否会接受我。所以我慢慢走向他，拿下帽子致意说："如果我没错的话，你是利文斯敦医生吧？"这样做的我是多么懦弱和自大啊！

"我是。"他说，脸上扬起一个和蔼的笑容，轻轻举起了帽子。

我们先后戴上帽子，互相紧握双手，然后我大声说："谢天谢地，医生，我很荣幸见到你。"

他回答说："不胜感激，欢迎到来。"

周围的阿拉伯人异口同声喊着"Yambo"向我致意，我转向他们，拿下帽子表示感谢，医生一一为我介绍了他们的名字。然后，我和利文斯敦转头向他的小屋走去。我们忘记了身后的人群，也忘记了和我一起历险的人们。

他指向宽阔的屋檐遮蔽下的长廊，确切地说，那是个泥土做成的平台，平台上是他的特别座位：一个稻草垫子。垫子上面铺着一块山羊皮，还有一块山羊皮被钉在墙上，以免他的背与冰冷的泥土接触。这个座位让我清楚地看出了他的年龄和他在非洲的经历。他指着座位请我坐下，虽然我再三反对，但医生毫不退让，我只好坐了下来。

我和医生靠着墙坐下来，阿拉伯人坐在我们左边。我们前方的广场上密密麻麻挤满了超过一千名当地人，他们沉溺于好奇之中，互相议论着两个白人在乌吉吉见面的事——他们一个刚从西部的曼越马回来，而另一个来自东部的乌尼亚尼扬贝。

交谈开始了，但我敢说我早就忘记我们谈了些什么。哦，我们应该互相问了这些问题：

"你是怎么到这儿来的？""这么长时间你去哪儿了？全世界都以为你已经死了。"没错，我们就是这样开始的，但我没办法一字不差地把医生和我之间的谈话记下来，因为整个过程中我一直凝视着他，默默将这名伟大的男人记在心里。此时此刻，我在中非，就坐在他的身边。

自从我被告知"带上你想要的一切，只要能找到利文斯敦"，我就如此渴望得到他的消息。现在，属于他的每一根须发、他脸上的每一条皱纹和表达情绪的方式以及他疲态微露的外貌,都在向我传递着有关他的消息。我从中看到了我非常关注的一面,也看到了质朴的真实。我边听边写,这些无声的见证者会向我讲述什么样的故事呢?

(亨利·M. 斯坦利)

How Franklin Learned to Write

Mr. Matthew Adams, who had a pretty collection of books, and who frequented our printing-house, took notice of me, invited me to his library, and very kindly lent me such books as I chose to read. I now took a fancy to poetry, and made some little pieces; my brother, thinking it might turn to account, encouraged me, and put me on composing occasional ballads.

One was called The Lighthouse Tragedy, and contained an account of the drowning of Captain Worthilake, with his two daughters. The other was a sailor's song, on the taking of Teach (or Blackbeard) the pirate.

They were wretched stuff, in the Grub-street-ballad style; and when they were printed he sent me about the town to sell them. The first sold wonderfully, the event being recent, having made a great noise.

This flattered my vanity; but my father discouraged me by ridiculing my performances, and telling me verse-makers were generally beggars. So I escaped being a poet, most probably a very bad one; but as prose writing had been of great use to me in the course of my life, and was a principal means of my advancement, I shall tell you how, in such a situation, I acquired what little ability I have in that way.

About this time I met with an odd volume of the Spectator. It was the third. I had never before seen any of them. I bought it, read it over and over, and was much delighted with it. I thought the writing excellent, and wished, if possible, to imitate it.

With this view I took some of the papers, and making short hints of the sentiment in each sentence, laid them by a few days. Then, without looking at the book, I tried to complete the papers again, by expressing each hinted sentiment at length, and as fully as it had been expressed before, in any suitable words that should come to hand. Then I compared my Spectator with the original, discovered some of my faults, and corrected them.

But I found I wanted a stock of words, or a readiness in recollecting and using them. This I thought I should have acquired before that time if I had gone on making verses.

In verse the continual occasion for words of the same value, but of different length, to suit the measure, or of different sound for the rhyme, would have laid me under a constant necessity of searching for variety. Verse would also have tended to fix variety in my mind, and make me master of it.

Therefore I took some of the tales and turned them into verse. After a time, when I had pretty well forgotten the prose, I turned them into prose again.

I also sometimes jumbled my collections of hints into confusion, and after some weeks endeavored to reduce them into the best order, before I began to form the full sentences and complete the paper. This was to teach me method in the arrangement of thoughts.

By comparing my work afterwards with the original, I discovered many faults and amended them; but I sometimes had the pleasure of fancying that, in certain particulars of small import, I had been lucky enough to improve the method or the language, and this encouraged me to think I might possibly in time come to be a tolerable English writer.

(Benjamin Franklin)

译文

富兰克林是怎么学写作的

马修·亚当先生家中藏书丰富，他经常光顾我们的印刷所，并且对我颇为关照。他邀请我去他的藏书室，还慷慨地将我想读的书借给我。那时候我十分喜爱诗歌，自己也写些小诗；我哥觉得写诗可以赚点钱，便鼓励我时不时地写些叙事诗。

我写了两首叙事诗。一首叫作《灯塔悲剧》，讲述的是沃斯莱克船长与他的两个女儿溺水身亡的故事。另一首是水手歌，讲的是捉拿海盗铁柯（外号黑胡子）的经过。

这两首诗没什么水准，都是些葛拉布街诗（译注：葛拉布街是伦敦一条旧街，过去为穷苦潦倒文人的聚居地；因此文中将低劣的诗歌叫作"葛拉布街诗"）。印好之后，哥哥叫我拿到小镇上去卖。第一首诗卖得很好，毕竟讲的是近期发生的、轰动一时的事情。

这使我沾沾自喜，然而我的父亲反对我写诗，他嘲笑我的作品，说诗人都是穷光蛋。如此，我成为诗人（极可能是个低劣的诗人）的路便被切断了。但是，写散文却让我十分受益，并且成了我提升自己的一种基本手段，接下来我将告诉你，在这种情况下，我是如何获得我现有的这点小小才能的。

大约在那时候，我偶然看到了《旁观者》的零售本，是第三册，在此之前我从未看过这一系列的书。我把它买了下来，一遍又一遍地反复品味，爱不释手。这本书写得好极了，我想或许我也能模仿它写点什么。

于是我挑了几篇文章，摘录出要点，搁置几天后，再自己想出合适的词句将这些要点表述成文，与原版对照，找出自己的错误和不足，加以修改。

这样我便发现了自己词汇贫乏的问题，或者说，我不能很快地找到适当的词来用，我不禁想，假如我以前没有放弃写诗的话，那么现在我的词汇一定会丰富得多了。

如果我写诗的话，我得不断地寻找意思相同而长度不同的词，或是不同音素的词去凑韵脚，这会迫使我不断地搜索形式不同的同义词，这会有助于我记忆并掌握这些不同的词。

于是我选取了一些故事，改编成诗歌。过了一段时间，当我把原来的散文忘得差不多的时候，再把自己改编的诗歌改写成散文。

有时候我会把我摘录的思想打乱，几个星期以后，再设法把它们用最恰当的次序排列起来，然后再把它们写成完整的句子，凑成文章。这样做是为了学习如何组织思想。

完成这件事之后，再拿我的文章与原文比较，会发现许多错误和不足之处，我便加以改正。

但是有时候我不禁觉得：在某些小细节上，我侥幸地改进了原文的条理和语言，这样的想法鼓励了我，使我相信，在将来，我或许能成为一个不错的英文作家。

（本杰明·富兰克林）

♪ 作者介绍

　　本杰明·富兰克林出生于美国波士顿，著名的作家、科学家、爱国者。十岁时，他到哥哥经营的印刷所当学徒。后来他到了费城，开始了自己的写作事业。之后便声名鹊起，成了著名的作家及公众精神领袖。富兰克林进行了一项著名的实验：在雷雨天气中放风筝，证明了雷电是由电力造成的，这一发现使他在欧洲科学界名声大噪。美国独立战争开始时，他作为美国大使访问法国；他的努力推动了法国承认美国作为独立国家的独立性。

　　富兰克林的《自传》和《穷查理宝典》收录了他的大量作品。

Longfellow

When my acquaintance with Longfellow began, he had written the things that made his fame, and that it will probably rest upon: "Evangeline", "Hiawatha" and "Courtship of Miles Standish" were by that time old stories. But during the eighteen years that I knew him he produced the best of his minor poems, the greatest of his sonnets, the sweetest of his lyrics.

He rarely read anything of his own aloud, but in three or four cases he read to me poems that he had just finished, as if to give himself the pleasure of hearing them with the sympathetic sense of another. "Elizabeth" in the third part of "Tales of a Wayside Inn" was one of these, and he liked my liking its form, which I believed one of the best adapted to the English subject, and which he had used himself with so much pleasure and success.

Longfellow so rarely spoke of himself in any way, that one heard from him few of those experiences of the distinguished man in contact with the undistinguished, which he must have had so abundantly. But he told, while it was fresh in his mind, an incident that happened to him one day in Boston at a tobacconist's, where a certain brand of cigars was recommended to him as the kind that Longfellow smoked.

"Ah, then I must have some of them; and I will ask you to send me a box," said Longfellow, and he wrote down his name and address. The cigar-dealer read it with the smile of a worsted champion, and said, "Well I guess you had me, that time."

Sometimes people were shown by the poet through Craigie House, who had no knowledge of it except that it had been Washington's Headquarters. Of course Longfellow was known by sight to every one in Cambridge. He was daily in the streets while his health endured, and as he kept no carriage, he was often to be met in the horse-cars, which were such common ground in Cambridge that they were often like small invited parties of friends when they left Harvard Square.

I fancy that he was somewhat shy of his fellow-men, as the scholar seems to be, from the retired habit of his life; but I think Longfellow was incapable of marking any difference between himself and them. I never heard from him anything that was patronizing, when he spoke of people, and in Cambridge, where there was a great deal of contempt for the less lettered, and we liked to smile though we did not like to sneer, Longfellow and Longfellow's house were free from all that. Whatever his feelings may have been toward other sorts and conditions of men, his manner was one of entire democracy.

Once your friend, Longfellow was always your friend; he would not think evil of you, and if he knew evil of you, he would be the last of all that knew it to judge you for it. This may have been from the habit of his mind, but I believe it was also the effect of principle, for he would do what he could to defend others from judgment, and would soften the sentence passed in his presence.

As for his goodness, I never saw a fault in him. I do not mean to say that he had no faults, or that there were no better men but only to give my knowledge concerning him. But as a man shows himself to those often with him, and in his known relations with other men, he showed himself without blame. In the years when I began to know him, his long hair and the beautiful beard mixed with it were of iron-gray, which I saw blanch to a perfect silver. When he walked, he had a kind of spring in his gait, as if now and again a buoyant thought lifted him from the ground.

It was fine to meet him coming down a Cambridge street; you felt that the encounter made you a part of literary history, and set you apart with him for the moment from the poor and mean. You could meet him sometimes at the market, if you were of the same provision-man as he; Longfellow remained as constant to his tradespeople as to any other friends.

He rather liked to bring his proofs back to the printer himself, and we often found ourselves together at the University Press, where the Atlantic Monthly used to be printed. But outside of his own house, Longfellow seemed to want a fit atmosphere, and I love best to think of him in his study, where he wrought out his lovely art with a serenity expressed in his smooth, regular, and perfect handwriting.

His writing was quite vertical, and rounded with a slope neither to the right nor left. At the time I knew him first, he was fond of using a soft pencil on printing paper, though commonly he wrote with a quill. Each letter was distinct in shape, and between the verses was always the exact space of half an inch. I have a good many of his poems written in this fashion, but whether they were the first drafts or not I cannot say. Toward the last he no longer sent his poems to the magazines in his own hand, but they were always signed in autograph.

(William Dean Howells)

译文

朗费罗

《伊凡吉琳》《海华沙之歌》和《迈尔斯·斯坦狄什的求婚》，都是根据当时的老故事写成的，应该就是它们成就了朗费罗的名声。在朗费罗写完这几部作品之后，我才开始跟他熟悉起来。不过，他那些小诗、十四行诗和情诗当中的佼佼者，都诞生在我认识他的十八年里。

朗费罗很少大声朗读自己的作品。也有例外，有三四次吧，他曾在我面前朗读了他刚刚写好的诗。仿佛有知音在侧，并与他一同倾听，便是乐事一件。他曾朗读过的一篇，就是选自《路畔旅舍的故事》第三部分的《伊丽莎白》。我很赞赏它的形式，朗费罗对此感到很高兴。我认为这是英语体裁的最佳改编之一，他也因此收获了成功与快乐。

朗费罗作为杰出人士，却经常去接触普通人，因为他很少谈论自身，别人是很难从他嘴里听到这些经历的。但他曾说过一个他觉得很新奇的经历。一天，波士顿的一个烟草商向他推荐某个香烟牌子，并说，这就是朗费罗吸的烟。

"啊，那我是得有一些这种烟，你要送我一箱才是。"朗费罗说完，写下了自己的名字和地址。烟草商看到之后，露出一个挫败的笑容，说："好吧，我猜你以前吸的就是我的烟。"

去克雷吉公寓参观的人，只知道这里曾是华盛顿的指挥部，却不知道大诗人朗费罗就住在这里。有时候，朗费罗甚至会充当他们的导游。但在剑桥，人人一看见他，就知道他是大诗人朗费罗。身体条件允许时，他天天都在街上，虽然不坐车，但他常被邀上马车与人会面。人们离开哈佛、到了剑桥后，邀朋友在马车会晤的现象非常普遍，马车俨然成了小派对的所在。

从朗费罗退休后的生活习惯和他的表现来看，我猜朗费罗在某种程度上面对同胞会表现的腼腆，就想许多学者一样，但是他不会制造出与同胞的差异。他会摆出高高在上的姿态跟别人说话，这种事我闻所未闻，即便在剑桥这样普遍歧视没文化的人的地方也一样。我们都喜欢，但我们不喜欢讥笑。朗费罗和他的家人从来没有讥笑过别人。不论面对何种人，不论他们遭遇怎样的情况，不论对他们怀有何种观感，朗费罗都始终维持完全民主的态度。

朗费罗一旦把你当朋友，他便永远把你当成朋友，再不会把你往坏处想。如果他知道了你的劣迹，那他肯定是知道这件事的人当中最后一个评判你的人。这也许是因为他的思维习惯，不过我更相信是由于他心中的原则。他会竭尽所能维护他人，使其免受批判，也会尽可能地软化自己对他人的评判。

他确实优秀，我从来没看过他犯错误。我不是说他没有缺点，也不是说没有比他更好的人，我只能把注意力放他身上。但是，对待那些经常跟在他身边的人，或者是其他他熟识的人，他的行为举止落落大方。我开始认识他的那些年，他有着铁灰色的长发美髯，现在已彻底被岁月漂白成了银色。他在走路的时候，步伐总是充满活力，好像时常飞扬的思绪已经载着他从平地升起似的。

在剑桥街上遇见他，是一件妙事。在那一瞬间，他会带着你离开贫穷与卑劣，你会感觉他让你变成了文学史的一部分。有时，如果恰巧你和他在同一个人那里买东西，你也能在市场看见他。朗费罗对待那些摊贩的方式，和对待朋友毫无二致。

朗费罗很喜欢亲自去印刷工那里把书稿的校样带回来。我们经常能在学校的出版社相遇，《大西洋月刊》就是在这儿印刷出来的。在家外面的地方，他似乎想要的是一个合适的氛围。我最喜欢想象他在书房里的样子。也就是在这里，他那些可爱的作品，不动声色地在流畅、规律而完美的书写之下流泻出来。

　　他的字体挺直圆润，既不向左斜，也不向右歪。我刚开始认识他的时候，他就喜欢用一支软芯铅笔在印刷纸上写字。不过在写作的时候，他更常使用一支羽毛笔。他写的每个字母都清晰可辨，诗的每小节之间，都会留下一厘米多宽的固定空白。我手里有许多他的诗作，书写风格便是如此，至于到底是不是初稿，我不敢肯定。后来，他寄去杂志社的稿件，就不再是他亲笔书写的了，但是他一定会亲自签上落款。

（威廉·迪恩·豪威尔斯）

Saluting Mount Vernon

The United States dispatch-boat *Dolphin* was making her way up the Potomac from the sea to Washington. The captain, navigator, and officer of the deck were on the bridge piloting the vessel carefully through the many turns and bends of the river.

They kept a sharp lookout for the landmarks and buoys, and followed the course of the ship on the chart spread out on its stand. The navigator, looking up from the chart, turned to the captain, who was trying to make out a buoy not far form the ship.

"Mount Vernon is just ahead, sir," he said.

"Very well, call all hands to quarters," was the captain's reply.

"Sound to quarters, sir," this to the officer of the deck from the navigator.

"Ave, ave, sir. Bugler, sound to quarters!" rang out the voice of the young officer.

A moment's pause, and the assembly call rang out over the silent current of the river, and echoed back from the heights above its banks. The white pillars of Washington's beautiful home flashed out through the deep green of the trees high above the ship.

The officers and men, hurrying form all parts of the vessel, ranged themselves at their quarter. "From on the port side, facing outboard!" came the sharp order from the bridge, and later, "Sound attention!"

The bugle again broke the stillness. The Dolphin was now abreast of the historic home of the first chief magistrate of the country; all hands were lined up along the port side of the ship, standing at attention, and facing the shore.

As the order, "Salute!" came, sharply cut and abrupt, from the bridge, the right hand of every officer and man was raised to his cap, and there remained while the ship's bell rang out twenty-one slow, solemn strokes, one for each gun of a national salute.

The venerable mansion, with the white pillars of its porch, like giant sentinels on guard, looked down from the heights through a framework of majestic trees to the river below. As a gray-beared patriarch receives the homage of youth, so this dignified monument to the first head of the government seems to receives the homage of youth, so this dignified the passing salute of the representation of the government to-day.

With the last stroke of the bell came the order, " Sound the retreat!"

The bugle answered, and as the last note came back from the shore, Mount Vernon disappeared behind the green of the trees.

Every vessel of war of the United States passing the home of Washington observes this impressive ceremony. The effect upon one seeing it for the first time is thrilling, and it loses none of its dignity and beauty by repetition.

It is a good custom and tends to keep alive in the hearts of our country's defenders on the sea a spirit of veneration and love for the one whom every schoolboy learns to consider the first soldier and statesman of the country's history.

(John F. Urie, adapted)

译文

致敬弗农山庄

美国通信船海豚号正从波托马克河开往华盛顿海域。船长、领航员和值更官，正站在舰桥上小心翼翼地驾着轮船驶过一个个河流的转角。

他们时刻留心着地标和浮标，谨慎地按照航海图上计划的航线行驶着。领航员把目光从航海图上收回，转向船长。船长正在辨认不远处的一个浮标。

"先生，弗农山庄就在前面了。"领航员说道。

"很好，通知所有船员，鸣笛示意！"船长说道。

"吹号角！先生！"领航员对值更官说。

"遵命，先生。喇叭手！吹号角！"年轻的船员放声喊。

一阵短暂的静默之后，号角声在寂静的河流上响起，在山川之间回响。

船员们的目光穿过浓密翠绿的树丛,华盛顿美丽的白色柱子渐渐映入眼帘。

船员们全神贯注,坚守岗位,全速前进。"朝着船外面对的港口的另一边前进!"船长在舰桥上铿锵有力地发出命令,"吹号角!大家注意!"

号角声再一次划破了沉寂。海豚号将经过这个国家历史上第一位总统的故居。所有船员整齐地站在面对港口的船边,全神贯注地看着海岸。

另一声铿锵有力的命令下达:"敬礼!"坚定的声音从桥上传来。一瞬间,所有船员的右手举到帽檐,船铃缓缓地响了二十一声,庄严而有力,每一声都代表着向国家致敬的一声枪响。

在那座庄严的公馆里,白色的柱子伫立在走廊上,像巨大的守卫,从高处俯览,从雄伟壮丽的树林直到树林下方的河流。

一位白胡子的老人接下了领导众青年人的使命,成为第一届美国独立政府的领袖,这座为纪念他而建造的纪念碑闪烁着荣耀的光芒,至今为后人敬仰。

随着,最后一声鸣笛命令的响起,"退后"!

海岸也传来最后一声号角的回应,弗农山庄渐渐消失在身后,隐没在绿色的树丛中。

每一艘路经华盛顿的美国战舰都会举行这样意义深远的仪式。每一位第一次看见这种仪式的人都会激动万分,心中充满着自豪与骄傲;即使看过好几次的人也不会感到厌烦,每一次都能体验到它庄严隆重的美与深远的意义。

这是一个优良的传统,并且在国家海岸保卫者心中一代一代地传承。这是美国独立精神的体现,受到每个曾学习过美国开拓者与领导者历史的人的深切热爱。

(约翰·F.尤里,有删改)

Scott and His Home

It is among the very earliest recollections of my school-days, that the master told us youngsters, that the great author Sir Walter Scott was dead. And I think some lout of a boy down the bench, who was a better hand at marbles than he ever was at books, said in a whisper that two or three of us caught, "I wonder who he was?"

It was at a later day that we boys began to catch the full flavor of "Waverley" and the "Heart of Midlothian" and of that glorious story of battles and single-handed fights in which the gallant Saladin and the ponderous Richard of the Lion Heart took part.

We may possibly have read at that age his "Tale's of a Grandfather"; and we may have heard our kinsfolk talk admiringly of the "Lady of the Lake" and of "Marmion"; but we did not measure fairly the full depth of the school-master's grave manner, when he told us, in 1832, that Walter Scott was dead.

For my part, when I did get into the full spirit of "Guy Mannering" and of "Ivanhoe", some years later, it seemed to me a great pity that a man who could make such books should die at all,——and a pity that he should not go on writing them to the latest generation of men.

That feeling, I think, I had not wholly shaken off when I wandered twelve years later along the Tweed, looking sharply out in the Scotch mist for the gray ruin of Melrose Abbey.

I knew that this beautiful ruin was near to the old homestead of Walter Scott, toward which I had set off on a foot pilgrimage, a day before, from the old border-town of Berwick-upon-Tweed. I had kept close along the river, ——seeing shepherds at sheep-washing on Tweed-side, ——seeing old Norham Castle, and Coldstream Bridge, and the palace of the Duke of Roxborough.

I had slept at Kelso, had studied the great bit of ruin which is there, and had caught glimpses of Teviotdale, and of the Eildon Hills. I had dined at the drover's inn of St. Boswell's.

I had trudged out of my way for a good look at Smaillholme Tower, and at the farmhouse of Sandy Knowe, both of which you will find mentioned if you read (as you should) Lockhart's "Life of Scott".

Dryburgh Abbey, with its gloom, and rich tresses of ivy vines, where the great writer lies buried, came later in the day. At last, in the gloaming I toiled into the little town of Melrose. There is not much to be seen there but the Abbey in its ghostly ruin. I slept at the George Inn, dreaming—— as I dare say you would have done——of "Ivanhoe" "Rebecca" and "Old Mortality".

Next morning after breakfast I strolled two miles or so down the road, and by a little green foot-gate entered upon the grounds of Abbotsford. This was the home that Walter Scott created, and the home where he died.

The forest trees under which I walked were those which he had planted. I found his favorite out-of-door seat, sheltered by a thicket of arborvitae trees, from which there could be caught a glimpse of the rippled surface of the Tweed, and a glimpse of the many turrets that crowned the house of Abbotsford.

But, pray, where Tom Purdy, and Laidlaw, and Maida, and Sibyl Gray? For you must remember I was, in that day, fresh from a first reading of Lockhart's "life of Scott" in which all these, and many more, appear, and give life and stir to the surroundings of his home at Abbotsford.

You will read that book by Lockhart some day, and you will find in it, that Tom Purdy was an old out-of-door servant of Scott, who looked after the plantation and the dogs, and always accompanied the master upon his hunting frolics and his mountain strolls. Laidlaw did service in a more important way in-doors,——reading and writing for the master of the house.

Maida was a noble , whom Scott loved almost as much as any creature about him, and of whom he has left a charming portrait in old Bevis,——whose acquaintance you will make whenever you come to read the tale of Woodstock. As to Sibyl Gray, that was the name of the stout nag which carried Scott safely through fords and fens.

(Donald G. Mitchell)

◈ 译文

司各特和他的家园

在我求学的时候,老师告诉我们这些年轻人,伟大的作家沃尔特·司各特先生去世了。这是我对学校生活的最早的回忆之一。我记得一个有些笨拙的男孩滑下了长凳,他不怎么喜欢读书,很喜欢玩弹珠。我们听见他低声说了一句"我想知道这个人是谁"。

直到后来,我们这些男孩才开始领略《威弗利》《米德罗西恩的监狱》的意味,醉心于那些享有盛名的故事。我们在这些书里读到了英勇的萨拉丁和强壮的"狮王心"理查德的故事,读到了他们凭一己之力领导的反抗和战斗。

我们在某个年纪可能会读到他的《祖父的传说》;我们可能听到我们的亲人怀着敬仰谈起《湖上夫人》和《玛米恩》。但是当1832年学校老师告诉我们沃尔特·司各特去世时,我们并没有完全领会他那种沉重的态度。

一些年之后,我才能够完全领悟《盖伊·曼纳林》和《艾凡赫》等书中的思想,对创作出这些伟大作品的人的离世感到非常惋惜。更令人惋惜的是,他再也不能继续为下一代创作更多的作品了。

我想,就算时间已经过去了十二年,我仍然没有完全摆脱那种情绪。当时,我正沿着特威德河畔漫步,在苏格兰的薄雾里试图看清梅尔罗斯修道院的灰色遗迹。

我知道,这座美丽的废墟靠近沃尔特·司各特的故居,因为就在前一天,我从特威德河畔贝里克的旧边界出发,靠着河边前行。沿途能看见牧羊人在特威德河畔给绵羊刷毛,看到了诺勒姆城堡、冷溪桥和罗克斯伯勒公爵的官殿。

我住在凯尔索,仔细观察了那里的重要遗迹的断瓦残垣,匆匆游览了蒂维厄特河谷和艾尔登山,还在圣鲍斯威尔的德罗佛旅馆用了餐。

中途,我好好参观了斯梅尔霍姆塔和桑迪诺伊农舍。如果你读了洛克哈特的《司各特传》,你会发现里面提到了这两个地方。你真应该读读这本书。

随后我来到了这位伟大作家的埋身之地——德莱堡修道院。修道院里爬满了常春藤，看上去很昏暗。最后，我在暮色之中走进了梅尔罗斯小镇。那里除了隐身在幽灵般废墟中的修道院，没有太多可看的景致。我在乔治旅馆过夜，梦到了——我敢说你也会做这样的梦——《艾凡赫》《丽贝卡》以及《修墓老人》。

第二天用过早餐后，我顺着马路逛了大约三千二百米，然后通过一扇小小的绿色底门进入了阿伯茨福德。这是沃尔特·司各特的家园，也是他去世的地方。

我从他种植的那些树林下走过。柏树丛的背后，藏着他最心爱的座位。坐在那里，他可以瞥见特威德河面上的波光和阿伯茨福德大宅上耸立的塔楼。

但是，请问汤姆·珀迪、莱德劳、梅达和西比尔·格雷在哪里？我想你一定还记得第一次读到洛克哈特《司各特传》时的那股新鲜劲儿。传记讲述了这些人的故事，他们为阿伯茨福德奉献了一生。

如果你哪天读到洛克哈特的《司各特传》，你会发现，汤姆·珀迪是他的户外佣人，负责照看种植园和狗，经常陪着他的主人打猎消闲、漫步山间。莱德劳扮演更重要的角色，他是室内佣人，负责为宅子的主人读书、写字。

梅达是一条血统高贵的猎犬，司各特很爱它，并按梅达的形象栩栩如生地塑造成了老毕维斯这个角色。如果你读过《伍德斯托克》，你就会知道。西比尔·格雷是一匹好马，司各特曾经骑着它，安然渡过了浅滩和沼泽。

（唐纳德·G. 米切尔）

♪ 作者介绍

唐纳德·米切尔用伊克·曼威的笔名写了一些轻松有趣的小说和随笔。米切尔先生的大多数作品中都有一种幽默的反转。除此之外，他还懂得怎样用优美的语言抒发纤细的情感。他一直热爱大自然，并且在康涅狄格州纽黑文附近的艾奇伍德农场生活了许多年。本文选自《关于讲故事的老人》一书。米切尔先生所有作品中最知名的是《单身汉的白日梦》这部小说。他在艾奇伍德所做的关于生命的自然研究也很出色，这些成果由查尔斯·斯克里布纳父子出版公司集结再版。

The Coronation of the Czar and the Czarina

The coronation was much more beautiful than any one could possibly have imagined that it was going to be. The tribune to the right of the thrones was the one most closely crowded. It held the grand-duchesses and the ladies of the court, who were in the native costume of the country, and who wore the diamonds for which Russia is celebrated.

On the tribune immediately behind the throne stood the Russian senators in magnificent coats of gold, with boots to the hip and white leather breeches, and with ostrich feathers in their peaked hats. With them were the correspondents, the Germans and Russians in military uniforms, the Englishmen in their own court dress, and the Frenchmen and Americans in evening dress.

The diplomats and their wives, and the visiting commanders-in-chief and generals of armies from all over the world, occupied the third tribune to the left of the throne, and formed the most splendid and gorgeous group of all. Around the platform itself were the princes and grand-dukes glittering with the chains and crosses of the imperial orders. Between the screen and the platform the priests moved to and fro in jeweled miters as large as a diver's helmet, and in robes stiff with gold and precious stones, their vestments flashing like the scales of goldfish.

But nothing in the whole drama of the morning presented so impressive a picture as did the young Empress when she first entered the chapel and stood before her throne. Of all the women there, she was the most simply robed, and of all the women there, she was by far the most beautiful. A single string of pearls was he only ornament, and her hair, which was worn like that of a Russian peasant girl, fell in two long plaits over her bare shoulders. Her robe of white and silver was as simple as that of a child going to her first communion.

The most interesting part of the ceremony, perhaps, was when the Czar changed from a bareheaded young officer in a colonel's uniform, to an emperor in the most magnificent robes an emperor could assume, and when the Czarina followed him, and from the peasant girl became a queen, with the majesty of a queen.

When the moment had arrived for this transformation to take place, the Czar's uncle, the Grand-Duck Vladimir, and his younger brother Alexander lifted the collars of the different orders from the Czar's shoulders. They then fastened upon him the imperial of gold cloth, which is some fifteen feet in length, with a cape of ermine, and covered with the double eagle of Russia in black enamel and precious stones.

Over this they placed the broad diamond Collar of St. Andrew, which sank into the bed of snowy white fur, and lay glimmering and flashing as the Emperor moved forward to take the imperial diadem from the hands of the Metropolitan of St. Petersburg.

The crown was a marvelous thing, fashioned in two halves to typify the eastern and western kingdoms. It was formed of white diamonds, and surrounded by a great glowing ruby, above which was a diamond cross. The Czar lifted this globe of flame and light high above him, then lowered it to his head, and took the scepter in his right hand and the globe in his left.

When he had seated himself upon the throne, the Czarina stood up and walked to a place in front of him. There she sank upon her knees at his feet, with her bare hands clasped before her. He rested his crown for an instant upon her brow, and then replacing it upon his head, lowered a smaller crown of diamonds upon hers. Three ladies-in-waiting fastened it to her hair with long gold hair-pins, the Czar watching them with deepest interest as they did so.

Then, as they retired, two of the grand-dukes placed a mantle similar to the Czar's upon her shoulders, and hung another diamond collar upon the ermine of her cape. When this was done, the Czarina stepped back to her throne of ivory, and the Czar to his throne of turquoise.

The supreme moment had come and gone, and Nicholas the II and Alexandra Feodorovna sat crowned before the nations of the world.

Some one made a signal through the open door, and the diplomats on the tribune outside rose to their feet, and the crush of moujiks below them sank on their knees, and the regiments of young peasant soldiers flung their guns at salute, and the bells of the churches carried the news over the heads of the kneeling thousands across the wall of the Kremlin to where one hundred and one cannon hurled it on across the river and up to the highest hill of Moscow, where the modern messengers of good and evil began to tick it out to Odessa, to Constantinople, to Berlin, to Paris, to the rocky coast of Penzance, where it slipped into the sea and hurried on under the ocean to the illuminated face in the Cable Company's tall building on Broadway [New York City], until the world had been circled, and the answering congratulations came pouring into Moscow while the young Emperor still stood under the dome of the little chapel.

After the congratulations the ceremony was continued by the priests alone, who chanted and prayed for nearly two hours, during which time the Czar and Czarina took little part in the services beyond crossing themselves at certain intervals. At last the priests ceased, and the most solemn ceremony of the coronation was reached. The Czar passed from sight through the jeweled door of the screen, while his young wife, who could not enter with him, waited, praying for him.

When he came forth again, the tears were streaming down his cheeks. One could see in his face, white and drawn with hours of prayer and fasting, how strongly he was moved. And one could imagine what he felt when he looked forward into the many years to come and again saw himself as he was at that moment, a young man of twenty-eight, taking in his hands the insignia of absolute sovereignty over the bodies of one hundred million people and on his lips the most sacred of oaths to protect the welfare of one hundred million souls.

(Richard Harding Davis)

✍ 译文

沙皇和皇后的加冕

加冕仪式要比任何人所能想象的华丽得多。王座右面的礼台上挤满了人，大公夫人和宫廷中的贵妇都在那里，她们穿着本国的服饰，佩戴着俄国闻名遐迩的钻石。

俄罗斯的参议员们站在王座正后方的礼台上，他们身着华丽的金色上衣和白色皮裤，脚蹬高及臀部的长靴，头上戴着顶部插有鸵鸟羽毛的帽子。和他们站在一起的是各国记者，有穿着军事制服的德国人和俄国人，穿着自己国家宫廷服饰的英国人，还有身着晚礼服的法国人和美国人。

外国使节和他们的妻子，以及到访的世界各地的军队总司令和将军们占据了王座左边的第三个礼台。这群人最为光彩夺目。王子和大公们站在礼台的四周，佩戴着熠熠生辉的帝国勋章。牧师们戴着镶有珠宝，有如潜水员头盔那般大的法冠，在帷幕和平台间来回穿梭。金饰和珠宝将他们的长袍坠得笔挺，让法衣像金鱼的鳞片那般闪闪发亮。

但整个早晨的仪式中，最让人印象深刻的是年轻的皇后第一次步入礼堂，站在她宝座前的那一刻。所有在场的女士中，她穿着最为简朴，但绝对是最漂亮的一位。一小串珍珠是她唯一的饰物，她的头发就像俄罗斯农村女孩那样，编成两股垂在光溜溜的肩上。她那银白色的袍子就像第一次领圣餐的小孩穿的那样朴素。

也许，沙皇从一个光着脑袋穿着上校制服的年轻军官，变成身着最华丽长袍的皇帝，而皇后跟随着他，从乡村女孩化为具有王权的皇后的那一刻是整个仪式中最有意思的部分。

当这一蜕变的时刻来临时，沙皇的叔叔弗拉迪米尔大公和他的弟弟亚历山大按顺序取下沙皇肩上的项链，然后把皇帝的金色衣装穿在他身上。这件衣服大约有四米多长，带有貂皮披肩，上有饰宝石、着黑色珐琅的俄罗斯双头鹰。

他们把大钻石"圣安德烈项链"挂在衣服的最上面，它陷入那雪白的毛皮中，随着皇帝的步伐闪闪发亮。随后皇帝走上前去，从圣彼得堡大主教手中接过皇冠。

皇冠是一样非凡的东西，被设计成两半来代表东部和西部王国。它由白色钻石制成，钻石周围环绕着一圈映着红光的红宝石，最顶上立着一个钻石的十字。沙皇将这个闪耀着光芒的圆球高高地举过头顶，然后放下来托在头前，最终右手拿起权杖，左手托着皇冠。

当他在王座落座后，皇后就站起身来走到他面前，然后屈膝跪下，在身前握着双手。他举着自己的皇冠在她额前稍作停留，随后戴在自己的头上，并把一个稍小的钻石皇冠戴在她的头上。在沙皇最关切的注视下，三位侍女用长长的金发卡把皇冠扣紧在皇后的头发上。

当她们退下后，两位大公就把一件跟沙皇的类似的大衣披在皇后肩上，并把另一串钻石项链戴在她的貂皮披肩之上。所有这一切结束后，皇后便坐回到她那象牙宝座上去，而沙皇则坐在他那绿松石王座上。

那至高无上的时刻就这样开始，这样结束。尼古拉二世和亚历山大德拉·费奥多萝芙娜已戴着皇冠坐在全世界面前。

有人向敞开的大门外发了个信号，外面礼台上的外国代表们就站起身来，而挤在台下的庄稼汉们则跪了下来，大群年轻的农民战士们挥枪致敬。教堂的钟声载着这个消息飘过千万个跪着的人的头顶，翻越克里姆林宫的围墙。一百零一门礼炮把它投射过河流，送到了莫斯科最高的山上。在那里，带有善意或敌意的现代报信者们将这个消息用电报发送到敖德萨、君士坦丁堡柏林、巴黎，还有彭赞斯那满是岩石的海边。从那里，它跃入海中在大洋底下飞速前行，传到了纽约百老汇大道上电报公司大楼内还在灯火下工作的人的手中，一直到全世界都知道了这个消息。当这个年轻的君王还站在礼堂的穹顶之下时，回复的贺词已向莫斯科涌来。

祝贺完毕，仪式由牧师们单独继续进行，他们会歌颂、祈祷近两个小时。在这期间，沙皇和皇后不怎么参与，只是间歇性地各自划着十字。最后，牧师停止了祷告，加冕仪式中最庄严的一刻到来了。沙皇走进了珠宝交织的帷幕之后，此刻他年轻的妻子也不能跟随入内，只能等待着为他祈祷。

当他再次出现时，已是满颊热泪。可以从他那由于好几小时祷告、斋戒而显得苍白而又憔悴的脸上看出他有多么激动。人们可以想象，当他所期待的多年过去以后，回过头来会如何看待此刻的自己：一个二十岁的年轻人，手中掌控着一亿人民身体上的绝对统治权,并在口中作出了最神圣的誓言,要去守护那一亿个灵魂的幸福。

(理查德·哈丁·戴维斯)

Chapter 5

Stories of Children ｜ 孩子们的故事

A Poet at Home

预习

chary /ˈtʃeri/ 谨慎的

concordance /kənˈkɔːrdəns/ 一致

consequence /ˈkɑːnsəkwens/ 结果

felicitous /fəˈlɪsɪtəs/ 极为适当的

formidable /ˈfɔːrmɪdəbl/ 可怕的

thermometer /θərˈmɑːmɪtər/ 温度计

unfledged /ʌnˈfledʒd/ 没经验的；尚未成熟的

vocabulary /vəˈkæbjəleri/ 词汇

  One day Julia had an adventure——not "a wildly exciting one", as some of the girls liked to describe what had happened to them, but one that she was always to remember with pleasure. It was a windy day in early January, and there was a fine glaze on the ground from a storm of the day before. As she was slipping along down Beacon Street, on her way home from school, it was all that she could do to hold her footing.

  Luckily she had no books to carry, and so when suddenly she saw some sheets of letter paper whirling past her, she was able to rush on and pick them up as they were dashed against a lamp-post. Then she naturally looked around to see to whom they belonged. The owner was not far away, for just a few steps behind her was an old gentleman not very tall, dressed all in black with a high silk hat.

  Under his arm the gentleman carried a book, and as he held out his hand toward her, Julia had no doubt that he was the owner of the wandering manuscript. "Thank you, my child," he said, as she held the sheets towards him. "Another gust, and I should have had to compose a new poem to take the place of this one."

"Why, sir?" Julia began to say; then looking up in his face, she suddenly gave a start. Surely she had seen that face before. But where? In an instant she recognized the owner of the papers. He was certainly no other than Dr. Oliver Wendell Holmes, the famous Autocrat of the Breakfast Table, several of whose poems she knew almost by heart. "Were——were they some of your own poems?" she managed to stammer. "It would have been dreadful if they had been lost."

"Not half so dreadful," he replied smiling, "as if they had been written by some one else. As a matter of fact they were sent to me by an unfledged poet, who wished me to tell him whether he would stand a chance of getting them into a publisher's hands. He told me to take great care of them as he had no copy. I read his note at my publisher's just now, and I felt bound to carry the manuscript home. But I'm not sure that it would not have been a good thing to lose a sheet or two to teach him a lesson. He should not send a thing to a stranger without making a copy."

When Julia repeated this later at the table, her aunt was much interested. "What else did he say?" she inquired.

"Oh, he thanked me again for picking up the papers, and when he heard that I had not been long in Boston, he asked me to call some afternoon to see him. I walked along until he reached his door. Do you know that he lives near here?"

Her aunt knew, and approved of her making the call. A few afternoons later Julia and her friend Edith walked up the short flight of stone steps to the poet's front door. Their hearts sank a little. To make a call on a poet was really a rather formidable thing, and they pressed each other's hands as they heard the maid opening the door to admit them.

"Just wait here for a moment," said the maid, after they had inquired for the master of the house. In a moment she returned and asked them to follow her. At the head of the broad stairs they saw the poet himself standing with outstretched hand to meet them. When Julia mentioned

Edith's name, he made them sit down beside him, one on each side, while he occupied a large leather armchair drawn up before his open fire, and asked them one or two questions about their studies and their taste in literature.

As Dr. Holmes talked, Julia's eyes wandered to the little revolving bookcase on which she could not help noticing a number of volumes of his own works. The old gentleman, following her glance, said, "They make a pretty fair showing for one man, but my publishers are getting ready to bring out a complete edition of my works, and that, well that makes me realize my age." After a moment, he asked quickly, "Does either of you write poetry?"

"Oh, no, sir," answered Edith quickly, "we couldn't."

"Why, it isn't so very hard," he said, "at least I should judge not by the numbers of copies of verses that are sent to me to examine. Poetry deals with common human emotion, and almost any one with a fair vocabulary thinks that he can express himself in verse. Words and expression seem very felicitous to the writer, but he cannot expect other persons to see his work as he sees it."

"It depends, I suppose," said Edith shyly, "on whose work it is."

"Do you really have a great deal of poetry sent you to read?" Julia asked.

"Every mail," he answered, "brings me letters from strangers,—— from every corner of the globe. Some are accompanied by long manuscripts on which my opinion is asked. I am chary now about expressing any opinion, for some publishers have a way of quoting very unfairly in their advertisements. If I write 'your book would be very charming, were it not so carelessly written', the publisher quotes merely 'very charming', and prints this in large type."

Both girls smiled at the expression of droll sorrow that came over the poet's face as he spoke.

"And I am so very unfortunate myself," he added, "when I try to get an autograph of any consequence. Now I sent Gladstone a copy of a work on trees in which I thought that he would be interested. He returned the compliment with a copy of one of his own books. But——" here he paused, "he wrote his thanks on a postcard!" Again the girls laughed. "Dear me!" he concluded. "This cannot interest young creatures like you; do you care for poetry?"

"Oh, yes, indeed we do," cried Julia, "and we just love your poetry."

"Well, well," said the poet, with a twinkle in his eyes, "perhaps you would like to hear me read something?"

The beaming faces that met his glance were a sufficient answer, and taking a volume from the table, Dr. Holmes began,

"This is the ship of pearl, which, poets feign,
Sails the unshadowed main,
The venturous bark that flings
On the sweet summer wind its purpled wings
In gulfs enchanted, when the Siren sings,
And coral reefs lie bare,
Where the cold sea maids rise to sun their streaming hair."

When he had finished the stanza, he looked up inquiringly.

"The Chambered Nautilus," murmured Julia.

"Ah, you know it then?" said the poet.

"Oh, yes, I love it," she answered.

Then with a smile of appreciation, adjusting his glasses, Dr. Holmes read to the end of the poem in his wonderfully musical voice. When it was finished, the girls would have liked to ask for more, but the poet rose to replace the volume. "Come," he said, "you have listened to the poem which of all I have written I like the best, now I wish to show you my favorite view."

Following him to the deep bay window, they looked out across the river. It was much the same view to which Julia was accustomed in her uncle's house, and yet it was looking at the river with new eyes to have the poet pointing out all the towns, seven or eight in number, which he could see from that window.

"In winter," he said, "there is not much to see besides the tug-boats and the gulls. But in the early spring it is a delight to me to watch the

crews rowing by, and an occasional pleasure-boat. Ah! I remember——"
But what it was he did not say, for as Edith turned her eyes toward an oil painting on the wall near by, he said, "Of course you know who that is; of course you recognize the famous Dorothy Q.

"Now look at the portrait closely, and tell me what you think of that cheek. Could you imagine any one so cruel as to have struck a sword into it? Yet there, if your eyes are sharp enough, you will see where a British soldier of the Revolution thrust his rapier."

When both of the girls admitted that they could not see the scar, "That only shows," he said, "how clever the man was who made the repairs."

Before they turned from the window he made them notice the tall factory chimneys on the other side of the river, which he called his thermometers, because according to the direction in which the smoke curled upwards he was able to tell how the wind blew, and decide in what direction he should walk.

"Remember," he said, "when you reach my age always to walk with your back to the wind," and at this the girls smiled, feeling that it would be many years before they should need to follow this advice. Yet during their call how many things they had to see and to remember! He let each of them hold for a moment the gold pen with which he had written Elsie Venner and the Autocrat papers, and Julia turned over the leaves of the large Bible and the concordance on the top of his writing table. As she looked about, she thought that she had seldom seen a prettier room than this with its cheerful rugs, 'massive furniture, and fine pictures, all so simple and yet so dignified.

Then before the girls could realize it Dr. Holmes placed in the hand of each of them a small volume in a white cover, and bidding them open their books, said, "Well, I must put something on that bare fly-leaf." So seating himself at his table with a quill pen in his hand, he wrote slowly and evidently with some effort, the name of each of them, followed by the words," With the regards of Oliver Wendell Holmes," and then the year, and the day of the month.

As he handed them the books, the girls turned toward the door. With a word or two more of half-bantering thanks to Julia for her assistance on that windy day, Dr. Holmes opened the door, and bowed them down the stairs.

(Helen Leah Reed)

译文

一位居于家中的诗人

有一天，朱莉娅经历了一场奇遇——不是那种像一些女生喜欢描述自己所经历的"疯狂而又刺激"的奇遇，而是一种她会永远带着快乐去回顾的经历。那是一月初一个刮风的日子，前一天的暴风雨淋过，地面上仿佛铺上了一层光滑的釉。她正从学校返回家，沿着比肯街快速前行，尽可能地控制着双脚不打滑。

幸运的是，她不用带书回去，所以当她突然看到几张信纸在面前打着旋儿飘过的时候，才能跑上去捡起来，防止它们撞向路灯。之后，很自然的，她四处张望看看这些信纸是谁的。信纸的主人就在不远处，她身后几步远的地方就站着个不算很高的老绅士，穿一身黑色衣服还戴了一顶大礼帽。

老绅士的胳膊里夹着一本书，而当他向她伸出手时，朱莉娅就肯定他正是这随处漫游的手稿的主人了。她把信纸递过去。"谢谢你，孩子，"他说，"又是一阵风，我应该再作一首新诗来代替这首的。"

"为什么呢，先生？"朱莉娅开口说；当时她抬头看向他，突然这样发问。她敢肯定自己见过这个人。但是在哪儿见过呢？那一刹，她认出来了这信纸的主人。不是别人，正是奥利弗·温德尔·霍姆斯，那个出名的"早餐桌上的霸主"，他的好几首诗她都铭记于心呢。"这——这些也是你写的诗吗？"她变得结结巴巴的，"要是弄丢了的话，可是会令人很心痛的。"

"没那么痛心，"他笑着回答，"就当是别人写的好了。事实上，那些确实是一个尚未成熟的诗人给我的，他想问问我那些诗是否有希望送到出版商的手中。他还让我收好这些诗，因为他手里没留副本。我刚在我的出版商那看到了他的名字，所以觉得应该可以把这些手稿带回去了。但我不知道，弄丢一两张给他点教训是不是件好事。他不应该把诗发给一个陌生人，自己却没留副本。"

朱莉娅在餐桌上重复这些话，她的姑妈对此十分感兴趣。"他还说什么了？"她询问道。

"噢，他对我捡起那些纸再次表示感谢，还有当他得知我刚到波士顿没多久后，他让我下午有空的时候去他家拜访。我们一路同行直到他到家门口。你知道他就住这附近吗？"

她的姑妈知道，并且赞成她去拜访。几天后的一个下午，朱莉娅和她的朋友伊迪丝走上通往诗人家的前门的那一小段石砌台阶，她们的心都沉甸甸的。按一位诗人家的门铃还真是件艰难的事。当听到女佣前来开门欢迎的声音时，两人不约而同地握紧了对方的手。

"在这稍等片刻。"女佣在得知他们想要见房子主人的请求后说。不久她就回来，并把她们领进去。在宽敞的楼梯顶端，她们看到了诗人，他站在那儿伸出手迎接她们。朱莉娅介绍完伊迪丝后，他就让她们坐在自己旁边，一边一个，而他自己坐在皮革扶手椅上，靠近炉火前。接着又问了一两个有关她们的学业和文学兴趣的问题。

霍姆斯先生讲话期间，朱莉娅的眼睛飘到那个小巧的旋转书架上，她忍不住去留意数不胜数的他的作品。老绅士随着她的视线看过去，说道："对一个人来说，这很不错了。但是我的出版商们准备出版一个我的作品的完整的版本，而这，恰恰让我意识到自己已经不年轻了。"过了一会，他迅速地问："你们中有谁写诗吗？"

"噢，没有，先生。"伊迪丝迅速回答道，"我们都不会。"

"为什么呢，这并不很难，"他说，"至少从人们送给我审阅的诗歌的数量上可以得出这个结论。诗歌描写的是朴素的人类情感，几乎任何有足够词汇量的人都觉得自己能用诗句表达自我。或许在作者看来字词和措辞都恰如其分，但他不可能奢求别人也能以同样的审美看待他的作品。"

"这得看情况，我认为，"伊迪丝害羞地说，"得看是谁的作品。"

"真的有特别多人把诗歌发给你阅读吗？"朱莉娅问。

"每封邮件，"他答道，"都会带来从世界每个角落寄给我的陌生人的书信。有的还附带些手稿来询问我的看法。现在我对表达任何看法都很谨慎，因为一些出版商总会以不正当的方式引用到他们的出版宣传中。比如我写，'要是你的书写得不那么随意的话，将会非常有吸引力'，出版商就只引用'非常有吸引力'，并且加粗字体印刷到书面上。"

女孩儿们都被这位诉苦的诗人脸上滑稽的悲伤表情逗笑了。

"我真是太不幸了，"他继续说，"尤其是在我想要得到任何出版成品的亲笔签名时。我之前送给格拉德斯通一本有关树木的书册，我相信他会对里面的内容感兴趣的。他寄回一本自己写的书作为回礼，但是——"他停顿了一下，"他把感谢语写在明信片上了！"女孩们又笑起来。"哎呀！"他总结道，"这个不能使你们这些小年轻感兴趣；你们喜欢诗歌吗？"

"哦，是的，我们很喜欢，"朱莉娅，"而且我们正好喜欢你写的诗。"

"好啊，好啊，"这位诗人眼睛炯炯有神地说着，"你们愿意听我读点东西吗？"

眼下那两张兴奋得放光的小脸蛋就是最好的答案。霍姆斯先生从桌子上拿来一卷诗，开始读：

"这是一艘，诗人捏造的，珍珠船，

航行在没有阴影笼罩的海——

这不顾险阻的帆船就这样乘风破浪

在晴朗的夏日里，收起她紫色的羽翼，

在附魔的深渊间，当海妖的歌声响起

而珊瑚礁露出赤裸枝干

那里，冰冷的少女从海中浮出，晒干她们柔顺的长发。"

读完诗的一节，他探询着抬眼看了看。

《洞穴里的鹦鹉螺》。"朱莉娅喃喃地说。

"啊，看来你知道这首？"诗人说。

"是啊，我喜欢这首。"她回答。

带着感谢的微笑，霍姆斯先生调整了下眼镜，然后用他美妙悦耳的嗓音接着读下去。读完后，女孩们想再听一首，但这位诗人却起身去换书了。"过来，"他说，"你们已经听了我写的所有诗中我最喜欢的那首，现在我想给你们看看我最喜欢的景色。"

两人跟随他来到窗台前，他们看向河对岸。这和朱莉娅在她叔叔家常看到的那片景色是差不多的，可是随着诗人新的视角看向河那边，他指出窗外能看到的所有小镇，有七八个。

"冬季里，"他说，"除了拖船和鸥鸟没什么太多的东西能看。但是在初春时节，观察划船经过的船员和偶尔路过的游船可是我的一大乐趣呢。啊！我记得——"后面的话他没说完，因为伊迪丝把视线转移到旁边墙上的一幅油画上了，他说："你肯定知道这是谁的作品；你肯定认出了著名的多萝西·Q的笔法。

"那么我们来仔细欣赏下这幅画像吧，说说看你们对脸颊这块有何看法。你们能想象曾有人能残忍地把剑刺进去吗？还有那儿，要是你们眼睛够尖的话，你们能看到曾有一个英国的革命士兵把十字剑插进去过。"

女孩们纷纷坦白看不出画像有何损伤。"那只能说明，"他继续说，"做画像修复的人实在是很高明啊。"

离开窗台前，他还让她们注意看河对岸高耸的工厂烟囱，他称之为"温度计"，因为他可以根据烟雾缭绕上升的方向推断出风向，从而决定他应该朝哪个方向走。

"时刻牢记，"他说，"等你们到我这个年纪的时候，要背对风向走路。"女孩们听后忍俊不禁，等到她们要遵循这条建议，恐怕是许多年之后的事了。而在她们拜访期间，还有好多值得一看，留下回忆的事！他让她们分别拿了一会儿他写《埃尔希文纳》和《早餐桌上的霸主》散文用的金笔，茱莉娅还翻看了那一大本圣经的书页和他写字桌的重要用语索引。小姑娘环顾四周，她从没见过这么漂亮的房间，那温馨的小地毯、厚重的家具、精美的画像都是如此简约而又尊贵。

女孩们还没反应过来，霍姆斯先生就在她们手里，一人给了一本白色封面的小书册，并嘱咐她们打开自己的书，说道："嗯，我必须在那空白的扉页写点东西。"于是他捏着一只鹅毛笔坐到自己的书桌前，缓慢而又明显有些努力地写下她们各自的名字，后面还写上几个词，"奥利弗·温德尔·霍姆斯致以问候。"然后是年、月、日。

女孩拿到书后便转身向门口走去。三言两语地半开玩笑地感谢茱莉娅刮风那日的帮助，霍姆斯先生拉开门，并鞠躬目送她们下楼离开。

（海伦·利娅·里德）

✍ 作者介绍

  海伦·利娅·里德出生于加拿大新不伦瑞克省的圣约翰市，成长于美国波士顿，毕业于拉德克利夫学院。她的作品有《布伦达，她的学校和俱乐部》《布伦达在罗克利度过的夏日》《布伦达在拉德克利夫的表亲》，这篇文章由利特尔&布朗出版社授权。

A Second Trial

☆ 预习

appreciate /əˈpriːʃieɪt/ 欣赏
automatic /ˌɔːtəˈmætɪk/ 自动的
concentrated /ˈkɑːnsntreɪtɪd/ 全神贯注的
humiliation /hjuːˌmɪliˈeɪʃn/ 耻辱
identified /aɪˈdentɪfaɪd/ 经鉴定的
kaleidoscope /kəˈlaɪdəskoʊp/ 万花筒
permutations /pɜːmjuːˈteɪʃnz/ 置换

It was commencement at one of our colleges. The people were pouring into the church as I entered it, rather tardy. Finding the choice seats in the center of the audience-room already taken, I pressed forward, looking to the right and to the left for a vacancy. On the very front row of seats I found one.

Here a little girl moved along to make room for me, looking into my face with large gray eyes, whose brightness was softened by very long lashes. Her face was open and fresh as a newly blown rose before sunrise. Again and again I found my eyes turning to the rose-like face, and each time the gray eyes moved half-smiling to meet mine. Evidently the child was ready to "make up" with me. And when, with a bright smile she returned my dropped handkerchief, and I said "Thank you". We seemed fairly introduced.

Other persons now coming into the seat, crowded me quite close up against the little girl, so that we soon felt very well acquainted.

"There's going to be a great crowd," she said to me.

"Yes," I replied. "People always like to see how schoolboys are made into men."

Her face beamed with pleasure and pride as she said, "My brother's going to graduate; he's going to speak; I've brought these flowers to throw to him."

They were not greenhouse favorites; just old-fashioned domestic flowers, such as we associate with the dear grandmother. "But," I thought, "they will seem sweet and beautiful to him for little sister's sake."

"That is my brother," she went on, pointing with her nosegay.

"The one with the light hair?" I asked.

"Oh, no," she said, smiling and shaking her head in innocent reproof, "not that homely one; that handsome one with brown wavy hair. His eyes look brown, too; but they are not-they are dark-blue. There! He's got his hand up to his head now. You see him, don't you?"

In an eager way she looked from me to him, and from him to me, as if some important fate depended upon my recognizing her brother.

"I see him," I said. "He's a very good-looking brother."

"Yes, he is beautiful," she said, with artless delight. "And he's so good, and he studies so hard. He has taken care of me ever since mamma died. Here is his name on the program. He is not the valedictorian, but he has an honor, for all that."

I saw in the little creature's familiarity with these college terms that she had closely identified herself with her brother's studies, hopes, and successes.

"His oration is a good one, and he says it beautifully. He has said it to me a great many times. I almost know it by heart. Oh! It begins so prettily and grandly This is the way it begins," she added, encouraged by the interest she must have seen in my face."Amid the permutations and combinations of the actors and the forces which make up the great kaleidoscope of history, we often find that a turn of Destiny's hand——"

"Why, bless the baby!" I thought, looking down into her bright proud face. I can't describe how very odd and elfish it did seem to have those big words rolling out of the smiling childish mouth.

As the exercises progressed, and approached nearer and nearer the effort on which all her interest was concentrated, my little friend became excited and restless. Her eyes grew larger and brighter, two deep-red spots glowed on her cheeks.

"Now, it's his turn," she said, turning to me a face in which pride and delight and anxiety seemed about equally mingled. But when the overture was played through, and his name was called, the child seemed, in her eagerness, to forget me and all the earth beside him. She rose to her feet and leaned forward for a better view of her beloved, as he mounted to the speaker's stand.

I knew by her deep breathing that her heart was throbbing in her throat. I knew, too, by the way her brother came up the steps and to the front that he was trembling. The hands hung limp; his face was pallid, and the lips blue as with cold. I felt anxious. The child, too, seemed to discern that things were not well with him. Something like fear showed in her face.

He made an automatic bow. Then a bewildered, struggling look came into his face, then a helpless look, and then he stood staring vacantly, like one in a dream, at the waiting audience. The moments of painful suspense went by, and still he stood as if struck dumb. I saw how it was; he had been seized with stage-fright.

Alas! Little sister! She turned her large dismayed eyes upon me. "He's forgotten it," she said. Then a swift change came into her face; a strong determined look; and on the funeral-like silence of the room broke the sweet, brave child-voice,

"Amid the permutations and combinations of the actors and the forces which make up the great kaleidoscope of history, we often find that a turn of Destiny's hand——"

Everybody about us turned and looked. The breathless silence; the sweet, childish voice; the childish face; the long, unchildlike words, produced a weird effect.

But the help had come too late; the unhappy brother was already staggering in humiliation from the stage. The band quickly struck up, and waves of lively music rolled out to cover the defeat.

I gave the little sister a glance in which I meant to show the intense sympathy I felt; but she did not see me. Her eyes swimming with tears, were on her brother's face. I put my arm around her, but she was too absorbed to heed the caress, and before I could appreciate her purpose she was on her way to the shame-stricken young man sitting with a face like a statue's.

When he saw her by his side the set face relaxed, and a quick mist came into his eyes. The young men got closer together to make room for her. She sat down beside him, laid her flowers on his knee, and slipped her hand into his.

I could not keep my eyes from her sweet pitying face. I saw her whisper to him, he bending a little to catch her words. Later, I found out that she was asking him if he knew his "piece" now, and that he answered "Yes".

When the young man next on the list had spoken, and while the band was playing, the child, to the brother's great surprise, made her way up the stage steps, and pressed through the throng of professors and trustees and distinguished visitors, up to the college president.

"If you please, sir," she said with a little courtesy, "will you and the trustees let my brother try again? He knows his piece now."

For a moment the president stared at her through his gold-bowed spectacles, and then, appreciating the child's petition, he smiled on her, and went down and spoke to the young man that had failed.

So it happened that when the band had again ceased playing, it was briefly announced that Mr.——would now deliver his oration——"Historical Parallels".

A ripple of heightened and expectant interest passed over the audience, and then all sat stone still, as though fearing to breathe lest the speaker might again take fright. No danger. The hero in the youth was aroused. He went at his "piece" with a set purpose to conquer, to redeem himself, and to bring the smile back into the child's tear-stained face. I watched the face during the speaking. The wide eyes, the parted lips, the whole rapt being said that the breathless audience was forgotten, that her spirit was moving with his.

And when the address was ended with the ardent abandon of one who catches enthusiasm in the realization that he is fighting down a wrong judgment and conquering a sympathy, the effect was really thrilling. That dignified audience broke into rapturous applause; bouquets intended for the valedictorian rained like a tempest. And the child, the child that had helped to save the day——that one beaming little face, in its pride and gladness, is something to be forever remembered.

(Sarah Winter Kellogg)

译文

再试一次的机会

我们的一个学院正要举行毕业典礼。人们像潮水一样涌入教堂。我到的时候,发现观众席中央的位置已经坐满了人,于是不得不继续向前挤。我左右张望着,想找一个空位,最后在前排座位中找到了一个。

一个小女孩挪了一下,给我让出行走的空间。她灰色的大眼睛凝视着我的脸,长长的睫毛让她明亮的双眼显得十分柔和。她脸上的神情坦诚而充满活力,就像日出前刚刚绽放的玫瑰。我的眼睛一次又一次瞥向这玫瑰般的脸蛋,而她的灰眼睛也总会浅笑着迎上我的视线。显然,这个孩子已经准备好要和我认识一下了。然后,当她带着明亮的笑容把我掉落的手帕还给我时,我说了一声"谢谢"。于是,我们似乎已经成了熟人了。

现在其他人也开始落座,我和这个小女孩不得不挤在一起,所以我们不久就感觉非常熟悉了。

她对我说:"好多人,真是太挤了。"

"是的。"我赞同地回答,"大家都愿意看着男孩子长成大人。"

她的脸上出现高兴和自豪的表情,说:"我哥哥就要毕业了,他会发表演讲。我买了这些花,准备抛给他。"

这些花不是花房最喜欢种的那种,只是传统的家庭用花,就像我们送给亲爱的祖母的那种花。"不过，因为小女孩，他一定会觉得这些花又美丽又芬芳。"我心里想。

她用花束指着方向，继续说："那是我哥哥。"

我问："是那个浅色头发的吗？"

"哦，不是。"她微笑着回答，天真无邪地摇头责备着，"不是那个，那个人不好看。我哥哥是那个棕色卷发的帅气小伙。看起来他的眼睛也是棕色的，但其实是深蓝色的。看，他就在那儿！现在他正举着两只手呢。你看见他了吧？"

她热切地在我和他之间转换视线，仿佛我认出他的哥哥这件事和什么至关重要的命运有关似的。

"我看见他了。"我说，"真是一表人才啊。"

"当然，他很帅。而且他很棒，学习很刻苦。自从妈妈去世后，都是他照顾我。流程表上有他的名字，就在这儿。他不是毕业生代表，但是因为他的表现，他获得了在毕业典礼上演讲的荣誉。"她说话时带着那种单纯的快乐。

我看出来这个小女孩很熟悉这些学校里面的词儿，她佩服哥哥的成绩，认同哥哥的希望，看到哥哥成功了，就好像自己获得了成功一样。

"他的演说词很棒，而且他讲得很好。他已经对我说过很多次了。我几乎都记住了。哦！他的开场白真是落落大方。那番话是这么说的——"她一定看到了我脸上浓厚的兴趣，鼓起勇气补充说："'瞬息万变的历史力量和人才辈出的英雄人物不断更替，造就了历史。在其中，我们经常会发现命运之手的翻覆——'"

"哎，上帝会保佑这孩子！"我想，低头看着她明亮自豪的脸蛋。她带着笑容和稚气，滔滔不绝地讲出那些深奥的词，我无法描述这种古灵精怪的感觉。

随着典礼的进行，演说时间越来越近了。我的这位小小的朋友变得兴奋又焦急，她的注意力都集中起来了，眼睛睁得更大，眼神更亮，脸颊上出现两片深深的红晕。

"现在轮到他了。"她转过身对我说，脸上带着一种自豪、高兴又担忧的表情。但是当序曲响起，台上点到了他的名字，这个热切的孩子忘记了我和她周围的世界。在他登上舞台走向演说台时，她站起来向前探着身体，想把他看得更清楚些。

听着她深深地呼吸，我知道她的心快要跳出来了；看着她哥哥走上舞台、走到前方的样子，我知道她也正紧张得发抖。他艰难地抬起手，脸色苍白，嘴唇发紫，像受了寒似的。我很担忧，小女孩也非常担心。她似乎看出来他有些不对劲，脸上出现了焦虑的表情。

他机械地鞠了一躬，表情显得既困惑又挣扎，接下来是无助。最后，他像做梦一样茫然地盯着等待的观众。难挨的最初几秒钟过去了，他仍然哑口无言地站着。我看出了事情的真相：对舞台的恐惧把他击垮了。

唉！他的小妹妹惊慌地转头看着我，说："他忘记演说词了。"接着她脸上的神情突然迅速改变了，显出一种坚定的决心。然后，她那甜美而勇敢的童音打破了空气中死一般的沉寂：

"瞬息万变的历史力量和人才辈出的英雄人物不断更替，造就了历史。在其中，我们经常会发现命运之手的翻覆——"

每个人都转身四下寻找我们。令人窒息的沉默，甜美的童音，幼稚的面孔，一段长长的、不带孩子气的说辞，这些因素加在一起，造成了一种怪诞的效果。

可惜这帮助来得太迟了。悲惨的哥哥已经带着耻辱蹒跚地从舞台上走了下去。乐队很快开始演奏，轻快的乐浪倾泻而出，掩盖了这次失败。

我看了小女孩一眼，想要用眼神表达我强烈的同情，但她没看见，她流着泪，盯着她哥哥的脸。我伸出手臂环住她，但她太专心，根本没留意我的拥抱。我还没来得及赞赏她坚强的意志，她就走向了那个如雕像一样面无表情地坐在那里、深感羞辱的年轻人。

看见她在身边，他的面部表情放松了，但眼睛里很快蒙上一层水雾。坐在那儿的年轻人们相互挤在一起，为她挪了个地方。她在哥哥旁边坐下来，把花束放在他的膝盖上，把手放在他手里。

我不能把目光从她那充满怜悯的、亲切的小脸上移开。我看见她低声说着什么，他低头弯腰，好把她的话听清楚些。随后，我发现她正问他现在是否记住他的"发言稿"了，他的回答是肯定的。

当流程表上的下一位年轻人结束发言之后，乐队奏起了音乐，哥哥惊讶地发现小女孩正向舞台走去。她从一大群教授、理事和重要的观礼人中挤了过去，径直走到学院主席的面前。

"先生，如果您允许的话，您和理事们可以再让我哥哥试一次吗？他现在能记起他的发言稿了。"她有点谦卑地说。

好一会儿，学院主席只是从他的金边眼镜后面盯着她看。然后，他对小女孩微笑起来，对她提出请求表示欣赏。他走到舞台下对那个失败的年轻人说了起来。

于是乐队再次停止演奏，主持人简单地说了几句，表示那位先生将发表他的演说——《历史的平行线》。

观众们兴趣高涨，满怀期待。所有观众都像石头般静静坐着，屏住呼吸，似乎生怕这名演讲者再次打怵。但这种担心是多余的。年轻人心中的勇士被唤醒了，他演讲的时候，心中有着坚定的目标。他要征服全场的观众，挽回自己的形象，让小妹妹满是泪痕的脸上重现笑容。演说过程中我一直观察着那张脸：睁大的眼睛，分开的嘴唇——忘记了所有屏住呼吸的观众，她的情绪随他一起变化。

年轻人以一种激烈纵情的姿态结束了演说。在实现梦想的过程中，他充满热忱，克服错误的判断，获得认同。演说效果真是非常震撼。静默的观众爆发出一阵狂热的掌声，为毕业生代表准备的花束像暴风雨一样落在他的身边。而那个设法挽救这一天的小女孩，她的小脸喜气洋洋，洋溢着自豪与高兴，我永远都不会忘记当时的景象。

（萨拉·温特·凯洛格）

Playing Theater at River Mouth

"Now, boys, what shall we do?" I asked, addressing a thoughtful conclave of seven, assembled in our barn one dismal, rainy afternoon.

"Let's have a theater," suggested Binny Wallace.

The very thing! But where? The loft of the stable was ready to burst with hay provided for Gypsy, but the long room over the carriage-house was unoccupied. The place of all places! My eye saw at once its possibilities for a theater. So here, in due time, was set up some extraordinary scenery of my own painting. The curtain, I recollect, though it worked smoothly enough on other occasions, invariably hitched during the performances; and it often required the united energies of the Prince of Denmark, the King, and the Grave-digger, with an occasional hand from "the fair Ophelia" (Pepper Whitcomb in a low-necked dress), to hoist that bit of green cambric.

The theater however, was a success, as far as it went. I retired from the business with no fewer than fifteen hundred pins, after deducting the headless, the pointless, and the crooked pins. From first to last we took in a great deal of this counterfeit money. The price of admission to the "River Mouth Theater" was twenty pins. I played all the principal parts myself,——not that I was a finer actor than the other boys, but because I owned the establishment.

At the tenth representation, my dramatic career was brought to a close by an unfortunate circumstance. We were playing the drama of "William Tell, the Hero of Switzerland". Of course I was William Tell in spite of Fred Langdon, who wanted to act the character himself. I would not let him, so he withdrew from the company, taking the only bow and arrow we had. I made a cross-bow out of a piece of whalebone, and did very well without him.

We had reached that exciting scene where Gessler, the Austrian tyrant, commands Tell to shoot the apple from his son's head. Pepper Whitcomb, who played all the juvenile and women parts, was my son.

To guard against mischance, a piece of pasteboard was fastened by a handkerchief over the upper part of Whitcomb's face, while the arrow to be used was sewn up in a strip of flannel. I was a capital marksman, and the big apple, only two yards distant, turned its russet cheek fairly towards me.

I can see poor little Pepper now, as he stood without flinching, waiting for me to perform my great feat. I raised my cross-bow amid the breathless silence of the crowded audience, ——consisting of seven boys and three girls, exclusive of Kitty Collies, who insisted on paying her way with a clothes-pin. I raised the bow, I repeat. Twang! Went the whipcord; but, alas! Instead of hitting the apple, the arrow flew right into Pepper Whitcomb's mouth, which happened to be open at the time, and destroyed my aim.

I shall never be able to banish that moment from my memory. Pepper's roar, expressive of astonishment, indignation, pain, is still ringing in my ears. I looked upon him as a corpse, and glancing not far into the dreary future, pictured myself led forth to execution in the presence of the very same spectators then assembled.

Luckily poor Pepper was not seriously hurt; but Grandfather Nutter, appearing in the midst of the confusion (attracted by the howls of young Tell), issued an order against all theatricals hereafter, and the place was closed; not, however, without a farewell speech from me, in which I said that this would have been the proudest moment of my life, if I had not hit Pepper Whitcomb in the mouth.

Thereupon the audience (assisted, I am glad to state, by Pepper) cried, "Hear! Hear!" I then attributed the accident to Pepper himself, whose mouth, being open at the instant I fired, acted upon the arrow much after the fashion of a whirlpool, and drew in the fatal shaft. I was about to explain how a comparatively small whirlpool could suck in the largest ship, when the curtain fell of its own accord, amid the shouts of the audience.

This was my last appearance on the stage. It was some time, though, before I heard the end of the William Tell business. Malicious little boys, who had not been allowed to buy tickets to my theater, used to cry after me in the street,——

"Who killed Cock Robin?

'I' said the sparrer,

'With my bow and arrer,

I killed Cock Robin.'"

The sarcasm of this verse was more than I could stand. And it made Pepper Whitcomb pretty angry to be called Cock Robin, I can tell you!

(Thomas Bailey Aldrich)

译文

河口剧院

"兄弟们，现在我们玩什么？"我问道。那是一个阴沉沉的午后，天上下着小雨，我们七个小伙伴聚在马厩里，进行一场意义非凡的"秘密会议"。

"我们组建一个剧院吧。"宾尼·华莱士提议。

对！我们就玩这个！但是在哪里演呢？马厩上的阁楼堆满了吉普赛人用的干草，但是马车车库楼上有一个长形的房间，目前还是空着的。太好了！我们就在这间房里玩！一眼望去，我就发现这里非常适合演话剧。于是，大家用我的画在这里搭起一些很特别的场景，时间刚刚好。我还记得那副窗帘，尽管平时它可以拉得很顺，但是在我们表演的时候，它就一定会卡住，而且丹麦王子、国王、盗墓者有时还会一起使劲拉动那一小块绿色的帆布，美丽的"奥菲利亚"（身着低领长裙的佩珀·惠特科姆扮演）偶尔也会加入其中。

然而，小剧场的生意却非常成功。在打烊的时候，除去那些钝的、没头的、弯曲的别针，我一共收下了一千五百多枚别针。从开始到结束，我们都把别针当成虚拟货币，一张"河口剧院"的门票是二十枚别针。我一直亲自充当老板一角，不是因为我的演技比其他小伙伴好，而因为是我亲手创建了这家剧院。

在演到第十场戏的时候，一件不幸的事情发生了，导致我的戏剧生涯告一段落。当时，我们正在演《瑞士英雄——威廉·特尔》，我扮演威廉·特尔，但是弗雷德·兰登也想演这个角色，因为没演成，就离开了剧院，还带走了我们仅有的弓和箭头。于是，我用鲸鱼骨做了一把十字弓，即使少了弗雷德·兰登，演出也很精彩。

最激动人心的一幕开演了。奥地利暴君盖斯勒命令特尔，射中他儿子头顶上的苹果。佩珀·惠特科姆扮演所有的少年、女性角色，在这部戏中，他扮演我的儿子。为了防止意外发生，惠特科姆脸蛋的上部有一块硬纸板，用手帕系在他的头上，箭头也用一条法兰绒布缝了起来。我扮演的是一位神射手，将近两米远的黄皮大苹果正对着我。

现在，我把目光投向可怜的小佩珀，他毫不畏缩，静静地站着，等着看我的精彩演出。喧闹的观众席里有七个小男孩，三个小女孩，还不算执意要用衣夹当门票的牧羊犬吉蒂，他们安静下来，屏住呼吸，此时，我举起十字弓，瞄准苹果，"砰"！弓弦弹出；但是，哎呀！那时佩珀·惠特科姆的嘴刚好张着，箭没有射中苹果，而是正中佩珀·惠特科姆的嘴，毁了我的表演。

那一刻，我终生难忘。佩珀吓呆了，怒气冲天，痛苦不堪，他咆哮的声音至今萦绕在我的耳边。我当时以为他已经死了，于是脑海里浮现了即将发生的一幕悲剧——我就要在这群观众面前被处死。

不幸中的万幸是，可怜的佩珀伤得不重，但他的一阵喊叫引来了纳特爷爷，面对眼前一片混乱的局面，还没等我发表告别演说，纳特爷爷就下令以后禁止演戏，封了这间房。然而，如果我没射中佩珀的嘴巴，这将是我人生中最引以为豪的一刻。

于是，观众喊道："听他说！听他说！"在佩珀的支持下，我开心地向大家解释刚刚发生的一幕，我把这场意外的发生归罪于佩珀，正是因为在我射箭的那一刻，他张着嘴，箭头如漩涡般飞速前进，才造成致命的伤害。在观众的呐喊声中，我刚要解释这和一个小漩涡能吞没一艘大轮船的道理一样，幕帘就自动关上了。

这是我在舞台上的最后一次演出，然而，我出演的威廉·特尔一角却深入人心。一个淘气的小男孩因为没被允许买我们剧院的门票，总是跟在我身后，一路上喊着——

"谁杀死了知更鸟？

'我'，麻雀说，

'用我的弓和箭,
我杀了知更鸟。'"

告诉你!我实在忍受不了这首诗的讽刺,而且佩珀·惠特科姆知道自己被叫知更鸟后,也十分生气。

(托马斯·贝利·奥尔德里奇)

♬ 作者介绍

托马斯·贝利·奥尔德里奇,美国诗人,小说家。在1881年至1890年期间,曾任《大西洋月刊》的编辑。他的作品包括小说、诗歌和散文,其中的一些作品富于幽默感,深受欢迎。他也善于给读者带来惊喜,趣味十足。如果你想知道为何,不妨读一读他的小说《马乔里·道》和《示巴女王》。他的一些诗歌广为年轻读者所熟知,大受追捧。《蒙茅斯剧院》出自《顽童故事》一书。

American Salmon

预习

enthusiasm /ɪnˈθuːziæzəm/ 热情

gaff /gæf/ 用尖锐的铁器戳一个洞用来钩住

harlequin /ˈhɑːrləkwɪn/ 滑稽角色

ponderous /ˈpɑːndərəs/ 沉重的

tense /tens/ 紧绷的

weir /wɪr/ 垂直置于水中的渔网

That was a day to be remembered. It had only begun when we drew rein at a tiny farmhouse on the banks of the Clackamas and sought horse feed and lodging, ere we hastened to the river that broke over a weir not a quarter of a mile away.

Imagine a stream seventy yards broad, divided by a pebbly island, running over charming "riffles" and swirling into deep, quiet pools, where the good salmon goes to smoke his pipe after meals.

The weir had been erected to pen the Chenook salmon from going farther up-stream. We could see them, twenty or thirty pounds in weight, lying by the score in the deep pools, or flying madly against the weir and foolishly skinning their noses. They were not our prey, for they would not rise at a fly, and we knew it Nevertheless, when one made his leap against the weir, and landed on the foot-plank with a jar that shook the board I was standing on, I would fain have claimed him for my own capture.

California sniffed up-stream and down-stream, across the racing water, chose his ground, and let the gaudy fly drop in the tail of a riffle.

I was getting my rod together, when I heard the joyous shriek of the reel and the yells of California, and three feet of living silver leaped into the air far across the water. The forces were engaged.

The salmon tore up-stream, the tense line cutting the water like a tide-rip behind him, and the light bamboo bowed to breaking. What happened there after I cannot tell.

In what appeared to be half a day, but in what was really little over a quarter of an hour, the fish sullenly came home with spurts of temper, dashing head on and dancing in the air, but home to bank came he, and the unpitying reel gathered up the thread of his life inch by inch.

We landed him in a little bay, and the spring weight in his glorious gills checked at eleven and one half pounds. Eleven and one half pounds of fighting salmon! We danced a war-dance on the pebbles, and California shouted, "Partner! Partner! This is glory! Now you catch your fish! Twenty-four years I've waited for this! "

I went into that icy-cold river and made my cast just above the weir, and all but foul-hooked a blue-and-black water snake with a coral mouth, which coiled itself on a stone and hissed.

The next cast——ah, the pride of it, the regal splendor of it! the thrill that ran down from finger-tip to toe! Then the water boiled. The salmon broke for the fly and got it. There remained sense enough in me to give him all that he wanted when he jumped not once, but twenty times, before the up-stream flight that ran my line out to the last half-dozen turns, and I saw the reel-bar of nickel glitter under the thinning green coils. My thumb was burned deep when I strove to stopper the line.

I did not feel it until later, for my soul was out in the dancing weir. As I bowed back, the butt of the rod on my left hip-bone, and the top joint dipping like unto a weeping willow, he turned and accepted every inch of slack that I could by any means get in as a favor.

There lie several sorts of success in this world which taste well in the moment of enjoyment. I question whether the steady theft of line from an able-bodied salmon, who knows exactly what you are doing and why you are doing it, is not sweeter than any other victory within human scope.

Like California's fish, he ran at me head on, and leaped against the line, but I had two hundred fifty pairs of fingers given me in that hour. The banks and the pine-tree danced dizzily round me. But I only reeled——reeled as for life——reeled for hours, and at the end of the reeling, continued to give him the butt while he sulked in a pool.

The first wild enthusiasm of capture had died away. We were both at work in deadly earnest now. I would rather have died among the pebbles than surrender my right to play and land a salmon, weight unknown, with an eight ounce rod. I dropped on a log to rest for a moment. As I drew breath, the weary hands slackened their hold, and I forgot to give him the butt.

A wild scutter in the water, a plunge, and a break for the head-waters of the Clackamas were my rewards. The weary toil of reeling in with one eye under the water and the other on the top joint of the rod was renewed.

"The father of all the salmon!" California shouted. "Get your trout to bank, Johnny Bull!"

But I could do no more. Even the insult failed to move me. The rest of the game was with the salmon. He suffered himself to be drawn, skipping with pretended delight at getting to the haven where I would fain bring him. Yet no sooner did he feel shoal water under his ponderous body than he backed like a torpedo-boat, and the snarl of the reel told me that my labor was in vain.

A dozen times, at least, this happened ere the line hinted that he had given up the battle and would be towed in. He was towed. The landing-net was useless for one of his size, and I would not have him gaffed. I stepped into the shallows and heaved him out with a respectful hand under the gill for which kindness he battered me about the legs with his tail, and I felt the strength of him and was proud.

California had taken my place in the shallows, his fish hard held. I was up the bank, lying full length on the sweet-scented grass and gasping in company with my first salmon caught, played, and landed on an eight ounce rod. My hands were cut and bleeding, I was dripping with sweat, spangled like a harlequin with scales, water from my waist down, nose peeled by the sun, but utterly, supremely happy.

The beauty, the darling, my salmon, weighed twelve pounds, and I had been seven and thirty minutes bringing him to bank. He had been lightly hooked on the angle of the right jaw, and the hook had not wearied him. That hour I sat among princes and crowned heads, greater than them all.

(Rudyard Kipling)

译文

美国鲑鱼

那是永生难忘的一天。我们在克拉克默斯边界的一座小农舍前勒住了马步，准备给马找一个歇脚进食的地方。但最后我们却冲向了一千六百米外的一条河，河的上方横跨着一道鱼梁。

一条六七十米宽的小溪，中央是一个满是卵石的小岛。溪水潺潺流淌，流过迷人的浅石滩，旋转着流进幽深的水洼里。不难想象，这里一定是鲑鱼饭后散心的地方。

鱼梁是一张垂直竖立在水里的渔网，作用是为了防止鲑鱼逆流而上，游到过远的地方。我们能看见那些鱼有的成群结队地在深深的水洼里游泳，有的则疯狂地撞向鱼梁，蠢笨地弄伤了它们的鼻子。这些鱼每一条都有十来千克重。我们没法抓到它们，因为它们不会为了一只苍蝇浮到水面上来。我们都知道，除非一条鲑鱼跳过鱼梁，"砰"一声落在桥面上，猛烈晃动我脚下的木板，否则我就无法轻易将它收入囊中。

加利福利亚跨过湍急的水流，在小溪上游下游查探，挑选自己的地盘，然后把一只苍蝇扔进了一片浅石滩的底部，这并没有什么用。我正想拿起我的鱼竿，突然听见绕线轮那里传来一阵声响，加利福尼亚大声嚷嚷着，然后一条三尺长的活泼银鱼越过水面，跃到了空中。战斗开始了。

这条鲑鱼分开了溪水，紧绷的鱼线切开了水面，激起浪花，轻巧的竹竿几乎要被拽断。接下来发生的事情简直无法用言语表达。

这条鱼绷紧身体，在空中冲撞跳跃，怒气冲冲地想要逃回去。它折腾了一刻多钟，但我感觉像是过了半天。不过，它还是被拖向岸边，无情的绕线轮正一厘米一厘米地卷起，它生命的线也在缩短。

我们把它放在一个小水湾里，用弹簧秤钩着它的两腮称了重量，刻度显示有两三千克重。一条两三千克重的活蹦乱跳的鲑鱼！我们在卵石上跳起了战阵舞，加利福利亚大声喊道："伙计！伙计！这真是太了不起了！我亲自抓到了鱼！我等这一天等了二十四年了！"

我走进冷冰冰的河水，把我的钓线从鱼梁上甩出去，但只钩上来一条珊瑚色嘴巴、蓝黑相间的水蛇。它盘在一块石头上，"嘶嘶"地冲我吐着蛇信。

但接下来的一次垂钓真是无与伦比，令人骄傲！一开始，我感到从手指尖到脚趾泛起一阵战栗，紧接着水面沸腾了！鲑鱼跃出水面咬住了苍蝇。它扑腾了二十来次，我非常明白它的用意，所以我任由它拉着我的钓线游向小溪上游，直到我的绕线轮只剩下最后六圈线，能看见薄薄的绿色线圈下镍质轮轴闪烁的光芒。我努力拽住钓线，却在大拇指上割了一道深深的口子。

我全神贯注，看着不停摇晃的鱼梁，很久之后才感到大拇指上传来的疼痛。我身体后仰，钓竿的尾部抵着我的左髋骨，顶部则像一枝垂柳般没入水中。它在水里翻腾，我仁慈地把钓线稍稍放松了一点，但无论如何我还是会捉住它。

世界上没有几种成功的喜悦能媲美此刻的欢乐。我想，没有什么比钓到一条强壮的三文鱼更快乐的事了，因为它完全知道你在干什么，也知道你为什么这么干。

像加利福利亚的鱼一样，它迎面向我冲来，妄图摆脱钓线，但我在那时如有神助。河岸和松树仿佛围着我起舞，令人头晕目眩，而我却只是拼命绕着线轮——仿佛那是我的生命之线一般——我绕了好几个小时，在它气势汹汹地跃进一个水洼时甩动钓竿。

刚开始捉鱼时的狂热已经消逝。我们如今都在非常认真地工作。我宁愿死在河滩上的卵石中间，也不愿意放弃用一根两百多克的鱼竿钓到一条重量未知的鲑鱼的乐趣。我找到一根木头坐下休息片刻。我歇口气的时候，受伤的手松开了钓线，我忘记拉动钓竿了。

结果，这条鱼拼命地猛冲了出去，钻到水中，重又回到克拉克默斯的河里。我不得不一只眼睛盯着河水，一只眼睛盯着竿顶，艰难而疲惫地重新开始绕线。

"这是一条鲑鱼之父！"加利福利亚大喊说，"约翰·布尔，把这条鱼钓上来！"

但是我累得动都不想动，哪怕受到侮辱，我也不想再动一下了，接下来就任由鲑鱼怎么折腾。它忍着疲惫，装作心甘情愿的样子跳到了一个"避难所"，在这个位置我很容易就能抓到它。不过，它笨重的身体刚刚碰到那滩浅水，就立刻像一艘鱼雷艇一样冲了回去。绕线轮刺耳的声音表明，我的努力又白费了。

你来我往地重复了十几次之后，该发生的还是发生了。我从钓线上就能感觉到，它放弃了抵抗，投降了。我把它拖出水面。袋网对这种尺寸的鲑鱼毫无用处，而我又不想用鱼叉插住它。于是我走到浅滩，一只手掐着鱼鳃把它举起来。它的鳃部一张一合，猛击我的手，还甩着尾巴击打我的腿。我感到这是一条有力气的鱼，我很自豪自己能逮住它。

加利福利亚取代了我在浅滩里的位置，艰难地举着他的鱼。我上了岸，完全展开身体躺在甜美芳香的草地上喘息。我用两百多克重的鱼竿钓到的第一条鲑鱼就放在我的身边。割伤的手还在流血，我汗流浃背，闪闪发光，像披着一身鱼鳞的小丑。我的下半身湿淋淋的，我的鼻子被太阳晒脱了皮，但我真的非常非常快乐。

我那条亲爱的漂亮鲑鱼重达五千克。我花了七个半小时才把它钓上岸。鱼钩轻轻地钩在它下颌右面的斜角里，没有把它弄伤。那一刻，我感觉自己比王公贵族还要伟大。

（拉迪亚德·吉普林）

练习

1. 把下列三句话，合并为一句话。

Wild scutter in the water was my reward.

A plunge was my reward.

A break for the head-waters of the Clackamas was my reward.

_____

2. 一个谓语拥有两个以上的主语，这样的形式称为复合主语。

分解复合主语句子，使每个句子只有一个主语：

The little man in green, and the minnows with silver tails taught Tom a lesson.

_____

A New England Boyhood

☞ 预习

asbestos /æsˈbestəs/ 石棉
lavishness /ˈlævɪʃnəs/ 浪费
phosphorus /ˈfɑːsfərəs/ 磷
radius /ˈreɪdiəs/ 半径范围
resource /ˈriːsɔːrs/ 资源
scientific /ˌsaɪənˈtɪfɪk/ 科学的
systematic /ˌsɪstəˈmætɪk/ 有系统的
tinder /ˈtɪndər/ 火绒

I. The Swimming School

Joy, joy, joy! On a hot summer day in June, when I was nine years old, I was asked how I would like to learn to swim. There is little doubt in the mind of any boy who reads this what my answer was. I and my elder brother, who was twelve, were to be permitted to go to the swimming school. This was joy enough to have that year marked with red in our history.

The swimming school was in water that flowed where Brimmer Street and the houses behind it are now built. It was just such a building as the floating baths are now, which the city maintains, but it inclosed a much larger space. Of this space a part had a floor; the depth was about five feet. To little boys like me it made little difference that there was this floor, for we could be as easily drowned in five feet of water as we could in fifteen.

As soon as you were dressed and ready——and this meant in about one minute——you took your turn to be taught. A belt was put around you under the arms; to this belt a rope was attached, and you were told to jump in. You jumped in and went down as far as gravity chose to take you, and were then pulled up by the rope. The rope was then attached to the end of a long belt, and you were swung out upon the surface of the water. Then began the instruction.

"O-n-e! ——Two! Three!" the last two words were spoken with great rapidity——"one" spoken very slowly. This meant that the knees and feet were to be drawn up very slowly, but were to be dashed out very quickly, and then the heels brought together as quickly.

Boys who were well built for it and who were quick, learned to swim in two or three lessons. Slender boys and little boys who had not much muscular force——and such was I——were a whole summer before they could be trusted without the rope. But the training was excellent, and from the end of that year till now I have been entirely at home in the water.

I think now that scientific and systematic training in swimming is a very important part of public instruction, and I wish we could see it introduced everywhere where there is responsible oversight of boys at school.

II. Out of Doors

For the half-holidays that were not otherwise provided for, my brother and I took care by using "the means which God and nature put into our hands". That is to say, we walked out of town to such woodland generally as we had not explored before, until we were personally acquainted with the whole country for a circle of fully five miles' radius around the State House.

We always kept for such expeditions what were known as phosphorus-boxes, which were the first steps in the progress that has put the tinder-boxes of that day entirely out of sight. Most of the young people of the present day have not so much as seen a tinder-box, and I do not know where I could go to buy one. But, in the working of the household, the tinder-box was the one resource for getting a light.

We boys, however, with the lavishness of boys, used to buy at the apothecary's phosphorus-boxes, which were then coming in. We had to pay twenty-five cents for one such box. These boxes were made in Germany; they were of red paper, little cylinders about four inches high and an inch in diameter. You could carry one, and were meant to carry it, in your breast pocket. In the bottom of the box was a little bottle, which contained asbestos soaked with sulphuric acid, and in the top were about a hundred matches, made, I think, from chlorate of potash. One of these you put into the bottle and pulled it out aflame. We never should have thought of taking one of these walks without a phosphorus-box.

When we arrived at the woodland sought, we invariably made a little fire. We never cooked anything that I remember, but this love of fire is one of the early barbarisms of the human race which dies out latest. I suppose if it had been the middle of the hottest day in August we should have made a fire.

So soon as the morning session of school was over, in the summer or autumn months, if it were a half-holiday, we would start on one of these rambles. Sometimes, if the walk was not to a great distance, we invited, or permitted, the two sisters to come with us. We had a tin box for plants, and always brought home what seemed new or pretty.

When, in 1833, the Worcester Railroad was opened, this walking gave way, for a family as largely interested in that railroad as we were, to excursions out of town to the point where the walk was to begin. The line to West Newton was opened to the public on the 7th of April, 1833, but from the day when the Meteor, which was the first locomotive engine in New England, ran on her trial trip, we two boys were generally present at the railroad, on every half-holiday, to take our chances for a ride out upon one of the experimental trips.

We knew the engine-drivers and the men who were not yet called conductors, and they knew us. My father was the president of the road, and we thought we did pretty much as we chose. The engine-drivers would let us ride with them on the engine, and I, for one, got my first lessons in the business of driving an engine on these excursions. But as soon as the road was open to passengers, these rides on the engine dropped off, perhaps were prohibited. Still we went to Newton in the train as often as we could, and afterwards to Needham.

There were varied cars in those days, some of them open, like our open horse-cars of to-day, and all of them entered from the side, as in England up to the present time. After this date our long walks out of town naturally ceased. Nothing was more common in our household than for the whole family to go out to Brighton or to Newton, and, with babies and all, to establish ourselves in some grove, where we spent the afternoon very much as God meant we should spend it, I suppose; returning late in the evening with such spoils of wild flowers as the season permitted.

(Edward Everett Hale)

译文

在新英格兰度过的少年时代

1. 游泳学校

耶耶耶！六月的一个炎炎夏日，九岁的我被问愿不愿意去学游泳。毫无疑问，任何一个读到这儿的男孩心里都很清楚我的答案是什么。我和我十二岁的哥哥被批准去游泳学校学习。这是件值得用红笔将这一年在我们的成长中记下来的天大喜事。

游泳学校建在一条河里，现在这个地方成了布里默街，后面建有房子。这所学校在城市中如同现在的那种漂浮泳池一般，只是要比漂浮泳池容积大得多。在这片空间里，有一部分是有池底的；虽然水深大约一米五，但对像我这样的小男孩来说，有没有这块池底没什么差别，因为在一米五的水里，和在四米多的水里一样容易溺水。

等你刚一换好衣服，做好准备——这大概要一分钟——就轮到你学游泳了。一根皮带会从你的手臂下方穿过，把你的身子缠住，上面连着一根绳子；然后他们就会让你跳进水里。等你跳进去后，你就会不断下沉，听任重力的摆布，然后你就被绳子拉了上去。绳子拉到长腰带的顶端，你也就从水面上浮出来了。之后就是指令。

"一！——二，三！"后两个字被极快地说出——"一"语调被拉长。这说明膝盖和脚要收得非常慢，但划出去的时候要非常快，脚后跟也要很快并拢在一起。

男孩们天生就是把好手，他们学起游泳来非常迅速，一两节课就会游了。纤细或瘦小的男孩们肌肉没有太多力量——像我就是——要一整个夏天才能使他们放心让我脱离绳子游泳。但是训练棒极了，从那年年末起到现在，我就一直把自己整个泡在家里的水里。

我想既然科学而系统的游泳训练是公共教育非常重要的一部分，那么我希望我们都能看到，游泳训练可以在那些能够负责任地看管校内男孩们的地方普及起来。

2. 在户外

对于没有其他安排的半日休假，我和哥哥都会用"上帝和大自然赐予我们的方式"谨慎行事。换句话说就是我们要走出城镇，到那些我们之前没怎么探索过的林地去。后来，我们亲自"视察"了以州议会大厦为中心、整整八千多米半径范围的整片"国土"，才停止了这种行为。

我们总是为这种远征探险保留一个叫作"磷盒"的东西，这个东西就是使当年的打火匣完全淡出人们视线之后，最先出现的替代品。如今大多数年轻人都没怎么见过打火匣了，我也不知道去哪可以买到。但是，在家庭的日常劳务里，打火匣是点亮灯火的一种办法。

我们男孩子，不管怎样，有着男孩的奢侈，过去常常在药剂师那儿买刚刚流行起来的磷盒。一盒要二十五美分。这些盒子是德国制造的。它们外面包着红色的纸，是有十厘米高的小圆柱体，直径为三厘米。如果你打算带上它，你可以把它挂在你的上衣口袋里。盒子底部是个小瓶子，里面装着用硫酸浸泡的石棉，而盒子顶部有大概一百来支火柴，我认为是由氯酸钾制的。你从其中拿一支放到瓶子里，拉出来就点燃了。我们总是记得带一个磷盒出行。

等我们到达要寻找的那片林地，我们总是会点上一把火。我记得我们从没煮过什么东西，但是对火种的这份热爱是人类种族的早期原始行为之一，至今仍未熄灭。我想，即使是八月最热那一天的正午，我们应该也会点火。

夏季或秋季里，学校上午的课一结束，如果有半天的休假，我们就会开始漫步。有时候，如果步途不算很远，我们就会邀请，或者说准许，两个妹妹同我们一起去。我们有个专门装植物的马口铁罐，总是会带些看起来新鲜或是好看的（植物）回家。

当1883年伍斯特铁路开通，这种徒步活动就让步于到小镇外的短途旅行了，因为我们全家都对铁路非常感兴趣。这条通往的西牛顿镇的路线在1883年4月7日才对外开放，但从新英格兰的第一台机车蒸汽机"流星号"试运行的那天起，我们两个小男孩每到有半日休假，就常常出现在铁路上。我们冒险之旅的一项活动，就是看能不能平安穿过铁路。

我们认识那些火车司机和那个还不能被称作指挥员的男人，他们也认识我们。我父亲是铁道部部长，而我们觉得自己行为非常棒。那些火车司机会让我们和他们一起骑在发动机上，我，作为其中之一，在这些短途出游中，上了从事驾驶机车的第一堂课。但是铁路一对乘客们开放，这些骑在发动机上的体验就结束了，大概因为这是被禁止的吧。但我们仍尽量每次都坐火车去牛顿镇，后来是去尼德姆镇。

在那个时候，火车和汽车一样，各种式样都有。有的火车是敞篷的。所有的火车都是从侧面的门进去的，就像英国至今还在做的那样。这个日子之后，我们出镇的远足自然也就停止了。在我们家，全家人一起去布莱顿或是牛顿镇是再平常不过的了，带上所有人，包括婴儿，一起到小树林里舒展身心；在那儿，我们挥霍午后的时光，我想，这是上帝旨意。我们傍晚才会迟迟返回，如果季节合适，还会带回些野花这样的战利品。

（爱德华·埃弗里特·黑尔）

❧ 作者介绍

爱德华·埃弗里特·黑尔，美国作家、编辑、神职人员，1822年出生于波士顿。他的父亲是内森·黑尔的外甥。身为美国的爱国人士，曾于1776年被英国人当作间谍接受刑罚。黑尔教授有《无国之人》《九十天的欧洲》《菲利普·诺兰的朋友》和若干男孩系列书，其中就有《在新英格兰度过的少年时代》。

✍ 练习

写一篇有关一些重要发明的报告。要求如下：

1. 发明者是谁？他的居住地？他如何想到这些发明的？他怎样改进他的第一计划的？

2. 这项发明替代了之前的什么东西？这项发明有什么优点？如何改进？

3. 这项发明如今的重要性？如果我们现在不能再使用它，会有什么坏处？

从下面的清单中选一个物体完成写作。

Locomotive   Steamboat
Stove   Street Light

4. 找出下面这些人的生活中最重要的事实，并写下来：

艾萨克·牛顿   伊莱·惠特尼
詹姆斯·瓦特   萨缪尔·F.B.摩尔斯
乔治·史蒂文森   赛勒斯·W.菲尔德
约翰·古藤贝格   托马斯·A.爱迪生
本杰明·富兰克林   乔治·威斯汀豪斯
罗伯特·富尔顿   威廉·马可尼

5. 把一些简单句组合成复合句。

A War-Time Adventure

After crossing the gully and walking on through the woods for what they thought a safe distance, Frank and Willy turned into the path.

They were talking very merrily about the General and Hugh and their friend Mills, and were discussing some romantic plan for the recapture of their horses from the enemy, when they came out of the path into the road, and found themselves within twenty yards of a group of Federal soldiers, quietly sitting on their horses, evidently guarding the road.

The sight of the blue coats made the boys jump. They would have crept back, but it was too late——they caught the eye of the man nearest them. They ceased talking as suddenly as birds in the trees stop chirping when the hawk sails over; and when one Yankee called to them, in a stern tone, "Halt there!" and started to come toward them, their hearts were in their mouths.

"Where are you boys going?" he asked, as he came up to them.

"Going home."

"Where do you belong?"

"Over there——at Oakland," pointing in the direction of their home, which seemed suddenly to have moved a thousand miles away.

"Where have you been?" the other soldiers had come up now.

"Been down this way," the boys' voices were never so meek before. Each reply was like an apology.

"Been to see your brother?" asked one who had not spoken before——a pleasant-looking fellow. The boys looked at him. They were paralyzed by dread of the approaching question.

"Now, boys, we know where you have been," said a small fellow, who wore a yellow chevron on his arm. He had a thin mustache and a sharp nose, and rode a wiry, dull sorrel horse.

"You may just as well tell us all about it. We know you've been to see 'em, and we are going to make you carry us where they are."

"No, we're not," said Frank doggedly.

Willy expressed his determination also.

"If you don't, it's going to be pretty bad for you," said the little corporal. He gave an order to two of the men, who sprang from their horses, and, catching Frank, swung him up behind another cavalryman. The boy's face was very pale, but he bit his lip.

"Go ahead,"——continued the corporal to a number of his men, who started down the path. "You four men remain here till we come back," he said to the men on the ground, and to two others on horseback. "Keep him here," jerking his thumb toward Willy, whose face was already burning with emotion.

"I'm going with Frank," said Willy. "Let me go." This to the man who had hold of him by the arm.

"Frank, make him let me go," he shouted, bursting into tears, and turning on his captor with all his little might.

"Willy, he's not going to hurt you,——don't you tell!" called Frank, squirming until he dug his heels so into the horse's flanks that the horse began to kick up.

"Keep quiet, Johnny! he's not going to hurt him," said one of the men kindly. He had a brown beard and shining white teeth.

They rode slowly down the narrow path, the dragoon holding Frank by the leg. Deep down in the woods, beyond a small branch, the path forked.

"Which way?" asked the corporal, stopping and addressing Frank.

Frank set his mouth tight and looked him in the eyes.

"Which is it?" the corporal repeated.

"I'm not going to tell," said he firmly.

"Look here, Johnny; we've got you, and we are going to make you tell us; so you might just as well do it easy. If you don't, we're going to make you."

The boy said nothing.

"You men dismount. Stubbs, hold the horses." The corporal himself dismounted, and three others did the same, giving their horses to a fourth.

"Get down!"——this to Frank and the soldier behind whom he was riding. The soldier dismounted, and the boy slipped off after him and faced his captor, who held a strap in one hand.

"Are you going to tell us?" he asked.

"No."

"Don't you know?" he came a step nearer, and held the strap forward. There was a long silence. The boy's face paled, but took on a look as if the proceedings were indifferent to him.

"If you say you don't know," said the man, hesitating in the face of the boy's resolution. "Don't you know where they are?"

"Yes, I know; but I'm not going to tell you," said Frank, bursting into tears.

"The little Johnny's game," said the soldier who had told him the others were not going to hurt Willy. The corporal said something to this man in an undertone, to which he replied,

"You can try, but it isn't going to do any good. I don't half like it, anyway."

Frank had stopped crying after his first outburst.

"If you don't tell, we are going to shoot you," said the little soldier, drawing his pistol.

The boy shut his mouth close, and looked straight at the corporal. The man laid down his pistol, and seizing Frank, drew his hands behind him, and tied them.

"Get ready, men," he said, as he drew the boy aside to a small tree, putting him with his back to it.

Frank thought that his hour had come. He thought of his mother and Willy, and wondered if the soldiers would shoot Willy, too. Then he thought of his father, and how proud he would be of his son's bravery when he should hear of it. This gave him strength.

"The knot——hurts my hands," he said.

The man leaned over and eased it a little.

"I wasn't crying because I was scared," said Frank.

The kind-looking fellow turned away.

"Now, boys, get ready," said the corporal, taking up his pistol.

How large it looked to Frank! He wondered where the bullets would hit him, and if the wounds would bleed, and whether he would be left alone all night out there in the woods, and if his mother would come and kiss him.

"I want to say my prayers," he said faintly.

The soldier made some reply, which he could not hear, and the man with the beard started forward; but just then all grew dark before the boy's eyes.

Next, he thought that he must have been shot, for he felt wet about his face, and was lying down. He heard some one say, "He's coming to"; and another replied, "Thank God!"

He opened his eyes. He was lying beside the little branch with his head in the lap of the big soldier with the beard, and the little corporal was leaning over him, throwing water in his face from a cap. The others were standing around.

"What's the matter?" asked Frank.

"That's all right," said the little corporal kindly. "We were just a-fooling a bit with you, Johnny."

"We never meant to hurt you," said the other. "You feel better now?"

"Yes; where's Willy?" He was too tired to move. "He's all right. We'll take you to him."

"Am I shot?" asked Frank.

"No! Do you think we'd have touched a hair of your head——and you such a brave little fellow? We were just trying to scare you a bit and carried it too far, and you got a little faint,——that's all."

The voice was so kindly that Frank was encouraged to sit up.

"Can you walk now?" asked the corporal, helping him and steadying him as he rose to his feet.

"I'll take him," said the big fellow, and before the boy could move, he had stooped, taken Frank in his arms, and was carrying him back toward the place where they had left Willy, while the others followed with the horses.

"I can walk," said Frank.

"No, I'll carry you, bless your heart!"

The boy did not know that the big dragoon was looking down at the light hair resting on his arm, and that while he trod the Virginia wood-path, in fancy he was at home in Delaware; or that the pressure the boy felt from his strong arms, was a caress given for the sake of another boy far away on the Brandywine. A little while before they came in sight of the other soldiers, Frank asked to be put down. The soldier gently set him on his feet, and before he let him go, kissed him.

"I've got a curly-headed fellow at home, just the size of you," he said softly.

Frank saw that his eyes were moist. "I hope you'll get safe back to him," he said.

"God grant it!" said the soldier.

When they reached the squad at the gate, they found Willy still in much distress on Frank's account; but he wiped his eyes when his brother reappeared, and listened with pride to

the soldiers' praise of Frank's "grit", as they called it. When they let the boys go, the little corporal wished Frank to accept a five-dollar gold piece; but he politely declined it.

(Thomas Nelson Page)

译文

战时历险记

弗兰克和威利穿过了一条溪谷,在树林中走呀走,终于感到安全了,才转向了一条林荫小道。

他们愉快地讨论着将军、休和他们的朋友米尔斯,讨论着那些不切实际的计划,想从敌人手中夺回自己的战马。当他们走回大道时,发现他们离联邦士兵仅有十八米左右的距离,那些士兵骑着马,一丝不苟地在道路上巡视。

看到这些士兵，孩子们吓了一跳。他们想要爬回去，但是太迟了——离他们最近的那个士兵发现了他们。就像雄鹰飞过，鸟儿就停止了鸣叫一般，这些孩子都不吭声了。一个士兵向他们走来，严厉地叫道："站住！"他们紧张得心都提到了嗓子眼。

"你们这些小孩子要去哪儿？"他一边问道，一边向他们走来。

"回家。"

"你们家在哪？"

"就在那——在奥克兰。"他们指了指家的方向，仿佛一瞬间就能够飞到千里之外的地方似的。

"那你们从哪儿来？"另一个士兵也追上来。

"从那一条路过来的。"男孩回答道，声音前所未有的谦恭，每一句话都像是在道歉。

"去找你的兄弟么？"另一位没说过话的士兵问道，他看起来非常和善。孩子们看着他，被这个问题吓呆了。

"现在，小伙子们，我们知道你们要去哪里了。"一位个子稍矮的下士说道，他的肩上别着一枚袖章，留着细细的山羊胡，骑着一匹结实的暗栗色的马。

"你最好还是告诉我们详细情况，我们知道你们已经见过他们了，带我们去他们那儿吧。"

"不，我们不会的。"弗兰克固执地说道。

威利也附和着，表明自己的态度。

"如果不答应，那你就要遭殃了。"下士说。他一声令下，另外两个人从马上跳了下来，抓住了弗兰克，把他拎到下士的后面。小男孩脸都白了，紧咬着嘴唇。

"去吧，"下士继续对其中一个士兵说道，并且走向了那条小径，"你们四个在这等着，等我们回来。"他对站在地上的两个人，以及骑在马上的另外两个人说。"把他留在这。"他情绪激动，脸上像火烧着一般，用颤抖的大拇指指着威利。

"我要和弗兰克一起去，"威利说。"让我去。"他对抓住他手臂的那个士兵说。

"弗兰克，叫他让我去。"他叫着，眼泪奔涌而出，用尽全部力量想要挣脱那个士兵的手。

"威利，他不会伤害你的——难道你看不出来么？"弗兰克说，摇摆着身体，用脚后跟狠狠地踢了马肚子一脚，马高高地扬起了前蹄。

"安静点，小伙子！他们不会伤害他的。"一个士兵温和地说，他长着棕色的胡须，牙齿很白。

他们骑着马沿着那条狭窄的小路缓慢地走着，士兵拽着弗兰克的大腿。在树林的深处，小路分成了两股。

"哪条路？"下士停下来问弗兰克。

弗兰克紧闭着嘴，紧盯着他的眼睛。

"到底走哪条路？"下士又重复了一遍。

"我不会说的。"他坚定地说道。

"听着，小伙子，我们抓住你了，我们会有办法让你说出来的，所以你还是直接说了吧，如果你不说的话，我们就要逼你了。"

小男孩还是没有说。

"你们下马吧，斯塔布斯，牵着这些马。"下士自己从马上下来，其他三人也立刻下了马，把马缰给了斯塔布斯。

"下来！"他对抓着弗兰克的士兵说道，士兵下了马，弗兰克滑下了马，正好面对着那个下士，下士的手上握着一根鞭子。

"你说不说？"他问。

"不说。"

"你是不知道么？"他向前走了一步，把皮带放在身前。沉默良久。男孩的脸十分苍白，似乎对这一切都漠不关心。

"如果你说你不知道——"下士说着，停顿下来看着男孩的脸色，"你是真不知道他们在哪儿吗？"

"我知道，但我不会告诉你的。"弗兰克说，眼泪也随之落了下来。

"小男孩的把戏。"那个说其他人不会伤害威利的士兵说。下士对那个士兵小声说了些什么，然后他回答道：

"你可以试试，但是不会有用的，总之，我也不喜欢你这个态度。"

在士兵说第一句话的时候，弗兰克停止了哭泣。

"你不说的话，我们就一枪毙了你。"下士说着，掏出了自己的手枪。

小男孩紧闭着嘴，眼睛直勾勾看着下士。下士放下自己的手枪，抓住弗兰克，把他的手紧紧反绑起来。

"准备好吧。"他说，同时把小男孩拽到一棵小树旁，让他背对着小树。

弗兰克觉得他的死期到了。他想到了他的母亲和威利，想着那些士兵会不会把威利也毙了。接着，他想到了他的父亲，如果父亲听到这件事，会感到很自豪吧！这都给了他力量。

"这个结——弄伤了我的手。"他说道。

那个人俯身过来帮他松了松结。

"我没有哭，因为我吓坏了。"弗兰克说。

看起来很善良的那个士兵转过了身。

"现在，小伙子，准备好吧！"下士一边说，一边掏出手枪。

弗兰克觉得，那只手枪真大呀！他在想，子弹到底会打在哪儿，伤口会不会流血，他一个人留在这儿，晚上会不会孤单，妈妈会不会过来亲吻他。

"我想祷告一下。"他淡淡地说道。

士兵做了回答，但是他没有听见。一位留着胡须的士兵向他走来，就在此时，他的眼前变得一团漆黑。

他想，自己一定是中枪了，他脸上湿湿的，人也倒了下来。有个人说："他醒过来了。"另一个人回答道："谢天谢地！"

他睁开眼。发现自己躺在小路上，头枕在那个长着胡子的士兵腿上，下士也侧着身子在看他。其他人站在周围。

"怎么回事？"弗兰克问

"一切都好。"下士温柔地说。"小伙子，我们只是和你开了一个玩笑。"

"我们没打算伤害你。"另一个士兵说道，"你是不是觉得好一些了？"

"好多了，威利在哪？"他太累了，根本动不了。"威利很好，我们会把他带到你这儿来的。"

"我中枪了没？"弗兰克又问。

"当然没有！你觉得我们会动你一根头发丝吗——尤其是像你这么勇敢的小伙子？我们只是想吓吓你，但是玩笑开得有点大，你昏迷了一小会儿——就这样。"

士兵的嗓音听起来非常和善，弗兰克备受鼓舞，坐了起来。

"你现在能走吗？"下士一边问，一边帮他站起来。

"我来帮他吧！"另一个大块头说，弗兰克还不能走路，他便弯腰背上弗兰克，一直背到弗兰克和威利分别的地方，其他人则骑着马跟在后面。

"我能走。"弗兰克说。

"哎呀，不，还是让我抱着你吧，老天保佑你！"

弗兰克不知道，这个大块头骑兵正看着自己浅色的头发，那些头发就垂在他的胳膊上。也不知道这位骑兵走在这片弗吉尼亚林荫道上，心里想象着自己正在特拉华的家里。这位骑兵胳膊上传来的力量，也是对另一个远在布兰迪维因的小男孩的爱抚。不一会儿，他们看见了其他的士兵，弗兰克要求下来。士兵温柔地把他放下来，并且在他离开之前亲吻了他。

"我家里有一个满头卷发的小家伙，和你差不多大。"他温和地说。

弗兰克看见他的眼眶湿润了。"我希望你能平安回到他身边。"他说。

"上帝保佑！"士兵说。

当他们看见在小路上的部队时，发现威利仍然为弗兰克临走前的那番话感到苦恼。但威利睁大了眼睛，才发现自己的兄弟又出现在眼前，还听到士兵们夸奖他"有勇气"（士兵们是这么说的）。士兵们放他们走的时候，下士给弗兰克的一枚五美元金币，被弗兰克礼貌地拒绝了。

（托马斯·尼尔森·佩吉）

作者介绍

托马斯·尼尔森·佩吉生于弗吉尼亚州奥克兰的一个种植园，他和兄弟们在种植园中度过了童年。南北战争爆发后，北弗吉尼亚军队有两年冬天都在这个种植园附近扎营。因此，他还是个孩子的时候，就见识了真实的军营生活，因此得知了无数的战争故事。佩吉把这些故事写入小说《两个小伙伴》中（本文即节选自此书），以及《营地之间》《枪的葬礼》和《被抓获的圣克劳斯》。同时，他还写了《古老的弗吉利亚》《夫人》《红色岩石》等有趣的故事和小说。本文由出版商查尔斯·斯克里布纳之子授权使用。

A Wolf-Hunt

🖉 预习

canter /ˈkæntər/ 马慢跑
comprehend /ˌkɑːmprɪˈhend/ 充分理解
exhilarating /ɪgˈzɪləreɪtɪŋ/ 令人振奋的
fugitive /ˈfjuːdʒətɪv/ 逃亡的
impatiently /ɪmˈpeɪʃntli/ 不耐烦地
impede /ɪmˈpiːd/ 妨碍
irritated /ˈɪrɪteɪtɪd/ 恼怒的
partially /ˈpɑːrʃəli/ 不公平地
unabated /ˌʌnəˈbeɪtɪd/ 不减弱的

  The light from the faintly yellow east had begun to fill the room when the sound of a galloping horse, rapidly approaching from the south, wakened Lincoln Stewart, and then a whistle mingled with the trample of the horse brought to a halt.

  "That's Milton Jennings!" he cried, leaping from his bed into the frosty air, and hurriedly dressing.

  When Lincoln got outdoors, the horseman was at the gate, seated on a restless gray colt.

  "Aren't you up early for a Seminary chap?"

  "Oh, I guess I haven't lost all my stamina with one term o' school," laughed Milton.

  "Had breakfast?"

"Yes."

"Well, I haven't, so you put Mark in the barn, and wait while I eat."

After a hasty breakfast, the boys brought out the colts. Mark came first, snuffing and alert, and Milton put one toe into the stirrup and swung gracefully into the saddle. Lincoln followed with Cassius, wild already, as if he smelled the game.

As Lincoln seized the pommel of his saddle, the horse plunged and reared and flew away sidewise, but the boy hung to the bridle and mane, and as he whirled, leaped into his seat and had the wild brute in hand before he could make a second rush. He was too good a horseman to be irritated by high spirits in a horse.

As they rode, the sun rose, and its rays, striking along the horizon, changed the level prairie into a flat basin, with the horsemen low in the center. To the east the line of timber seemed to rise far out of its normal position. Ten miles to the west, the larger and deeper forest seemed only three or four miles away.

"Will the boys be on hand?" asked Lincoln.

"Oh, yes! This snow will bring them out. It was the signal. We'll find them at the school house."

Some miles to the north, and just over the state line, a big square of wild land still lay. Upon it, as upon an island, the wolves, foxes, and badgers had taken refuge, and the Iowa boys had made several hunting trips " across the line," but Lincoln had never before taken part in them. Rance Knight, who always had a hand in any expedition of this kind, had been in two wolf-hunts, and was the natural leader of this one.

As the boys rode steadily on, three horsemen could be seen making easy way along another lane. When Milton caught sight of them, he rose in his saddle and uttered a wild whoop, which made a remarkable change in the pace of the other horsemen.

Answering yells rose, and a fine race took place. Lincoln let the rein loose on Cassius, dug his heel into his flank, and was off before Milton's protest could reach him.

Milton held Mark down to an easy lope, and watched the race

between Lincoln and the nearest horseman mounted on a black horse. Lincoln was a little nearer to the goal, but had a ravine to cross; and though the iron-sided Cassius did his best, the black turned in just a neck ahead.

When Milton cantered calmly up to the crowd, they all yelled.

"He isn't any good, that gray horse! Why didn't you let him out?"

"You'll find out why, later in the day," responded Milton coolly. "When the rest of your horses are all winded, Mark will be fresh as a daisy."

"That's so! That's a fact. Didn't think of that," the rest replied.

Soon, Rance, too, turned up, riding Ladrone, and in a few minutes they were all mounted. "Now we must be off," said Rance. "Keep behind me, don't race, and don't make too much noise. We strike for the big popple grove. All ready——into line. March."

He wheeled his horse and rode away at an easy gallop, followed by his laughing, jostling troop, along the road between fields, leading to the north. The day promised to be bright; the snow was just right; deep enough to aid in detecting the wolves, and not so deep as to interfere with the speed of the horses.

It was about ten o'clock when Rance pulled up on the edge of the range. "Now, then, Lineoln, you take Milt and Cy, and strike into that patch of hazel bush to the right, and remember, if you start a wolf, don't try to run him down, unless you're close on him. He'll run in a circle—— and while you're after him, fire a shot to let us know, and well cut across lots. When we strike his trail, you pull right off, and cut across behind us. If he turns to the right or left, let us know."

It was exhilarating to breathe the keen prairie air, to feel under one's thigh the powerful swing of muscles firm as iron, to know that at any moment a wolf might start up from the bush. The horses caught the excitement, champed their bits impatiently, and spurned the glittering snow high into the air.

Soon a shot was heard, and wild yells from the right division. A moment later, out from behind a popple grove leaped a wolf, followed by a squad of horsemen. Instantly all the captain's commands were forgotten. Everybody joined pursuit, whooping, laughing, firing, without an idea of order.

The wolf was surprised, but seemed to grasp the situation. In less than ten seconds the whole troop were in a huddle and riding fast, except Rance, who was now on the extreme left, cutting diagonally across. He fired his gun to interrupt his mob of excited hunters, and rode right into their front.

"Halt! Hold on there!"

He waited until they all came back around him.

"Now, what way of doing business is that? How many wolves are you going to kill by winding every horse in the crowd the first jump? You'll kill more horses than wolves. Listen to me: We don't want more than three horses after the wolf at the same time. The others must cut him off. Don't be in a hurry——wait and see where he's heading."

The boys were silent.

"Milt and Lincoln were all right. They started the game. But the rest of you were all wrong. Now, the wolf is in that big tow-head there. Cy, you go to the right, Milt, you go to the left, I'll take the center, and we'll see if we can go at this man-fashion."

In a few minutes they had partially encircled the grove and were moving down on it. Again the wolf broke cover, and started to the left. He was not aware of Milton and Lincoln, because they were hidden by a hunch of aspens, and Lincoln gave a wild whoop as the yellow-brown grizzled creature darted around the grove, almost under his feet, and entered the brush before the boy could collect himself.

Cassius leading, the party of four rushed into the brown hazel patch, a rushing, snorting squadron. The brush impeded and bewildered the wolf and he doubled on his track, bursting out on the prairie again, at an oblique angle to the course of the other horsemen.

The chase became magnificent. The wolf seemed to float along the ground, his long tail waving, his ears alert. Rance was riding like mad, to intercept him, and the wolf did not seem to understand, but he did: just as Ladrone seemed upon him, he disappeared. Rance reined sharply to the left, and waved his hat to Lincoln, who comprehended the situation. The wolf had entered a deep ravine, which ran to the southeast, and was doubling again, seeking his den.

"He's going back!" shouted Milton, letting Mark out for the first time. The grand brute, snorting with delight, slid over the ground, light as the wolf himself. The rider sat him as if he were standing still, but exulting to feel the vast power and pride of his horse.

"See that horse run!" shouted Lincoln in delight. The majestic colt swept down upon the wolf, as if all eyes were upon him, and his honor at stake. Milton could see the head of the wolf. It seemed as though Mark must run him down, so certainly equal were the distances, but Mark thundered down the slope and into the swale a few rods in advance.

The wolf whipped out behind. Milton fired twice, but the fugitive kept on. He reined Mark sharply to the right, with unabated speed, and rode back up the slope, waving his hat to show the way that the wolf had gone.

But the others had seen the change in course, and were driving down on the wily fugitive in a body. Ed Blackler was in the lead, his gun ready, guiding his horse by the pressure of his knees. He was upon him with a rush, and fired.

The wolf leaped into the air, rose, avoided the rush of the black, and started into the brush. Now was Lincoln's opportunity, and striking Cassius with the flat of his hand, he swept upon the wolf like a whirlwind. The wounded beast fell under the feet of the wild-eyed Cassius, who would have trampled fire in his excitement.

When Milton rode up to the circle of panting horses and excited boys, Lincoln was handing the tail to Ed Blackler, and Rance was saying :—

"The ears are yours, Link. That crazy horse of yours did the business."

The hoys were delighted with the result. Everybody praised the superb run made by Mark, the good shooting done by Ed Blackler, and the mad courage of Cassius, who bore the marks of the wolf's teeth on his legs.

(Hamlin Garland)

译文

猎狼记

旭日初升,熹微的晨光渐渐铺满了房间。林肯·斯图尔特被一阵从南边飞驰而来的马蹄声吵醒了。接着一声口哨混杂在马蹄声中响起,马停住了脚步。

"是弥尔顿·詹宁斯!"他喊起来,跳下床,在寒冷的空气里匆忙穿上衣服。

林肯走出门的时候,弥尔顿就在门边,骑在一匹焦躁不安的灰毛雄马上。
"你难道是为了一个塞米纳里的家伙才起这么早的吗?"

弥尔顿笑着说:"哦,我想,我还不至于上了一个学期的学,就一点精力都没有了。"

"吃过早饭了?"

"吃过了。"

"好吧,我还没吃,所以你得把马克牵到马棚里,然后等我吃完。"

林肯匆匆用完早餐后,男孩们把马儿牵了出来。马克第一个出来,它警觉地"呼哧呼哧"喷着气。弥尔顿一只脚尖踩进马镫,优雅地翻身上了马鞍。林肯带着卡修斯跟在后面。它似乎闻到了游戏的味道,已经野性毕露。

林肯刚抓住马鞍的前鞍,他的马就俯冲向前,抬起后背,从侧面飞奔了出去。林肯身上挂着缰绳,紧抓住马鬃,一个旋转,就跳上了他的马鞍,在马第二次冲锋前控制住了这只狂野的牲畜。他是一个很好的骑士,不会被马的情绪激怒。

在他们纵马前行的时候,太阳升起来了。阳光沿着地平线向前推进,平整的大草原看起来跟盆地似的,骑手们就在这个"盆地"的中央前行。东面地平线上的森林显得更加遥远了。西面那广袤幽深的森林离我们一万六千多米,现在好像只有几千米而已。

"男孩们都在附近吗?"林肯问。

"哦,当然!这场雪就是一个信号,他们会出来的。我们能在校舍里找到他们。"

数千米外的北面，就在州际线那里，有一大片野地。狼、狐狸和獾会到这里避难，仿佛把此处当成了一座安全岛。艾奥瓦州的男孩们曾为了打猎穿越州际线，但林肯之前从没有参与过这种活动。兰斯·奈特总是热衷于此，还曾经两次猎狼，他自然是这次狩猎的领袖。

男孩们稳稳地骑在马上，看见三名骑手在另一条小道上骑着马缓缓前行。弥尔顿一看见他们，立刻从马鞍上站了起来，发疯似的大叫了一声。这明显改变了骑手们的步调。

骑手们答应着，策马奔跑起来。林肯放松了卡修斯的缰绳，用脚跟刺了刺马儿的侧腹，弥尔顿还没来得及阻止，他就疾驰而去。

弥尔顿控制着马克的速度，好看清林肯和一名黑马骑手之间的比赛，这名骑手离他最近。林肯距离终点稍微近一点儿，但还要越过一道沟壑。虽然勇敢的卡修斯尽了最大努力，但仍落后黑马一段距离。

弥尔顿沉着地策马小跑过去，人群里很热闹，大家都在叫喊着说话。

"那匹灰马不怎么样！你为什么不放开它？"

"过会儿你就明白为什么了。"弥尔顿冷静地回答，"当你们的马全都喘不上气来的时候，马克还是生气勃勃的，跟朵小雏菊似的。"

"事实就是，想都不要想！"其他人回道。

不久，兰斯也出现了，他骑着一匹叫莱德隆的马。他们几分钟内就全都上了马。"现在我们必须要行动了。"兰斯说，"跟在我后面，不要比赛，也不要弄出太大的动静。我们朝那片杨树林进军吧。全体准备——列队前进，出发！"

他调转马头，轻快地飞奔出去，身后跟着欢声笑语、你挤我撞的骑士们。他们沿着野地之间的道路朝北前进。天色明亮，积雪深度正好：既有利于发现狼的足迹，又不会妨碍到马的速度。

上午十点，兰斯在猎区的边缘停了下来，开始排兵布阵："林肯，你带着弥尔顿和塞浦路斯去右边那片榛树丛。记住，如果你发现一头狼，距离很近的时候再跟过去。狼会绕着圈子跑，你追它的时候要鸣枪示意，我们得到消息，就抄小路切断它的后路。等我们追踪它的时候，你就离开右路，抄小路跟在我们后面。如果这匹狼左转或者右转了，告诉我们一声。"

呼吸着清新的草原空气，感受着震颤的大腿肌肉像钢铁一样充满力量，知道一头狼可能随时会从灌木丛中窜出来。这一切都太令人兴奋了！马儿们也感受到了这样的氛围,不耐烦地咬着嚼口,把银光闪闪的雪高高地踢向天空。

不久,一声枪声响起,从右边传来了震耳欲聋的叫喊。片刻之后,一头狼从后面的杨树林里跳了出来,一队骑手紧追其后。顿时,大家把首领的命令忘得一干二净,人人争相追赶,只听到呼声、笑声以及毫无章法的射击声。

狼受了惊,但看上去仍能掌握主动权。不到十秒的时间,整个队伍发力狂奔,乱作一团,只有兰斯例外。他在队伍最左边,从对角斜穿过小路,开枪让手下这帮兴奋的猎手们暂停行动。然后,他策马来到这群人的正前方。

"停!在这里停下!"

他等着他们重新聚集到他的身边。

"看看,怎么能这样做事呢?这群马跳一下就喘不过气来了,这样你还觉得能杀几头狼?你们累死的马会比你们杀死的狼还多。听我说,一头狼不需要三匹以上的马同时去追。其他人必须切断它的后路。不要着急,耐心等着,看清它朝哪个方向跑。"

男孩们全都安静下来了。

"弥尔顿和林肯做得对,他们开始了狩猎。但你们其他人都做错了。现在,狼跑到那边的一大片沙洲里去了。塞浦路斯,你去右边;弥尔顿,你去左边,我在中间。我们来看看,这种大人的做法是否奏效。"

几分钟内他们就分开包围了树林,向这个地方挺进。那头狼再次窜了出来,朝着左侧奔逃。弥尔顿和林肯藏在一堆杨树后面,狼并没有察觉。这只黄棕相间的家伙绕着树林横冲直撞,几乎就从林肯的脚下跑过,他还没来得及抓住它,它就跑进了灌木丛。林肯大喊了一声。

卡修斯率领剩下的四个人冲进了棕色的榛树丛。他们飞奔着,喷着鼻息,秩序井然。灌木丛挡住了狼的去路,它一时不知所措,于是从侧面溜出了骑手们的地盘,又一次在草原上飞奔,加速逃亡。

追逐的场面非常壮观。狼飞奔的时候就好像漂浮在地面上,长尾巴摆个不停,耳朵警觉地竖了起来。兰斯策马狂奔,想拦住这头狼。狼似乎并不明白他的打算——但实际上并非如此:莱德隆刚刚靠近它,它就消失了。兰斯猛然勒马,冲向左面,对着林肯挥舞帽子。林肯明白是怎么回事了。狼跑进了一道深沟,这条沟正对着东南方。狼再一次加快了速度,寻找它的避难所。

弥尔顿大喊道:"它要逃回老巢了!"说着,他第一次放开了马克的缰绳。

这匹马愉悦地打着响鼻，像狼一样轻轻跳着，一溜烟地跑了起来。骑手稳稳地坐在马鞍上。他感到了马的力量，心中十分欣喜，为他的马感到十分自豪。

林肯高兴地喊道："看那匹马，跑着呢！"健壮的小雄马向狼发动了袭击。所有的目光都注视着它，它的荣誉在此一举。弥尔顿能看见狼的头部。他们之间距离相当，看来马克要先追上它了。但是马克以迅雷不及掩耳之势奔下斜坡，抢先几步到了洼地。

狼迅速逃离，弥尔顿开了两枪，但它并没有停下脚步，继续逃跑。弥尔顿也没有减速，他猛然把马勒向右边，策马奔回斜坡，挥舞着帽子，示意那头狼的去向。

其他人见机而动，一起策马追赶那头狡猾的狼。艾德·布莱克一马当先，时刻准备开枪，用膝盖的压力引导马儿前进。他突然加速，靠近狼，然后开了一枪。

狼跳向半空，避过了黑马的冲撞，然后逃进了灌木丛。林肯的机会来了！他拍了一下卡修斯，像一阵旋风般扫倒了那匹狼。野性大作的卡修斯兴奋极了，对着那匹受伤的野兽又踩又踏。

男孩们激动万分，马儿都气喘吁吁，他们围成一个圈，当弥尔顿策马奔到的时候，林肯正把狼尾巴递给艾德·布莱克。他听见兰斯说：

"林肯，狼耳朵归你。你的那匹疯马是位功臣。"

男孩们对这个结果十分满意。每个人赞不绝口地谈论着马克的奔跑追逐是多么迅速、艾德·布莱克的射击有多么及时，以及卡修斯那疯狂的勇气是多么可嘉，卡修斯的腿上还留着那头狼的牙印呢。

（哈姆林·加兰德）

✍ 作者介绍

哈姆林·加兰德出生于威斯康星州，他的少年时代是在爱荷华州度过的。他还是个孩子的时候，课余时间就在农场里工作。他创作的大多数故事和小说都围绕西部和西部的人展开。本文选自《草原上的男孩生活》，这是一本男孩们喜欢的书。《大路条条》一书集结了加兰德先生最好的一些故事。《鹰之心》和《草原上的人》也很受欢迎。本文选自《草原上的男孩生活》第一版，由麦克米兰公司授权。

练习

1. 省略now, then, too, nevertheless, however, and to be sure阅读这些句子。这些短语可以独立使用。

1)Now, what way of doing business is that?

2)Now, then, Lincoln, you take Milt and Cy.

3)Rance, too, turned up, riding Ladrone.

4)Nevertheless, he distinguished at his feet a man of poor appearance.

5)After all, however, his fish were great curiosities.

6)Fishing, to be sure, is not easy.

2. 想一想，单词和词组怎样从句子的其他部分分离出来独立使用？

3. 写一写你曾经历过的户外活动：

在海滨的一天。

在城市的一天。

收集坚果。

一次野餐。

游览一处名胜。

在乡下的一天。

在公园里玩耍。

收集浆果。

钓鱼。

度假。

On a Higher Level

Jack Dunn stood in the door of his home on a crag of Persimmon Ridge and loaded his old rifle. Suddenly there came from the valley the baying of a pack of hounds in full cry. The boy looked wistful as he heard it, and then frowned.

"Those Saunders men have gone off and left me," he said reproachfully. "Here I've been kept chopping wood and pulling fodder until they have had time to get up a deer."

Then taking his rifle as the shadows grew long, he set out for the profit and the pleasure of still-hunting. Following the course of the mountain stream, which was swollen by heavy rains, and was now rushing and foaming far out of its banks, he came to an old and ruined mill.

No human being could live there, but in the doorway appeared a boy dressed like Jack in an old brown jeans suit and a shapeless white hat. This was Andy Bailey.

"Have you been hunting?" asked Jack. Andy nodded assent. Jack walked down into the rickety mill and stood leaning against the rotten old hopper. "What did you get?" he said, looking about for the game.

"Well," drawled Andy, with much hesitation, "I haven't been started out long." He turned from the door and faced his companion rather sheepishly.

"I hope you haven't been popping off that rifle of yours along the deer-path down in the hollow, and scaring off all the game," said Jack. "If I were as poor a shot as you are, I'd go a-hunting with a bean-pole instead of a gun, and leave the game to them that can shoot it."

For a mountain-boy, Andy was a poor shot and, therefore, the scoff of Persimmon Ridge.

"I've seen many a girl who could shoot as well as you, ——better," continued Jack jeeringly. "But la! I needn't go down there into the hollow expecting to get a deer to-day. They are all off in the woods a-smelling the powder that you have been wasting."

Andy was pleased to change the subject. "It seems to me that the water is scuttling along tolerably fast," he said, turning to the little window through which the stream could be seen.

It was running fast, and with a tremendous force. Logs and branches shot by, half hidden in foam. The old mill, whose wooden supports were now completely under water, trembled and throbbed with the rushing stream. As Jack looked toward the window, his cheek paled, and he sprang to the door with a frightened exclamation.

Too late! The immense bole of a fallen tree, shooting down the channel with force and velocity, struck the tottering supports of the crazy, rotting building.

It careened, and quivered in every fibre. There was a crash of falling timbers, then a mighty wrench, and two boys, clinging to the window-frame, were driving with the wreck down the river.

The old mill thundered against the submerged rocks, and at every concussion the timbers fell. It whirled around and around in eddying pools. Where the water was clear, and smooth, and deep, it shot along with great rapidity.

The clinging boys looked down upon the black current, with its sharp, treacherous, half-seen rocks and ponderous driftwood. The wild idea of plunging into the tumult and trying to swim to the bank faded as they looked. Here in the crazy building there might be a chance. In that frightful swirl there lurked only a grim certainty.

The boys were caged, as it were. The door-way was filled with the heavy debris, and the only possibility of escape was through that little window. It was so small that only one could pass through at a time, —— only one could be saved.

Jack had seen the chance from far up the stream. There was a stretch of smooth water close to the bank, on which was a low-hanging beech-tree, ——he might catch the branches.

They were approaching the spot with great rapidity. Only one could go. He himself had discovered the opportunity, ——it was his own.

Life was sweet, ——so sweet! He could not give it up; he could not now take thought for his friend. He could only hope with a frenzied eagerness that Andy had not seen the possibility of deliverance.

In another moment Andy lifted himself into the window. A whirlpool caught the wreck, and there it eddied in dizzying circles. It was not yet too late. Jack could tear the smaller, weaker boy away with on strong hand, and take the only chance of escape.

The shattered mill was dashing through the smoother waters now; the great beech-tree was hanging over their heads; an inexplicable, overpowering impulse mastered in an instant Jack's temptation.

"Catch the branched, Andy!" he cried wildly.

His friend was gone, and he was whirling off alone on those cruel, frantic waters. In the midst of the torrent he was going down, and down, and down the mountain. Now and then he had a fleeting glimpse of the distant ranges.

The familiar sight, the recollection of his home, brought sudden tears to his eyes. On, on, in this mad rush he went down to the bitterness of death.

Even with this terrible fact before him, he did not reproach himself with his costly generosity. It was strange to him that he did not regret it; perhaps, like that mountain in its sunset glory, he had suddenly taken up life on a higher level.

The sunset splendor was fading. The whole landscape seemed full of reeling black shadows, ——and yet it was not night. The roar of the torrent was growing faint upon his ear, and yet its speed was not checked. Soon all was dark and all was still, and the world slipped from his grasp.

"They tell me that Jack Dunn was nearly drown when the men fished him out of the pond at the sawmill down in the valley," said Andy Bailey, recounting the incident to the fireside circle at his own home. "They saw the rotten old timbers come floating into the pond, and then they saw something like a person hanging to them.

"The water was smooth, there, so they had no trouble in swimming out to him. They couldn't bring him to, though, at first. They said in a little more he would have been gone. Now "pridefully" if he had had the grit to catch a tree and pull out, as I did, he wouldn't have been in such a danger."

Andy never knew the sacrifice that his friend had made. Jack never told him. Applause is at best a slight thing. A great action is nobler than the monument that commemorates it; and when a man gives himself into the control of a generous impulse, thenceforward he takes up life on a higher level.

(Mary N. Murfree)

译文

升华

  杰克·邓恩站在柿子岭悬崖边自己的屋子里，正往那老旧的来复枪内装着子弹。突然，从山谷里传来一群猎犬的高声咆哮。这位男孩听到声音后露出了不快的表情，皱了皱眉。

  "那些桑德斯人已经离开了，留下我一个人。"他愤愤地说，"我可是在这里不停地砍树，准备饲料，才让他们有时间去猎鹿。"

  傍晚时分，影子越来越长，他拿起猎枪出发去伏击猎物，这既有钱赚又有意思。山间的溪流由于暴雨已经涨溢起来，呼啸地向前狂奔，溅起的泡沫已经越过了堤岸。他顺着溪流往前走，来到了一座废弃的破旧磨坊跟前。

  没有人住在这里，但一个同杰克一样穿着旧棕色牛仔衣、戴着难看的白帽子的男孩在门口，他是安迪·贝利。

  "你在打猎吗？"杰克问。安迪点了点头。杰克走进了破旧的磨坊，靠着朽烂的料斗说道："你打到了什么？"说着便环顾四周，寻找着猎物。

  安迪略有迟疑地说："我还没开始多久呢。"他从门口转过身来，羞怯地面对着小伙伴。

  "我希望你没有在山谷下满是鹿的道上丢下你的来复枪，然后吓得跑回来。"杰克说，"如果我像你那样枪法不准，我宁可使用一根杆子而不是猎枪，让那些会射击的人们自个儿玩去吧。"

作为一个山里的孩子，安迪枪法很差，因此也成了柿子岭的一个笑柄。

"我看到过不少女孩的枪法和你一样准，或许还更准。"杰克继续嘲弄着他，"不过也罢，今天我也不指望去下面的山谷逮到一只鹿了，它们闻到你浪费的火药的味道，全都逃进树林了。"

安迪想转换个话题，"在我看来，这水真是流得相当的快啊。"他说着打开了一扇能看到河流的小窗。

河流真是在飞奔着，携带着巨大的力量。原木和枝条被水冲击，有一半已被吞没在了泡沫之中。老磨坊的木头支架已经完全淹没在水中，随着河水的冲击而摇摇晃晃。杰克朝窗口看了一眼，吓得脸都白了，他害怕地惊叫着向门口窜去。

太晚了！一根掉落在水中的巨大树干带着力量和速度顺着水道冲了下来，撞在了破旧小屋那摇摇欲坠的底架上。

小屋倾倒了，每根木条都在颤抖。木头"噼里啪啦"地掉落下来，随后又是一阵强力的扭曲，接着两个紧紧抓住窗框的孩子就随着屋子的残骸一起被冲入河中。

撞上暗礁时，老磨坊会发出惊雷般的巨响，每次撞击都有木条掉落下来。在漩涡中，它会不停地打转。水流深且清澈，无比顺畅，带着小屋以极快的速度向前奔去。

紧贴在屋子里的孩子们向下望着黑色的河流，里面充满了若隐若现的危险的尖利岩石，还有漂浮着的巨大浮木，他们打消了跳进涡流并试图游到岸边的荒唐念头。待在这个疯狂的屋子里面或许还有生机，而跳入吓人的漩涡中肯定只有悲惨的结局。

就这样，孩子们被困在屋中。门口已经被大量残骸碎片堵上了，那扇小窗户是唯一逃脱的希望。但它太小了，一次只能允许一个人通过。只有一个人能够得救。

杰克在远远的上游处看到了一个机会。一处河岸边有一股奔腾的水流，水面上低垂着一棵山毛榉，他可以抓住那棵树。

他们正以飞快的速度接近那个地点。只有一个人能够出去。是他发现了这个机会，是他自己。

生命是美好的，太美好了！他不能放弃它；他现在不能替朋友着想，只能热切地希望安迪没有发现这个获救的机会。

那一刻，安迪正向窗上爬去。屋子的残骸遇上了一个漩涡打起了转转，让人头晕目眩。这还不算晚，杰克可以用强有力的手把那矮小瘦弱的男孩拉下来，得到这仅有的逃脱机会。

被撞得粉碎的磨坊正在那片较为平静的水面上飞速前进，那颗绝妙的山毛榉已经悬在了他们的头上。突然，一种难以名状而又不可阻挡的冲动一下子压倒了杰克的求生欲望。

"安迪，抓住那根树枝！"他大声叫道。

他的朋友逃了出去，而他独自在发狂的水流中翻腾着。他在洪流之中向山下冲去，不断向下、向下，不时能短暂地瞥见远处的景象。

那熟悉的景象以及自家的回忆一下子让他满眼泪水。近了，更近了。在这发狂的奔流中，他正冲向那令人痛苦的死亡。

但即使面对这个可怕的现实，他依然没有为那个代价昂贵的慷慨而责备自己。他感到奇怪，自己并没有为此感到后悔。也许就像那大山在落日中映出一片光辉那样，他的生命在那刻得到了升华。

落日的光芒褪去了，所有的景象笼罩在一片黑影之中，现在还没到晚上。咆哮着的奔流变得震耳欲聋，而它的速度依然没有得到控制。不一会儿，一切都变成了黑色的死寂，他失去了对这个世界的所有意识。

"他们告诉我，当人们在山谷下锯木厂的池塘中把杰克·邓恩捞上来时，他几乎都快淹死了。"安迪·贝利在家中的火炉边描述着发生的事情，"他们看到了水池中漂浮着的老朽木料，然后发现了上面好像挂着一个人。

"水面比较平静，所以他们毫不费力地游过去把他带了出来。但他们一开始没能让他恢复意识，并说他撑不了多久了。"安迪自豪地说："如果他像我那样勇敢地抓住大树把自己拉出来，本不会遭遇如此险境。"

安迪一直不知道他朋友所做出的牺牲，杰克从来没有告诉过他。掌声只是微不足道之物，一个伟大的举动要比纪念这一行为而建立的丰碑更为高贵。一个人会把自己交由慷慨的冲动来控制，从那刻起他的生命得到了升华。

（玛丽·洛丽兹·默弗里）

作者介绍

玛丽·洛丽兹·默弗里的笔名是查尔斯·埃格伯特·克拉多克，以下是她写的一部分著名的书籍：《在陌生人的国家》《大烟山的先知》《田纳西的群山中》和《基登悬崖的故事》。此处节选文章的出版已经得到了霍顿米夫林公司的同意。

练习

1. 把这个故事里的英雄和小吉芬、伊丽莎白·赞恩以及缪尔镇学院里的男孩们相比，谁是最勇敢的？写下你的理由。

2. 写一个关于勇敢行为的故事。这个行为因何而起？它做了些什么？结果呢？

"Muskratting"

One November afternoon I found Uncle Jethro back of the woodshed, drawing a chalk-mark along the barrel of his old musket, from the hammer to the sight.

"What are you doing that for, Uncle Jeth?" I asked.

"What for? For muskrats, boy."

"Muskrats! Do you think that they'll walk up, while you knock them over with a stick?"

"Go away! What I take you possumin' des dozen winters for when you dunno how to sight a gun in the moon yet? I am going muskratting by the moon tonight, en I won't take you."

Of course he took me. We went out about nine o'clock. Entering the zigzag lane behind the barn, we followed the cow-paths down to the pasture, then cut across Lupton's Pond, the little wood-walled lake that falls over a dam into the wide meadows along Cohansey Creek.

The big moon was riding over the meadows as we tucked ourselves snugly out of sight in a clump of small cedars on the bank. The domed houses of the muskrats——the village numbered six houses——showed plainly as the moon came up. When the full flood of light fell on the still surface of the pond, we could see the "roads" of the muskrats leading down through the pads to the open space about the dam.

These houses are so placed along a water-hole that the dweller can dive out and escape under water when danger approaches. The muskrat first chooses for his bedstead a large tussock of sedge that stands well out of the water. Now, from a foundation below the water, thick walls of mud and grass are erected inclosing the tussock; a thick thatch is piled on; the channels leading away from the doors are dug out; a bunch of soaking grass is brought in and made into a bed on the tussock, and the muskrat takes possession.

Here, in the single room of their houses, one after another will come, until the walls can hold no more; and curling up after their night of foraging, they will spend the frigid days blissfully rolled up into one warm ball of dreamful sleep.

Unless roused by the sharp thrust of a spear, the muskrat will sleep until nightfall. You may skate around the lodge, and even sit down upon it, without waking the sleepers; but plunge a stick through the top, and you will hear a smothered plunk, plunk, plunk, as one after another dives out of bed into the water below.

While Uncle Jethro and I waited that night, there was a faint plash among the muskrat houses. The village was waking up, and soon we saw swimming silently and evenly towards us, the round, black head of a muskrat.

A plank had drifted against the bank, and upon this the little creature scrambled out, as dry as the cat at home under the roaring kitchen stove. Down another road came a second muskrat, and joined the first comer on the plank. They rubbed noses softly, and a moment afterward began to play together.

They were out for a frolic, and the night was splendid. Keeping one eye open for owls, they swam and dived and chased each other through the water, with all the fun of boys in swimming.

On the bottom of this pond were mussels, which the muskrats reckon sweetmeats. They are hard to get, hard to crack, but worth all the cost. I was not surprised, then, when one of the muskrats sleekly disappeared beneath the surface, and came up directly with a mussel.

There was a squabble on the plank, which ended in the other muskrat's diving for a mussel for himself. Having finished this course of big-neck clams, they were joined by a third muskrat. Together then they filed over the bank and down into the meadow. Shortly two of them returned with calamus-blades.

The washing followed. They dropped their loads upon the plank, took up the stalks; pulled the blades apart, and soused them up and down in the water, rubbing them with their paws until they were as clean and white as the whitest celery one ever ate. What a dainty picture! Two little brown creatures, humped on the edge of a plank, washing calamus in moonlit water!

One might have taken them for half-grown coons as they sat there scrubbing and munching. Had the big owl from the gum swamp come along then, he could easily have bobbed down upon them, and might almost have carried one away without the others knowing it.

Muskrats, like coons, will wash what they eat, whether washing is needed or not. It is safe to say, I think, that had these found clean bread and butter upon the plank instead of muddy calamus, they would have scoured it just the same.

Before the two on the plank had finished their meal, the third muskrat returned, dragging his load of mud and roots to the scrubbing. He was just dipping into the water when there was a terrible explosion in my ears. As the smoke lifted there were no washers upon the plank; but over in the quiet water floated three long, slender tails.

"No man going standing shot, boy, just see a muskrat wash his supper," and Uncle Jethro limbered his stiffened knees and went chuckling down the bank.

(Dallas Lore Sharp, adapted)

译文

"逮水耗子"

十一月的一个下午，我在柴房后面发现了杰斯罗叔叔，他正给他的老步枪做记号。他沿着枪膛，用粉笔从扳机画到了准星。

"杰叔叔，你为什么要做这个呀？"我问。

"为啥子？为了逮水耗子呀小子！"

"水耗子！你觉得它们会走上来，然后你就可以趁机用棍子敲它们了吗？"

"滚蛋！这见鬼的大冬天我逮水耗子带你去干啥？夜里只照着月光，你懂得咋用枪瞄准吗？今晚有月光，我是要去逮水耗子，不过甭想我带你去。"

但是，他还是把我带去了。大约九点，我们出了门。我们走到牛棚背后的之字形小道上，顺着牛平时走去牧场的路，抄捷径到了勒普顿的池塘。池塘很小，围着木围栏，池塘的水通过一个水坝流进了宽阔的草地里。科汉西河就沿着这些草地流淌而过。

　　大大的月亮在草场上空照耀着，借着岸上的一丛雪松，我们把自己彻底地隐蔽起来。月亮刚升起来的时候，就能把水耗子的窝看得一清二楚。窝是半球形的，共有六个，形成了一个小小的群落。当潮水一般的月色完全倾泻在池塘表面时，我们还能看到那些通往水坝附近空地的"路"，都是水耗子用爪子挖出来的。

　　水耗子都是沿着水边做窝的，当危险来临，它们就可以跳入水中，从水底下逃走。因为莎草可以很好地在水面浮起，水耗子首先用一大丛莎草做自己的床架。然后，它用泥巴和草环绕着床架，糊成厚实的墙，再往上面垒起厚厚的草。接着，它又从洞口开始挖隧道，最后把一大丛草带进洞里，堆在莎草上做成了床。如此一来，水耗子就可以住进去了。

　　在一只水耗子的洞会住进一只又一只的水耗子。在墙被挤垮之前，都会一直有水耗子继续住进来。觅完食的夜晚，它们会蜷缩着身子，卷成一个温暖的球，幸福地进入梦乡，从而度过寒冷的日子。

　　只要不被锥子扎屁股，水耗子会一直睡到第二天傍晚。你可以在水耗子的窝上面溜过，甚至坐在上面，都不会把它们吵醒。要是从窝的顶部戳进一根棍子，你就会听见"啪、啪、啪"的声音闷闷地响起，水耗子就会一个接一个地从床上跳进水里。

　　那天晚上，我和杰斯罗叔叔正等待着。水耗子的几个窝之间溅起了小小的涟漪，它们已经醒了。不久，我们就看见它们圆圆的黑脑袋浮在水面，正静悄悄、齐刷刷地向我们游来。

　　一块板子自岸边漂浮过来，一个小家伙爬上去。就跟家里厨房的猫似的，因为待在烧得很旺的炉子底下，身上干燥得很。第二只从另一边过来了，跟第一只一样，爬上了板子。它们温柔地蹭着鼻子，过了一会儿，它们开始一起玩耍起来。

　　这是个很棒的夜晚，它们就是出来嬉戏的。它们跳入水中，就可以在水里游着泳，相互追逐嬉戏，只要稍微提防猫头鹰就行。它们和男孩子们游泳时一样充满了欢乐。

　　池塘底下有蚌，在水耗子心里，蚌像糖果一样美好，并且很难得到，也很难打开，却值得为之付出所有。一只水耗子滑溜地在水面消失，钻进了水底，马上又出现了。不出我所料，它带回来一只蚌。

板子上的两只水耗子起了争执，直到另一只水耗子跳进水中自己去找蚌，争执才停止。得到了肥美的蚌以后，有第三只水耗子加入了它们。三只水耗子排着队穿过了堤岸，然后跳进了草地里。不一会儿，其中的两个回来了，带着一些菖蒲的叶子。

接着，清洗就开始了。它们把叶子放在板子上，抓着茎干分开叶片，把它们浸入水中再提起来，同时爪子不断摩擦着叶片，直到变得又白又干净为止，白得跟以前吃的最白的芹菜梗一样。这画面真是赏心悦目！板子的边上，两只棕色的小家伙弯着背，在映着月光的水里洗刷着菖蒲。

它们坐在那里洗东西和嚼东西的样子，很容易会让人觉得它们是半大的浣熊。要是有身躯庞大的猫头鹰从黏稠的沼泽那边飞来，自上面朝它们飞下去，就能轻易带走它们其中的一个，几乎不会被另外几只水耗子察觉。

水耗子和浣熊一样，不论是否需要，它都会把食物洗一遍。我想我可以很肯定地说，就算它们发现的是干净的面包和黄油，不是这些沾满泥巴的菖蒲，水耗子照样会在板子上冲洗它们。

在板子上的两只水耗子吃完它们的晚餐之前，第三只水耗子回来了。它拖着一堆泥巴和草根，也开始了清洗的工作。它刚刚跳进水里，我的耳边就响起了可怕的枪声。板子上有烟冒了出来，但那些洗东西的家伙们已经不在那里了。平静的水面上，浮起来三根细长的尾巴。

"小子，看了水耗子把晚饭洗了个遍之后，哪个都不会想喂它们吃枪子儿了。"杰斯罗叔叔伸展着僵硬的膝盖，低声笑着，往岸边走去了。

（达拉斯·洛尔·夏普，有删改）

⚘ 作者介绍

达拉斯·洛尔·夏普是一个牧师，他生于1870年的新泽西州。自1901年开始，他成了《青年之友》杂志的编辑。他曾花费大量心力去研究大自然，写了许多关于动物和鸟类的文章。他的著书《家附近的野生动物》受到了很多大自然爱好者的喜爱。本文摘录于此，已获得世纪出版公司的授权。

🔖 朗读

The Perfect Life

It is not growing like a tree in bulk, doth make men better be,
Or standing long an oak, three hundred year,
To fall a log at last, dry, bald, and sear;
A lily of a day
Is fairer far in May;
Although it fall and die that night,
It was the plant and flower of light.
In small proportions we just beauties see;
And in short measure, life may perfect be.

🔖 译文

完美的人生

要成就更好的人生，不必像一棵巨树，
或者是一棵经历三百年时光的橡树，
倒下，干枯，枯萎，最终腐烂；
像一枝百合在五月盛开，
即使在夜晚凋敝，也比树木更高雅，
它是光明的植物，光明的花朵。
于细微之处，我们仍能看见美丽；
于短暂之时，我们仍能完善生命。

《美国语文》译者名录

钱志慧	南京师范大学
帕孜丽娅	暨南大学
尹吴娅琪	中南财经政法大学
侯艺东	南京师范大学
夏婕	南方医科大学
金晓寒	复旦大学
张佳佳	南京林业大学
杜子悦	华中师范大学
高倩	华东师范大学
蒋荟蓉	西南交通大学
赵艺珂	南开大学
苌婧	四川外国语大学
李颖	北京外国语大学

美工

彭慧	华东师范大学